EVERYMAN, I will go with thee,
and be thy guide,
In thy most need to go by thy side

The
English Poems
of
George Herbert

Edited by C. A. PATRIDES
G. B. Harrison Professor of English Literature,
The University of Michigan at Ann Arbor

Dent: London and Melbourne
EVERYMAN'S LIBRARY

© J. M. Dent & Sons Ltd 1974
All rights reserved

Made in Great Britain by
The Guernsey Press Co. Ltd, Guernsey, C.I.
for
J. M. Dent & Sons Ltd
Aldine House, 33 Welbeck Street, London W1M 8LX
First published 1974
Reprinted 1977, 1978, 1981, 1984

This book is set in 9pt Imprint 101, unleaded

No 1040 Paperback ISBN 0 460 11040 3

Contents

for Gerald Aylmer and Philip Brockbank

πολλὰ τὰ δεινὰ κοὐδὲν ἀνθρώπου δεινότερον πέλει

To The Reader

The editor of Herbert's poetry must walk circumspectly. His primary responsibility is to provide a reliable text; his secondary, to resist an excess of annotation; his third, to avoid the impertinence of mere paraphrases. True, unfamiliar words should be explained, obscure references clarified, and Biblical allusions identified *and* quoted; but to the extent that Herbert eschews the unduly remote, I demonstrate throughout this edition my conviction that ponderous annotation of his poetry would in fact severely restrict his meaning. The circumference of that meaning continues to expand as it is, witness the ever-increasing studies cited in the extensive bibliography and in my introduction. But the wise reader will know that the safest guide through Herbert's poetry is Herbert's poetry.

A Note on Abbreviations
References in brackets involving letters [e.g. *FEH*, *IW*, etc.] are expanded in the list of abbreviations, below, p. 214. References in brackets involving numbers preceded by the symbol § [e.g. § 14, § 173, etc.] are to the numbered entries in the bibliography, pp. 217-38.

Biblical quotations are from the King James ('Authorized') Version of 1611, unless otherwise stated. The place of publication is given only if it is other than London or New York.

A Note on the Text
The editor of Herbert's English poems must in the first instance decide on the relative authority of:

1 The first edition of *The Temple* in 1633;
2 The Bodleian Library's MS Tanner 307 ('The Original of Mr George Herbert's *Temple*; as it was at first Licenced for the presse')—hereafter abbreviated as *B*;
3 MS Jones B 62 in Dr Williams's Library, Gordon Square, London—hereafter abbreviated as *W*—which provides the text of sixty-nine out of the 164 poems in *The Temple* but also six poems lacking in both (1) and (2); and
4 Walton's *Lives* (1670) which provides the text of three poems not available elsewhere.

Except for the six poems in *W* and the three in Walton—all included in Appendix I, below, pp. 201-6—my primary authority is the first edition of 1633. *W* could not be regarded as authoritative since its sixty-nine poems are early versions of the poems

finally published (I quote, in the notes, some of *W*'s wording and
select stanzas so that the reader can study Herbert's approach to
revision: see especially Appendix II, pp. 207–8). Nor did I regard
B with favour since its frequently questionable wording and punc-
tuation tend to embarrass even its champions [see *passim* the
textual notes in *FEH*]. The first edition, on the other hand, was
prepared under the vigilant eye of the conscientious Thomas
Buck (see the title-page reproduced on p. 28) and can be com-
mended—as Hutchinson himself was obliged to acknowledge—
for its 'unusual excellence' [*FEH*, p. lxxiv; cf. J. Max Patrick,
below, p. 225].

The text of the first edition is nevertheless so amended here as
to include: the correction of the more obvious misprints, especially
if these were also corrected in the second edition;[1] the change of
'u' to 'v' where the latter is meant, and of 'i' to 'j' for the same
reason; the reduction of the second letter in each poem (originally
a capital like the first letter) to lower case; the introduction of
Latin numerals to differentiate poems with the same title (e.g.
'Jordan I', 'Jordan II'); and the amendment of the title 'The
23. Psalme' to 'The 23rd Psalme' (below, p. 177).

Acknowledgements
My foremost obligation is to the Librarian of Dr Williams's
Library who granted me permission to print the text of seven
poems from *W*—i.e. the six poems which Hutchinson also pro-
vides, and the seventh ('Perfection'/'The Elixer') which he does
not. These are now made available in Appendices I and II, pp.
201–8.

I am also grateful to the Custodian of the Department of Western
Manuscripts in the Bodleian Library for photographing the version
of 'The Elixer' in *B* needed to prepare Appendix II (p. 208), and
to the Trustees of the British Museum for granting me permission
to reproduce the title page of the 1633 edition of *The Temple*
(BM shelfmark: C. 58. a. 26). In connection with the poems
included in Appendix III (pp. 209–13), I am pleased to ack-
nowledge the permission of the Clarendon Press to reprint one of
The Poems English and Latin of Edward, Lord Herbert of Cherbury,
ed. G. C. Moore Smith (1923), and the first sonnet of *Astrophil
and Stella* from *The Poems of Sir Philip Sidney*, ed. William A.
Ringler, Jr (1962); also the permission of Harvard University
Press to reprint one poem each from *A Poetical Rhapsody* (1931)
and *England's Helicon* (1935), alike edited by H. H. Rollins; and
finally the permission of Oxford University Press to reprint the
'Song' attributed to the Earl of Pembroke in *The Poems of John
Donne*, ed. Herbert J. C. Grierson (1912).

---

[1] There were eleven editions of *The Temple* within the seventeenth
century: the first two in 1633, a third in 1634, and so on to the eleventh
in 1695 [all fully described in *FEH*, pp. lvi–lxii].

The preparation of this edition was substantially affected by several sustained studies of Herbert (notably those by Rosemond Tuve in 1952, Joseph H. Summers in 1954, and Mary E. Rickey in 1966) and the labours of editors who preceded me in annotating his poetry (notably G. H. Palmer in 1905, F. E. Hutchinson in 1941, J. H. Summers in 1967, Gareth Reeves in 1971, and Barbara K. Lewalski and Andrew J. Sabol in 1973). But when all is said I remain, as I must, primarily indebted to the *OED*.

I should finally record my gratitude to the staffs of the British Library and the Bodleian Library for their manifold courtesies and unfailing assistance; to Professor Peter Aston of the University of East Anglia for assisting me with the annotation of Herbert's musical terms; and to Mr and Mrs Peter Miles, and Mr Trevor Joscelyne, who provided me with out-of-print facsimiles of *The Temple*. Yet I must end where I should have begun, with an acknowledgement of the indispensable advice of three friends in particular: Professor Philip Brockbank of the University of York, Professor John R. Mulder of Drew University, and Professor Stanley Stewart of the University of California at Riverside.

University of York C. A. P.
January 1974

Postscript

Several reprints since the initial publication of this edition in 1974 have afforded me opportunities to make a few necessary corrections, to provide some addenda to the Bibliography (p. 238), and in a few cases to amend the annotation. Friends on both sides of the Atlantic have been extremely generous with their helpful observations, and I am particularly grateful for the sage counsel of Professor William B. Hunter of the University of Houston.

University of Michigan at C.A.P.
Ann Arbor
February 1981

An Outline of Herbert's Life
within the context of contemporary events

1593   Herbert born (3 April) in Montgomery in Wales, the fifth son of
Richard and Magdalen Herbert. Izaac Walton born. Death of
Marlowe. Hooker's *Of the Lawes of Ecclesiastical Polity* (Books
I–IV) published.

1595   Sidney's *Apologie for Poetrie* and Spenser's *Amoretti* and *Epithala-
mion* published. *Midsummer Night's Dream* first (?) acted; also
Richard II.

1596   Herbert's father dies; survived by his wife Magdalen, seven sons,
and three daughters. The eldest son Edward matriculates at
University College, Oxford. Spenser's *Faerie Queene* (Books
IV–VI) published; also his *Four Hymns*. *The Merchant of
Venice* first (?) acted.

1597   Bacon's first ten *Essays* published.

1599   Edward Herbert marries a cousin, Mary Herbert. Oliver Crom-
well born. Death of Spenser. *Julius Caesar* and *Henry V* first
acted.

1600   Death of Hooker. Fairfax's translation of Tasso published.
Hamlet first (?) acted.

1601   Execution of Essex. Lancelot Andrewes appointed Dean of
Westminster. Donne marries Anne More. *Twelfth Night* first
(?) acted.

1603   Death of Elizabeth I; accession of James I. The Millenary
Petition.

1604   Richard Bancroft appointed Archbishop. The Hampton Court
Conference. *Othello* first acted.

1605   Herbert attends Westminster School. Bacon's *Advancement of
Learning* published. The Gunpowder Plot. Sir Thomas
Browne born.

1606   *Macbeth*, Jonson's *Volpone* and Tourneur's *Revenger's Tragedy*
first (?) acted.

1608   Milton born. Robert Cecil created Earl of Salisbury, appointed
Lord Treasurer. Sylvester's translation of Du Bartas: 1st
complete edition. Herbert's mother marries Sir John Danvers.

1609   Herbert matriculates at Trinity College, Cambridge. Spenser's
Faerie Queene: 1st folio edition. Shakespeare's *Sonnets* pub-
lished.

1610   Johnson's *Alchemist* first acted; also Shakespeare's *Winter's Tale*
(1611?). Galileo reports on his telescopic view of the heavens.

1611   George Abbot appointed Archbishop. The King James ('Autho-
rized') Version of the Bible published. *The Tempest* first (?)
acted. Chapman's *Iliad* completed.

1612   Death of the heir apparent Prince Henry; Herbert contributes two
memorial poems in Latin, his first verses to be published. Death
of Salisbury. Robert Carr, later Earl of Somerset, in favour.

1613   Princess Elizabeth marries Frederick Elector Palatine. Sir Thomas
Overbury murdered. Crashaw born. Nicholas Ferrar visits the
Continent (to 1618).

1614 Ralegh's *History of the World* published. Webster's *Duchess of Malfi* first (?) acted.

1615 Donne ordained. George Villiers, later Duke of Buckingham, in favour.

1616 Death of Shakespeare. Herbert elected major fellow of Trinity College, Cambridge. Jonson's *Works* published.

1617 Death of Donne's wife.

1618 Herbert appointed Reader in Rhetoric at Cambridge. Ralegh executed. Bacon appointed Lord Chancellor. Cowley born.

1619 Edward Herbert appointed ambassador in Paris. Lancelot Andrewes appointed Bishop of Winchester.

1620 Herbert elected Public Orator at Cambridge (to 1628). Settlement of first New England colony by the Pilgrim Fathers. Bacon's *Novum organum* published.

1621 Bacon impeached. Donne appointed Dean of St Paul's. Burton's *Anatomy of Melancholy* published. Marvell born.

1622 Henry Vaughan born.

1623 The 1st Shakespeare Folio published.

1624 Herbert elected to represent Montgomery in Parliament (also in 1625). Edward Herbert's *De veritate* published in Paris.

1625 Death of James I; accession of Charles I who marries Henrietta Maria of France. Outbreak of plague. Nicholas Ferrar settles at Little Gidding in Huntingdonshire. Bacon dedicates his *Translation of Certaine Psalmes* to Herbert. Death of Webster.

1626 Herbert presented to a prebend in Huntingdonshire, four miles from Little Gidding. Death of Bacon; Herbert contributes a memorial poem in Latin. Death of Lancelot Andrewes. John Aubrey born.

1627 Death of Herbert's mother; the funeral sermon, delivered by Donne, was accompanied when published by commemorative poems including Herbert's *Memoriae matris sacrum*.

1628 Buckingham assassinated. William Harvey's discovery of the circulation of the blood published. Bunyan born.

1629 Marriage of Herbert to his stepfather's cousin Jane Danvers. Edward Herbert elevated to the peerage as Lord Herbert of Cherbury. Lancelot Andrewes's *XCVI Sermons* published.

1630 Herbert instituted to the rectory at Bemerton near Salisbury in April; ordained priest in September. Prince Charles (later Charles II) born. Emigrations to New England (1630 ff.).

1631 Death of Donne. Dryden born.

1632 Crashaw visits Little Gidding (1632 ff.).

1633 Charles I visits Little Gidding. William Laud appointed Archbishop. Donne's *Poems* published. 1 March: Herbert's death, of consumption, just before his fortieth birthday.

The Temple was published posthumously in 1633; Herbert's translation of Luigi Cornaro's *Trattato de la vita sobria*, in 1634 (appended to Leonardus Lessius's *Hygiasticon*); his 'Briefe Notes' on Juán de Valdés's *Hundred and Ten Considerations*, in 1638 (appended to its translation by Nicholas Ferrar); *Outlandish Proverbs*, in 1640 (enlarged edition as *Jacula prudentum*, 1651); *A Priest to the Temple*, in 1652 (as part of *Herbert's Remains*: see below, p. 235); and *Musae responsoriae*, in 1662 (as part of James Duport's *Ecclesiastis Solomonis*).

A Crown of Praise:
The Poetry of Herbert

'The Book is Praise, the parts are prayer. The name changes not the nature; Prayer and Praise is the same thing'.

John Donne, on the Psalter

I

On first looking into Herbert's poetry we note the grace, the artlessness, the self-conscious plainness. Recalling the ecstatic sentences in Izaac Walton's hagiography ('he seem'd to be marked out for piety, and to become the care of Heaven'*), we may also be persuaded of Herbert's seraphic reverence and steadfast holiness. But so far we would err.

The piety, the reverence and the holiness are never absent from Herbert. But they are dimensions of his religious experience which transform themselves when judged within the controlled turbulence of his larger utterance. The extent to which Walton remained a stranger to this quality need not surprise us: the exigencies of his art demanded a particular point of view, and he elected to observe in Herbert the self-abnegation of a pious individual, not the agony of a poet for whom humility was unattainable precisely because he was a great poet.

The grace, the artlessness and the plainness are by the same token responses which Herbert's poetry does initially elicit. But they are also responses in constant need of qualification. The grace will on reflection appear to be something more than a monotone, for Herbert's articulation invariably testifies to his remarkable tonal range. The artlessness will similarly emerge as less than artless in that Herbert's poetry possesses a dormant complexity not unlike Milton's or Marvell's. The self-conscious plainness, finally, will be observed to comprehend an all-pervasive consciousness of self that negates even the nominal 'plainness'.

The claims are large. Can they be substantiated?

II

'Thus he liv'd, and thus he dy'd like a Saint, unspotted of the World, full of Alms-deeds, full of Humility, and all the examples of a vertuous life' [IW, p. 319]. The conclusion of Walton's life of Herbert is by no means unique. Nicholas Ferrar's preface to The Temple in 1633 had already described Herbert as 'a companion to the primitive Saints' (below, p. 31); Vaughan's Mount of Olives in 1652 had canonized him even more enthusiastically as 'a most glorious true Saint'; while the rambling first hagiography

* [IW, p. 262]. The abbreviations in use throughout, are explained above, p. 1. The quotation from Donne in the headnote is from his Sermons, V, 270.

of Herbert by Barnabas Oley in the same year set the stage for
Walton's definitive performance in 1670. To deny Herbert's
holiness is obviously impossible, and in any case pointless. But
holiness, we should remind ourselves, does not necessarily exclude
violent upheavels in the saint's private universe. Quite the con-
trary indeed! Even Walton was obliged to report that the saintly
Herbert, when young, 'kept himself too much retir'd, and at too
great distance with all his inferiours: and his cloaths seem'd to
prove, that he put too great a value on his parts and Parentage'
[*IW*, p. 270]. In providing this report, Walton obviously meant to
emphasize Herbert's subsequent and reputedly total conversion.
But did the poet ever fully subordinate the way of the world to
his spiritual aspirations? Did he absolutely deny his parts and
parentage which, alike impressive, appeared to promise a public
career vastly different from his eventual translation to Bemerton's
'pittifull little chappell'?[1]

George Herbert belonged to an aristocratic family whose head,
after the death of his father, was his brother Edward, himself a
poet, an influential philosopher, and a public servant eventually
elevated to the peerage as Lord Herbert of Cherbury. Their
mother Magdalen was equally remarkable. One of the great ladies
of the late Elizabethan and early Stuart period 'Beauty's vision
to the world, the glass of God', Herbert called her later [*LPH*, p.
153]—she had chosen as her second husband the wealthy Lord
Danvers who was over two decades her junior. Her house in
Chelsea soon became one of the foremost centres of intellectual
activity: 'a *Court*, in the conversation of the best', to quote
Donne's judgement.[2] Emerging from such a context, Herbert
naturally aspired toward knowledge and, beyond knowledge,
position. 'I want Books extremely', he wrote to his young step-
father in 1618 [*FEH*, p. 364]. But books and his generous educa-
tion at Cambridge were means to that end which his election a
year later as the University's Public Orator appeared to fore-
shadow. The Orator, he pointedly informed his step-father,
'takes place next the Doctors, is at all their Assemblies, and
Meetings, and sits above the Proctors, is Regent or Non-regent
at his pleasure, and such like Gaynesses, which will please a
young man well'. The post is 'the finest place in the University,
though not the gain-fullest' [*FEH*, pp. 369–70]. The great ex-
pectations are patently obvious. Had not his predecessors attained
high political office, two of them—Sir Robert Naunton and
Francis Nethersole—having risen to become Secretaries of State?
After all, the king's favour had also been secured, especially after
Herbert had praised an oration by James I as superior to whatever
Greek and Roman 'hirelings' may have ventured [*FEH*, p. xxvii; cf.
LPH, pp. 58–9]. The flattered monarch returned the extravagant
compliment by describing Herbert as the University's 'Jewel' [*IW*,
p. 271]. No wonder that later, in 1675, Charles Cotton suspected that
Herbert was 'deeply tainted with Ambition'! [*FEH*, p. xliii].

Yet Cotton's suspicion was extreme. To ask whether Herbert's ambition like his pride was justified is to strike a less censorious note; for we would then observe that Herbert impressed himself not merely on a flattered king but on men of far greater perception, notably the saintly Lancelot Andrewes on the one hand, and the worldly Bacon on the other.[3] As Herbert counselled his younger brother Henry in 1618, 'be proud, not with a foolish vanting of yourself when there is no caus, but by setting a just price of your qualities: and it is the part of a poor spirit to undervalue himself and blush' [*FEH*, p. 366]. Herbert's progress, I am suggesting, was rather cumulative than strictly linear, not because he was ever utterly self-centred but because he was not. It is for this reason that he experienced, as he said, 'such spiritual Conflicts, as none can think, but only those that have endur'd them' [*IW*, p. 287]. How different was Donne's experience! For Donne would rear his mighty ego in order to exorcise it before his angry God. Not so Herbert, whose spiritual conflicts were all the more shattering in that they did not involve pride. They involved humility and *therefore* pride, to the extent that the practice of humility can be the most sinister form of pride. Donne displays pride in his highly personal diction, phrasing, and tone; yet Herbert in electing a plainer diction, simpler phrasing, and far more subdued tone, displays not humility but pride still. *The Temple* is the work of a humble man devoid of humility only because a great poet must set a 'just price' on his qualities.

III

On the face of it, Herbert's foremost quality is certainly his plainness, even his simplicity. But simplicity as such cannot account for Herbert's influence immediately on Crashaw and Vaughan, and later on such diverse poets as Hopkins and Emily Dickinson; nor does it explain either Coleridge's approbation of 'the great general merit of his Poems, which are for the most part exquisite in their kind' [§ 141], or T. S. Eliot's judgement that Herbert 'may justly be called a major poet' [§ 155]. Herbert's simplicity, it is clear, needs must be modified considerably.

But Herbert's approach to poetry, it may be objected, is plainly analogous to the parson's approach to the sermon so clearly delineated in *A Priest to the Temple*:

> The Parsons Method in handling of a text consists of two parts; first, a plain and evident declaration of the meaning of the text; and secondly, some choyce Observations drawn out of the whole text, as it lyes entire, and unbroken in the Scripture it self. This he thinks naturall, and sweet, and grave. Whereas the other way of crumbling a text into small parts, as the Person speaking, or spoken to, the subject, and object, and the like, hath neither in it sweetnesse, nor gravity, nor variety, since the words apart are not Scripture, but a dictionary, and may be considered alike in all the Scripture.   [*FEH*, pp. 234–5]

But opposition to a given practice—the practice of Lancelot Andrewes among others—need not enlist Herbert among those who preferred rather Senecan brevity than Ciceronian expansiveness, much less among those who endorsed mathematical plainness so that (as Hobbes said of Thucydides) 'the number of his sentences [i.e. thoughts] doth almost reach to the number of his words'.[4] Herbert's opposition is grounded on a decisive partiality not so much to any particular style as to Biblical precedents.

Herbert looked beyond the Bible for parodic purposes (see below, Appendix III, pp. 209–13), for the surprisingly numerous classical allusions which he promptly christianized [§ 204], and for the opportunities that the emblematic tradition afforded to render his poetry 'at once visual and intellectual' [§ 164; also §216, 'The Poem as Hieroglyph']. Otherwise, well-nigh every aspect of Herbert's poetry is traceable to the Bible. The evident lucidity—the 'terrifying lucidity', as one critic remarks with understandable awe [§ 156]—is Biblical. So is the omnipresent propensity toward understatement. Even more important, however, is the palpable influence of wisdom literature, of the Psalter, and of the parables embedded in the Gospels.

Herbert's interest in wisdom literature, especially the Book of Proverbs, is reflected in his own extensive collection of proverbial utterances. Simple in themselves, they prove less than simple on reflection, witness:

254. Providence is better then a rent.
381. We are fooles one to another.
462. To weepe for joy is a kinde of Manna.
540. Love is the true price of love.
792. Service is no Inheritance.

[*FEH*, pp. 323 ff.]

Thematically, the sanctified worldliness of wisdom literature affected Herbert's poetry rather adversely, if not in 'Charms and Knots' where the limit of sequentially arranged proverbs is reached expeditiously (p. 111), then certainly in 'The Church-porch', the unduly long introductory poem to *The Temple*, where the versified morality often contains excellent advice ('Never exceed thy income'!) but questionable poetry. Stylistically, on the other hand, Herbert's emulation of the Book of Proverbs afforded him the opportunity to indulge in that highly compressed, economic phrasing, whose precise impact on his poems we are yet to study. It is far otherwise with the Book of Psalms, not only because we are aware how crucial for Herbert were the translations by his relative Sir Philip Sidney [§§ 106, 166, 190], but because we know how often adaptations from the Psalter were the first fruits of poets who then proceeded, like Milton, to far more substantial harvests. Herbert himself, it will be noted, 'imitated' only one psalm, even though it is the celebrated twenty-third, 'The Lord is my shepherd' (quoted in full, for purposes of comparison, on

p. 178). Yet so profoundly was Herbert engaged with the Psalter
that its echoes reverberate across his poetry, to an extent unmatched
by any other poet in English literature. The primary attraction
of the psalms was, of course, that devotional nature which Herbert
celebrated in one of his Latin poems:

> O holy banquets! O soothing
> Oil of the spirit! Flakes of heaven, falling
> Droplets of a better world!
> [*LPH*, p. 35]

But Herbert was equally impressed by the Psalter as poetry. It is
not unwarranted to assume that he joined his contemporaries in
regarding David, to whose pen the psalms were traditionally
ascribed, as a great poet—'a better *Poet* than *Virgil*', as Donne
proclaimed with assurance.[5]

The parables also exerted a strong influence on Herbert, not
least because they are, like his poetry, 'the natural expression of a
mind that sees truth in concrete pictures rather than conceives it in
abstractions'.[6] We are reminded of the interest taken by Nicholas
Ferrar and his band of dedicated souls at Little Gidding in stories,
those 'divine interludes, dialogues and discourses in the Platonic
way' which eventually yielded the 'short moral histories' in-
corporated into the community's *Story Books*.[7] Herbert perceived
their uses readily enough. As he observes in *A Priest to the Temple*
of the parson's instruction of his parishioners,

> Sometimes he tells them stories, and sayings of others, according as
> his text invites him; for them also men heed, and remember better
> then exhortations.
>
> [*FEH*, p. 233]

True, the literary dimension of the parables is severely circum-
scribed: their claim as art cannot be pressed very hard. In *The
Temple*, however, parabolic teaching appears in many forms. It is
by no means confined to poems like 'Redemption', 'Christmas',
'Peace', or 'Love III' (pp. 60, 96, 136, and 192). Infinitely
pliable in Herbert's hands, it informs all the poems which involve
stories, among them 'Time' and 'Love unknown' (pp. 134 and
140). Moreover, given the dramatic nature of Herbert's verse, the
parable will be observed to have been significantly extended in
poems of dialogue or exchanges, for instance 'The Pulley' (p.
166), itself foremost among the productions whose apparent
naïvety is wont to elicit our condescending smiles. But Herbert's
method is the method of the Gospels in particular, and of the
Bible generally: 'unspeakable mysteries in the Scriptures', accord-
ing to Sir Thomas Browne's apposite reminder, 'are often de-
livered in a vulgar and illustrative way, not as they truely are, but
as they may be understood' (*Religio Medici*, I, 45). Prompt under-
standing of the central point is essential; but because the parable
is fundamentally an indirect discourse, total understanding is

reserved for those qualified to respond. It might therefore be said of Herbert's poetry what a Biblical scholar has asserted of parabolic teaching, that it possesses a complexity dormant within apparent simplicity.[8] As much is suggested by the New Testament in exclusively theological terms:

> Unto you it is given to know the mystery of the kingdom of God: but unto them that are without, all these things are done in parables (ἐν παραβολαῖς); that seeing they may see, and not perceive; and hearing they may hear, and not understand.
>
> (Mark 4.11–12)

In like fashion parables are parallelled in the Psalter with the 'dark sayings of old' (78.2), and in the apocryphal Ecclesiasticus with 'the secrets of grave sentences' (39.3). The metaphysical justification was best formulated by St Paul: 'now we see through a glass, darkly' (1 Corinthians 13.12).

The parabolic approach, then, represents tendencies in Herbert which argue his extensive indebtedness to Biblical precedents. But as much might be said of his tonal range, his polymorphic vocabulary, and his architectonic imagery, however pronounced the adjustment of each may have been under the impact of other influences. Herbert's tonal range, for instance, is the direct result of his training as an orator even while it is, demonstrably, the legacy of Donne. Yet it is no less the legacy of the Bible, especially in the studied understatement of a verse such as:

> My God, thou art all love.
>
> ('Even-song', l. 29)

There is no 'final' way of reading such a verse. Is it a contrite confession, or an exultant prayer? Does it involve passionate longing, absolute assurance, or profound amazement? The justly celebrated last lines of Herbert's poems often have the same effect. 'Redemption', for example, ends:

> Who straight, *Your suit is granted*, said, & died.

—which induces astonishment precisely because of its nominal simplicity, much as Milton's elaborate patterns in *Paradise Regained* are finally suspended with:

> Tempt not the Lord thy God; he said and stood.
>
> (IV, 561)

We observe elsewhere the significant extensions of the 'simple' Biblical language. The detected principle that 'the dominant emotion of each poem dictates its rhythmic form' [§ 139] is all too often not the rule but the exception. An emotion apparently dominant is likely to prove of secondary importance as the tone veers, sometimes abruptly, to accommodate even childish delight:

> He will be pleased with that dittie;
> And if I please him, I write fine and wittie.
>
> ('The Forerunners', ll. 11–12)

The technique of 'Deniall' and especially of 'The Collar' (pp. 96 and 161) is even more impressive, for the violent spasms in the internal arguments and external forms of both poems terminate in lines which, in their restored order, provide at last the neglected norm. We are again reminded of Milton, this time *Lycidas*, where the concluding ottava rima cancels the disorder of the casual rhymes, the half lines, the broken rhythm.

Herbert clearly belongs with Milton in manipulating the verse to reflect the thematic pattern. Yet in other poems he also belongs with Marvell in suggesting much more than the lucid texture seems to posit. The suggestiveness depends on the deployment of a vocabulary which, in appearance limited and even 'simple', expands outwardly in accordance with the given context. Just as the Bible qualifies familiar words, so Herbert is wont to amend the meaning of a word dramatically—as in 'winding' or 'twist',[9] but especially in the omnipresent 'rest' which appears with astonishing ingenuity as part of the sustained—and heavily ironic— imagery of gaming in 'The Church-Porch' (pp. 33 ff., ll. 227 and 297), with calculated ambiguity in the last line of 'The Answer' (p. 175), with suggestive orchestration in the rhyme scheme of 'Aaron' (p. 179), and with exceptional brilliance in the five instances of 'The Pulley' (p. 166), two of them almost totally submerged. We need only compare the argument of 'The Pulley' with the meditation on 'rest' by Sir John Hayward in 1623, to appreciate how a commonplace theme and even strikingly similar language were improved by Herbert. Hayward had thus urged his soul to cleave to God:

> Thou doest naturally desire nothing but him; the desire of worldy things is but a disease. Goe too then, tumble vpon the bed of honour, riches, or pleasure; thou shalt neuer find rest, because thou cariest thy disease within thee: ridde thee of thy sicknesse, and thou shalt finde reste only in GOD. The reason is plaine. GOD made thee only for himselfe; and therefore being thy last end, thou canst not find quiet, but onely in him . . .[10]

Herbert's articulation of the same theme is not only more economic; it is also more elliptical, in line with his frequent indulgence in word-play [§ 188] which accepts that verbal connections never look inwardly upon themselves. Herbert himself provides one lucid example, the traditional pun Son/sun: 'we give one onely name / To parents issue and the sunnes bright starre' ('The Sonne', ll. 5–6). Once juxtaposed, connections of this order intimate transcendent relationships best represented in the interlocked terms deployed in 'A Wreath' (p. 188), else the reiterated pattern of thine/mine in 'Clasping of Hands' (p. 164), and even the significant if apparently naïve rhyme schemes of 'Paradise' and 'Heaven' (pp. 143 and 191) which alike proclaim—as in delight/ light and persever/ever—the mystery veiled by familiarity. Herbert did not indulge in verbal pyrotechnics that 'burnish, sprout, and swell' ('Jordan II', l. 4) because, as he remarks in *A Priest to the Temple*, Jesus also confined himself to homely language, 'that by familiar things hee might make his Doctrine slip the more easily into the hearts even of the meanest' [*FEH*, p. 261].

'Familiar things' also inform Herbert's imagery, for its clusters are manifestly if not primarily Biblical. One notable exception is the imagery derived from music—'in which heavenly Art', Walton informs us, Herbert was 'a most excellent Master' [*IW*, p. 303; cf. § 216, Ch. VIII]. The deployment of musical imagery is, of course, a commonplace of literature generally as of Renaissance thought in particular: to quote Sir Thomas Browne again, 'there is musicke where-ever there is a harmony, order, or proportion' (*Rel. Med.*, II, 9). Yet it is a commonplace that Herbert's fertile imagination again transformed into a novelty. His frequent boldness is noteworthy, as when he remarks of Christ, 'His stretched sinews taught all strings, what key / Is best to celebrate this most high day' ('Easter', ll. 11–12)—a forceful reminder that Christ has not merely taught us to sound the appropriate music but provided the instrument as well: himself. Often, too, a musical image marks a transition in the tone. In the sonnet 'Prayer I', for instance, the initially elaborate endeavours to understand the nature of prayer yield to a musical reference that promptly affects the rhythm:

> A kind of tune, which all things heare and fear;
> Softnesse, and peace, and joy, and love, and blisse,
> Exalted Manna . . .

In 'Sunday', on the other hand, the joyful rhythm reflects the exuberance not of a child as of the man reborn into the kingdom of Christ:

> O let me take thee at the bound,
> Leaping with thee from sev'n to sev'n,
> Till that we both, being toss'd from earth,
> Flie hand in hand to heav'n!
>
> (ll. 60–3)

The Biblical burden of Herbert's other images is manifest in the light of Christ's habitual resort to 'the familiar things of daily life'—the moon and the stars, birds and sheep and fish, flowers and the vine, bread and water, door and keys.[11] In Herbert, accordingly, one cluster of pervasive images derives from the natural order. It marks the labours of the bee and next the flight of the dove, even as it measures the effect of dew and frost and rain and snow on fruit such as grapes, grain such as corn, and flowers like the rose. Man's life within the garden of the world—'Gods rich garden' ('Sunday', l. 27)—buds with joy, else withers in despair, and finally blooms again under the influence of implanted Grace. But other images expressly reminiscent of St Paul are also present, for example images of warfare as in 'Artillerie' (see below, p. 149), and especially images derived in the first instance from commercial and legal activities, and in the second from architecture. The relations between Redeemer and redeemed are most often set forth in commercial terms. Christ is said to have been 'sold' for us ('Antiphon II', l. 12; 'The H. Communion', l. 3; etc.), or to have taken 'the debt upon him' ('Love unknown', l. 61)—and so on through a vocabulary involving gain and loss, sales and bargains, rent and lease, bills and interest and the like. It sounds odd, not to say singularly inappropriate, until we recognize not only the Pauline terminology of Romans 3. 21–26 but the forensic language appropriate to the classic Protestant theory of the Atonement. In time that theory was to be enshrined in *Paradise Lost* (III, 80–415); but it had been formulated any number of times by major and minor theologians in statements of this order:

> Wee must then know that Christ is our Surety: and looke, as the debter is discharged by the payment performed by the Surety, and such payment made, is imputed to the Debtor, and reckoned as if hee had payed it himselfe: So God in sentence giuing, imputeth unto us that which our Surety hath done or suffered for us, and (whatsoeuer we are in our selues) respecteth us as if it had beene done by us, and so dischargeth us.[12]

The uniqueness of Herbert's adaptation of the commonly-held view resides not in that view but in its adaptation. One result is the sonnet 'Redemption' (p. 60); another, the triumphant proclamation of Christ's sacrifice

> Whose drops of blood paid the full price,
> That was required to make us gay
>
> ('Sunday', ll. 54–5)

—where the first line is a concession to tradition-bound thought, but the second marks Herbert's particular sensibility.

The last notable cluster of images favoured by Herbert is drawn from architecture. Extensively used by St Paul, architectural imagery is also basic to the fabric of the Bible at large. As Donne observed in one of his sermons,

> The Holy Ghost seemes to have delighted in the Metaphore of *Building*. I know no figurative speech so often iterated in the Scriptures, as the name of a *House*; Heaven and Earth are called by that name, and wee, who being upon earth, have our conversation in heaven, are called so too, (*Christ hath a House, which House wee are*). And as God builds his House, (*The Lord builds up Jerusalem*, saith *David*) so hee furnishes it, he plants Vineyards, Gardens, and Orchards about it, He layes out a way to it, (*Christ is the way*) He opens a gate into it, (*Christ is the gate*) And when hee hath done all this, . . . then he keepes house, as well as builds a house, he feeds us, and feasts us in his house, as well as he lodges us, and places us in it.[13]

The image is fundamental to several of Herbert's poems, for instance 'The World', 'Man', and 'Sion' (pp. 99, 106 and 120). But it also informs their collective title, *The Temple*.

IV

'*The Temple* is, in fact, a structure'. One tends to agree with T. S. Eliot's generalization [§ 155] only to disagree about its precise import. The constituent poems of *The Temple* have been observed to link in diverse ways, so that sequentially arranged poems (for instance 'Nature', 'Sinne I', 'Affliction I', 'Repentance', and 'Faith') intimate both in their titles and arguments the progress of the soul [§§ 191, 197]. But is the total structure meant to symbolize a pilgrim's progress under the care of the Church [§ 201], or possibly the divine order as reflected in the life of man within the Church [§ 216]? Is it perhaps based on the analogy between man's religious and aesthetic activities, themselves patterned after the activities of the Creator [§ 143]? Even more elaborately, does the threefold division of *The Temple* into 'The Church-porch', 'The Church', and 'The Church Militant', correspond to the tripartite division of the Hebraic temple into porch, holy place, and holy of holies, else to the three regions of the universe—the earth, the heavens, and the abode of God [§ 222]? To compound our difficulties, the first and the third of the collection's divisions—alike brutally moralistic—have not met with wide approbation: 'The Church-porch' is occasionally dismissed as dull [e.g. § 81], while 'The Church Militant' is generally regarded with stony silence. As a poem evidently pre-dating the rest of *The Temple*, 'The Church Militant' has even been said not to form an integral part of the collection [§§ 157, 263]. But it refuses to go away, stubbornly.

One analogy at least could not have been absent from Herbert's mind, for it was no less sanctified by tradition than it is implicit throughout *The Temple*: the analogy between Creator and poet. As George Puttenham (?) wrote at the outset of *The Arte of English Poesie* (1589),

> A poet is as much to say as a maker. And our English name well conformes with the Greeke word, for of ποιεῖν, to make, they call a maker *Poeta*. Such as (by way of resemblance and reuerently) we may say of God; who without any trauell to his diuine imagination made all the world of nought.[14]

A popular collection of commonplaces pronounced God a poet in even more sweeping terms:

> The begynner of meter was God, whych proporcioned the world, with all the contentes of the same, with a certain order, as it were a meter, for there is none (as *Pythagoras* taughte) that douteth, but that there is in thynges heuenly and earthely a kynde of harmonye, and onles it were gouerned, wyth a formall concorde and dys-cribed nomber, howe could it longe continue?[15]

On the widely-accepted metaphor of God the poet was often
superimposed the metaphor of God the architect. The Biblical
text usually cited was invoked from the apocryphal Wisdom of
Solomon: 'thou hast ordered all things in measure and number
and weight' (11.20). The creative method evident in the universe
at large was also said to have been applied within history when
the divine architect provided for Noah the proportions of the
Ark, for Moses those of the Tabernacle, and for Solomon those of
the Temple. In time the Solomonic Temple became the foremost
precedent for many medieval churches. As late as 1535 Francesco
Giorgi could write of the projected church of S. Francesco della
Vigna in Venice:

> We, being desirous of building the church, have thought it neces-
> sary, and most appropriate to follow that order of which God, the
> greatest architect, is the master and author. When God wished to
> instruct Moses concerning the form and proportion of the taber-
> nacle which he had to build, He gave him as model the fabric of
> the world [Exodus 25.8 ff.] ... And rightly so, because it was
> necessary that the particular place should resemble His universe . . .
> in proportion, which He wills should be not only in the material
> places, in which He dwells, but particularly in us of whom Paul
> says, writing to the Corinthians: 'ye are the Temple of God'
> [1 Cor. 2.16]. Pondering on this mystery, Solomon the Wise
> gave the same proportions as those of the Mosaic tabernacle to
> the famous Temple he erected.[16]

The argument is lucid in the extreme: all artistic endeavours rest
on a metaphysical foundation according to the precedent estab-
lished by God himself. Sir Thomas Browne once again provides
the appropriate generalization. 'In brief', he wrote, 'all things are
artificiall, for nature is the Art of God' (*Rel. Med.*, I, 16). Ob-
viously shared by Herbert, the assumption is most emphatically
evident in the poet's mimesis of the orderly pattern of words
emanating from God, the archetypal Logos or Word [§ 148]. But
the apprehension is not merely external. It is also an experience
within, in line with the several meanings that the Biblical witness
attaches to 'temple'.

The term, in the first and most obvious sense, designates the
house of the Lord—'an house of prayer for all people' (Isaiah
56.7). On other occasions, however, 'temple' is firmly differentiated
from any particular edifice: 'God that made the world and all
things therein, seeing that he is Lord of heaven and earth, dwelleth
not in temples made with hands' (Acts 17.24; cf. Matthew 12.6,
Acts 7.48). Metaphorically the term also appears as the natural
order in general (Psalms 29.9), more emphatically as the body of
Christ (Matthew 26.61, Mark 14.58, John 2.19), and by extension
as the body of man: 'ye are the temple of the living God' (2
Corinthians 6.16). By the early seventeenth century, moreover,
tradition had endorsed the application of 'temple' to the Church

at large. Donne explained in a sermon delivered in 1619 that the early Christians as well as 'all the *Fathers*' were wont to specify the Church by various terms, for instance *ecclesia* ('a company, a Congregation') and *dominicum* ('The Lords possession'). He added:

> But of all Names, which were then usually given to the Church, the name of *Temple* seems to be most large, and significant, as they derive it *à Tuendo*; for *Tueri* signifies both our beholding, and contemplating *God* in the Church: and it signifies Gods protecting, and defending those that are his, in his Church: *Tueri* embraces both.[17]

The reciprocal relationship between God and man stressed by Donne appears in Herbert through the communal sacramentalism of all his poems of dialogue if more particularly of the two poems alike entitled 'Antiphon' (pp. 72 and 108). But communal sacramentalism should not be mistaken for an act of worship performed solely in a given place at a given time. It is on the contrary the essence of things, the very nature of nature, in that it reflects the activities of the divine architect-poet both during his initial act of creation and his subsequent preservation of the world. 'Preservation', Herbert reminds us in *A Priest to the Temple*, 'is a Creation; and more, it is a continued Creation, and a creation every moment' [*FEH*, p. 281]. However traditional the basic concept,[18] its application by Herbert suggests the way the activities of the imitating poet are sanctified, the way language and even individual words look beyond themselves, the way the archetypal 'temple'—and each derivative 'temple' inclusive of structures like poems—possesses an external form even though it is fundamentally an internal experience: the 'frame and fabric', in his words, 'is within' ('Sion', l. 12). These diverse strands merge in Herbert's thought because they depend on a singular reality, the immanence of God in history through the sacrament of the Lord's Supper, the Eucharist.

V

The Eucharist is the marrow of Herbert's sensibility. Far more important than baptism, the only other sacrament recognized by Protestants, it had elicited ever since the Reformation violent disagreements as to the precise nature of Christ's 'presence' during its celebration. While Calvinists claimed that Christ is present solely through the communicant's faith, Roman Catholics asserted (as a rather crude formulation had it) that he is present 'not only to fayth, but also to the mouth, to the tongue, to the lips, to the flesh, to the bowells of all Communicants'.[19] Characteristically eschewing both extremes, Anglicans proclaimed in flexible if vague fashion that 'the Body and Blood of Christ are really and actually and substantially present and taken in the Eucharist, but in a way which the human mind cannot understand

and much more beyond the power of man to express'.[20] Herbert
agreed, but only after he had exorcised the partisan zeal he had
once displayed in a harsh tirade against a Puritan, to understand
at last the advantage of an irenic temper in the midst of his con-
temporaries' 'private Enthusiasmes'.[21] The Anglican formulation
of the Eucharist's *modus operandi*—'mystical, heavenly, and spirit-
ual', the elements present but 'figuratively and sacramentally'[22]—
became increasingly acceptable to Herbert, obliging him to ex-
clude from *The Temple* a rather militant meditation on 'The H.
Communion' (p. 201) in favour of a version far less explicitly
theological (p. 71). The larger consequence was poetry replete
with words reminiscent in their literal dimension of Roman
Catholic claims—*altar, table, board, repast, banquet, feast, store,
bread, meat, wine*, and especially *blood*, no less than the reiterated
verbs *taste* and *eat*—yet aspiring to intimate the mystery of 'the
pattern, the shadow, the type' of the ultimate reality.[32] It is of
course hardly accidental that the central division of *The Temple*,
'The Church', is preceded by the invitation of the 'Superliminare'
—i.e. the lintel over the entrance to the church—to 'approach,
and taste 1 The churches mystical repast' (p. 46). Within 'The
Church' proper, moreover, the first poem is 'The Altar', promptly
and significantly followed by the sixty-three stanzas of 'The
Sacrifice' (pp. 48 ff.) whose liturgical rhythms re-enact *and*
commemorate the original historical event, even as they suggest
the ideal response demanded of man. That response is also pro-
vided, at the other end of 'The Church', as the third of the poems
entitled 'Love' terminates with:

> You must sit down, sayes Love, and taste my meat:
>   So I did sit and eat.
>
> (p. 192)

If *The Temple* is indeed a 'structure', it is an eucharistic one. In
form as in content it is itself an 'eucharist', an εὐχαριστία or
'thanksgiving': the crown of praise offered, humbly, by 'A
Wreath' (p. 188).

The sacraments of the Eucharist and baptism were commonly
said to be 'visible signs of invisible Grace'.[24] Herbert's under-
standing of the nature of Grace involves in the first instance a full
awareness of the chaotic state of fallen man. All too often dis-
missed as mere dust, fallen man—man literally in-dependent of
God—is variously termed 'a poore clod of earth', 'a foolish
thing', 'an intangled hamper'd thing', 'a rotten tree', even 'a
silly flie'.[25] But in the divine scheme of the world's preservation
('a creation every moment'), Grace is not so much present as
omnipresent. Herbert would have agreed with the categorical
statement of one of his contemporaries that God 'giueth *Grace*
freely, conserueth *Grace* giuen, multiplieth *Grace* conserued,
and rewardeth *Grace* multiplied'.[26] But he would have added that
Grace is above all 'prevenient', anticipatory of man's behaviour by

virtue of Christ's presence in history. As much is attested by the
position of 'The Sacrifice' within *The Temple*, for its liturgical
stanzas 'prevent' (anticipate) the complaints to be heard in later
poems by placing them in advance of their articulation within the
context of Christ's Passion. To juxtapose 'The Sacrifice' and,
say, 'The Collar' (p. 161) is to realize how indirectly Herbert is
deploying his devastating irony. The convulsions in 'The Collar'
appear to refer solely to the agony of the individual speaker:

> Is the year only lost to me?
> Have I no bayes to crown it?

And:

> Have I no harvest but a thorn
> To let me bloud, and not restore
> What I have lost with cordiall fruit?

But the same language was already used by Christ in the vastly
different context of 'The Sacrifice':

> on my head a crown of thorns I wear ...

and especially:

> my blood [is] the onely way
> And cordiall left to repair mans decay ...

Christ's words in 'The Sacrifice' are significantly transferred to
the predicament of the individual sinner in the poem immediately
following 'The Thanksgiving' (p. 56), which also anticipates
(prevents) 'The Collar' in its deployment of words like store and
restore, thorns and flower, hand and blood. The principle is
articulated with characteristic clarity:

> Oh King of wounds! how shall I grieve for thee,
> Who in all grief preventest me?
> Shall I weep bloud? why, thou hast wept such store
> That all thy body was one doore.
> Shall I be scourged, flouted, boxed, sold?
> 'Tis but to tell the tale is told.
>
> ('The Thanksgiving', ll. 2–8)

Prevenient Grace in *The Temple* assumes numerous other forms
[cf. § 109]. Visually, it extends to the enactment of its dispensation
in 'Easter-wings' (p. 63); thematically, it embraces the recurrent
prayers that link verse to verse in a chain of pleas:

> O let thy graces without cease
> Drop from above! ..

> Lord, hunt me not ...

> O my God,
> My God, relieve me!

> Throw away thy rod . . .
>
> Lord restore thine image, heare my call . . .[27]

—'prevented' pleas all, answered by Grace even before they are voiced by man:

> Lord heare! *Shall he that made the eare,*
>   *Not heare?*
>   ('Longing', ll. 35–6)

The 'structure' of *The Temple* may be eucharistic, as claimed, but it is more generally charitological, centred on Grace—the invisible reality of which the Eucharist is the visible sign. Jointly central to Herbert's poetry, Grace and the Eucharist aver—to quote T. S. Eliot—'the absolute paternal care / That will not leave us, but prevents us everywhere'.[28]

Herbert's poetry celebrates the grace of Grace but is dominated by the love of Love. Crashaw who was not altogether unaware of the love that moves the sun and the other stars, rightly proclaimed of *The Temple*: 'Divinest love lyes in this booke'.[29] For Herbert, however, love was not the exuberant, inflammatory, even hysterical experience it proved for Crashaw. On the contrary love is a rationally apprehended obligation imposed by the very nature of love; for as St Paul had long since recognized, love 'constrains' (2 Corinthians 5.14)—or to use Herbert's significant word, it 'entices' ('Affliction I', l. 1), and more tellingly: it constitutes a 'crosse-bias' (*ibid.*, l. 53). While Donne thrived on contrary states, Herbert transcended them under the impact of irresistible love (e.g. 'The Crosse', last stanza, p. 170). 'I am he / On whom thy tempests fell all night', bears the unmistakable imprint of the self-centred elder poet; but Herbert wrote:

> O my onely light,
> It cannot be
> That I am he
> On whom thy tempests fell all night.
>   ('The Flower', ll. 38–42)

So, too, the numerous allusions in *The Temple* to history's *eschata* —'the four last things': death, judgement, heaven, hell—consistently avoid detailed references to 'the day of great vengeance' when Christ was traditionally expected to return 'in strength as a storme of haile, & as a whirlwinde breaking and throwing downe whatsoeuer standeth in his way, as a rage of many waters that flow and rush together. . . .'[30] Herbert composed merely two exclusively eschatological poems, 'Dooms-day' and 'Judgement', but they are alike arranged in low key as fourth and third from the end of the central division of *The Temple* (pp. 189–91). They are immediately followed by two parabolic visions, delivered as usual 'in a vulgar and illustrative way . . . as they may be understood': first a pointedly naïve glimpse of 'Heaven', and next the eucharistic banquet of 'Love III' we noted earlier:

> You must sit down, sayes Love, and taste my meat:
>   So I did sit and eat.
>   (above, p. 18)

Hell as the future abode of the damned, so thunderously present
in the consciousness of Herbert's contemporaries, is completely
bypassed in *The Temple*. The reality of its experience at any given
time is not denied; but in the end, Herbert suggests, Divine Love
overwhelms the terrors of history with mirth. The ultimate
realization is that 'All things are bigge with jest'.[31]

VI

For the modern reader the exclusively sacred burden of *The
Temple* is a serious stumbling-block. 'We hate poetry that has a
palpable design upon us' is a remark by Keats[32] not altogether
inapposite to Herbert's poetry. How is it possible to respond to
The Temple when its final aim is made so embarrassingly lucid in
the first stanza of 'The Church-porch'?

> A verse may finde him, who a sermon flies,
> And turn delight into a sacrifice.

It were relatively easy to dismiss the problem by reminding our-
selves that Herbert shares the widespread Renaissance assumption
that poetry teaches (as Milton wrote) 'the whole book of sanctity
and vertu through all the instances of example'.[33] Can an appeal
to traditional modes of thought allay our suspicions that Herbert's
poetry is less insistently propagandistic than it appears to be?

Hardly. On the other hand, what is the nature of Herbert's
'palpable design'? It is certainly explicit—militantly explicit—in
his Latin poetry, as in his vision of the Anglican Church under
James I:

>   See how
> The lovely Church outspreads its wings and sheds
> Its radiance as far as heaven. Far and wide
> The neighbour nations wonder, and, their minds adazzle,
> Want to learn a ritual in harmony with ours . . .
>   [*LPH*, p. 57]

Vestiges of such explicitness linger in both 'The Church-porch'
and 'The Church Militant'. But in so far as *The Temple* eschews
the declamatory for the dramatic, the impression is conveyed of
the presence in it of several voices and experiences so that the
reader finds himself—often to his surprise—at the very centre of
the given situation. Herbert's poetry, in other words, does indeed
have 'a palpable design upon us'; but it is a design woven aesthetic-
cally.

The presence in *The Temple* of several voices and experiences
can hardly be missed: the speakers range from Christ in 'The
Sacrifice' to a courtier in 'The Pearl', and from the narrator as
detached story-teller in 'The Pulley' to the narrator as participant

in 'The Collar'. The poems of *The Temple* could still be said to
emanate from a single if infinitely varied consciousness [cf. § 197],
yet they may not be regarded as so many ventures in autobio-
graphy. Composed at a time when dramatic literature had ex-
tended far beyond drama properly so called, they share with the
poems of Donne and Marvell and Milton a natural inclination to
dramatize in order to achieve an optimum of total range. Each
poem is an invitation to us sharply to differentiate between the
creating artist and the created artifact; for to be cognizant of the
total control that the poet exerted over his poetry is to appreciate
how far 'simplicity' conceals complexity, and apparent artlessness
the highest reaches of art. Herbert who had known 'such spiritual
Conflicts, as none can think, but only those that have endur'd
them', impresses not because he evinces those conflicts in his
poetry but because, all too often, he transcends them. The ex-
perience he had as man of 'the sicknesse that destroyeth at noone
day, (Ghostly pride and self-conceite)' [*FEH*, p. 238], could
not have been carried into his poetry unqualified; for that poetry
were else partial, incapable of displaying that controlled turbulence
which is among his foremost characteristics. Marvell who was to
share with Herbert a similar quality—turbulence so far controlled
in his case as to be subterranean!—discloses it both in 'Bermudas'
where nature's loveliness is qualified by the presence of huge
monsters within the roaring seas, and in 'To his Coy Mistress'
where a mere game is transformed into a nightmarish vision of
the passage of time.

I invoke Marvell when I might have invoked Donne. But we
have heard so much of Donne's decisive influence on Herbert—
and much more of 'the school of Donne' with its several obedient
students—that it may prove worthwhile to ascertain the individual
talent where earlier readers were content to seek the common
denominator. The generalization once confidently made that
Herbert is 'a metaphysical poet of the school of Donne with the
same undivided consciousness of his tribe' [§ 225], will no longer
serve; while the oracular pronouncement of T. S. Eliot that the
peculiar characteristic of the 'metaphysical' strain is 'a direct
apprehension of thought, or a recreation of thought into feeling',[34]
will mislead as often as it could enlighten. For how might either
claim apply to a poet whose self-effacement obliges us to discourse
rather in negative than in positive terms, much as he himself
does?

> My God, a verse is not a crown,
> No point of honour, or gay suit,
> No hawk, or banquet, or renown,
> Nor a good sword, nor yet a lute:
> ('The Quidditie', ll. 1-4)

A 'metaphysical' Herbert might have shared Donne's fondness for
cerebral pyrotechnics, Vaughan's pursuit of the single effect,

Crashaw's display of uninhibited explosiveness, and Traherne's indulgence in torrential lyricism. But he elected not to speak out loud and bold, aware that the range of experience incorporated in *The Temple* could best be attained by eschewing every given 'tribe'.

And the range was vital; for Herbert was much possessed with life.

[1] *Aubrey's Brief Lives*, ed. O. L. Dick, 3rd edn (1958), p. 137. Charles I with his usual perception thought it 'a very neate Curious Chappell' (C. Leslie Craig, *Nicholas Ferrar Junior* [1950], p. 50).

[2] *Sermons*, VIII, 89. Lady Danvers was the recipient of Donne's oequence of sonnets *La Corona*, together with their prefatory sonnet 'To Mrs Magdalen Herbert: of St Mary Magdalen'; see further the verse-letter 'To Mrs M. H.' ('Mad paper stay, and grudge not here to burn'). Her definitive portrait is provided by Walton [*IW*, pp. 263 ff.]; but see also Herbert's elegy in Latin and Greek, *Memoriae matris sacrum* [*LPH*, pp. 122–55], and for two accounts of her relationship with Donne: H. W. Garrod, 'Donne and Mrs Herbert', *RES*, XXI (1945), 161–73, and *The Elegies and the Songs and Sonnets*, ed. Helen Gardner (Oxford, 1965), pp. 251–8.

[3] *IW*, p. 273. Herbert addressed Latin poems to Andrewes [in *LPH*, pp. 4–5] and especially to Bacon [in *LPH*, pp. 166–73, as well as in Edmund Blunden's spirited translation in *E & S*, XIX (1933), 35–6].

[4] The statement, borrowed from Cicero's *De oratore* (II, xiii, 56), is quoted by Williamson [§ 123], p. 215, who also provides—on pp. 248–9—a context for the passage from *A Priest to the Temple* quoted above.

[5] *Sermons*, IV, 167. See also § 10.

[6] C. H. Dodd, *The Parables of the Kingdom* (1935), pp. 15–16.

[7] From John Ferrar's life of his brother Nicholas (quoted by Maycock, below, p. 224). The latter had given Herbert one of the 'short moral histories' entitled 'That God's Providence is unsearchable, from the Story of the Anchoret and the Angel' [*FP*, pp. 207–10].

[8] 'Simple as most of the parables seem to be, and easy to understand, when first read, there are many which are seen to be very difficult as soon as they are pondered over' (W. O. E. Oesterley, *The Gospel Parables in the Light of their Jewish Background* [1936], p. 13).

[9] 'Winding' describes in one poem the 'fashion / Of adoration' (p. 91, l. 27), yet in another is qualified as 'winding stair' (p. 75, l. 3) and in a third as 'winding sheets' (p. 112, l. 5). 'Twist' appears in one instance as 'a twist checker'd with night and day' (p. 130, l. 58), in another as 'twist a song / Pleasant and long' (p. 62, ll. 13–14), and in a third as 'with my yeares sorrow did twist and grow' (p. 66, l. 23). The sense of both words, moreover, is enacted in 'A Wreath' (p. 188).

[10] *David Teares* (1623), pp. 298–9. Hayward is better known as the author of the equally devotional *Sanctuarie of a Troubled Soule* (1604 ff.),

but also as an historian: his authoritative *Life and Raigne of King Edward the Sixt* (1630) was widely consulted, among others by Milton.

[11] Stephen J. Brown, *Image and Truth: Studies in the Imagery of the Bible* (Rome, 1955), p. 86. This is the most convenient summary of the metaphors in the Gospels and St Paul's epistles.

[12] Elnathan Parr, *The Grounds of Diuinitie*, 2nd edn (1615), p. 213. See also my studies of 'Milton and the Protestant Theory of the Atonement', *PMLA*, LXXIV (1959), 7–13, and *Milton and the Christian Tradition* (Oxford, 1966), Ch. V (iii). To be unaware of the traditional basis of Herbert's language is to misunderstand it totally [e.g. § 182], or ascribe it primarily to one theologian only [§ 133].

[13] *Sermons*, VII, 302–3. The Biblical quotations are, *seriatim:* Hebrews 3.6, Psalms 147.2, John 14.6, and Matthew 7.13.

[14] *Elizabethan Critical Essays*, ed. G. Gregory Smith (Oxford, 1904), II, 3. The etymology is also remarked by Sir Philip Sidney in *An Apologie for Poetrie*.

[15] Polydore Vergil, *An abridgemēt of the notable worke . . . conteygnyng the deuisers . . . of Artes, Ministeries* etc., abridged by Thomas Langley (1546), fol. 17–17v.

[16] Translated by Rudolf Wittkower, *Architectural Principles in the Age of Humanism*, 2nd edn (1952), p. 136.

[17] *Sermons*, II, 221. One of Herbert's Latin poems suggests the broad circumference of 'temple' by asserting its transformation by Christ into a world: 'non urbem . . . sed Orbem' [*LPH*, pp. 76–7]. For Milton's use of 'temple' see William B. Riggs, *The Christian Poet in 'Paradise Lost'* (Berkeley, 1972), pp. 42 ff., 164 ff.

[18] Cf. Peter Sterry: 'Learned men and Divines teach us; that the Preservation of the world is *continuata Creatio*, a continued Creation. In every moment of Time from the Beginning of the world to the end, the Divine Act of Preserving . . . is entirely the same with the Act of Creation' (*The Kingdom of God in the Soul of Man* [1683], pp. 409–10).

[19] Sylvester Norris, *An Antidote or Treatise of Thirty Controversies* (1622), p. 67; quoted by C. W. Dugmore, *Eucharistic Doctrine in England* (1942), pp. 28–9.

[20] William Forbes, in a treatise published posthumously in 1658 [in § 84, p. 471]. On the developing interpretations of the Lord's Supper, see the magisterial survey by Darwell Stone, *A History of the Doctrine of the Holy Eucharist* (1909), 2 vols, which discusses views current since the Reformation in Ch. IX et seq. See further below, p. 216.

[21] From his 'Brief Notes' on *The Hundred and Ten Considerations* of Juán de Valdés (Italian version, 1550; English translation by Nicholas Ferrar, 1638) [*FEH*, p. 308]. The Puritan in question was Andrew Melville; the tirade: *Musae responsoriae* [in *LPH*, pp. 2–61].

[22] Thus Bishop Overall and Archbishop Ussher, respectively; in Dugmore (as above, Note 19), pp. 40 and 54.

[23] From Edward Reynolds's definition of sacraments (1638), [in § 84, p. 411].

[24] I quote from the great Anglican apologist Richard Hooker [in § 84, p. 407]; but the phrase is a commonplace of Protestant theology.

25 Below, p. 34, l. 54; p. 114, l. 2; p. 122, l. 64; p. 84, l. 2; p. 116, l. 76; p. 118, l. 22; and p. 153, l. 8.

26 Daniel Price, *The Creation of the Prince* (1610), sig. C4ᵛ.

27 Below, p. 78, ll. 3–4; p. 105, l. 2; p. 99, ll. 29–30; p. 183, l. 1; and p. 59, l. 12.

28 'East Coker', ll. 160–1.

29 'On Mr G. Herberts books intituled The Temple', l. 2; in *Steps to the Temple* (1646).

30 George Hakewill, *An Apologie* (Oxford, 1627), p. 458.

31 'The Church-porch', ll. 239–40; see Sterne's use of these lines, quoted below, p. 39. Herbert often expounds the redemption of man in terms of 'mirth' (e.g. p. 125, l. 4; p. 93, l. 57), eliciting a response in kind (e.g. p. 127, ll. 3–4).

32 In a letter to John Hamilton Reynolds, 3 February 1818.

33 *The Reason of Church-Government* (1642), in *Milton: Selected Prose*, ed. C. A. Patrides (Penguin Books, 1974), p. 57.

34 From 'The Metaphysical Poets' (1921). Cf. Eliot's later statement: 'in Donne thought seems in control of feeling, and in Herbert feeling seems in control of thought' [§ 155].

A Note on Typology

Herbert's use of typology is so extensive that a general understanding of its nature and aims is advisable.

Typology is concerned with those events and persons in the Old Testament which are said to have foreshadowed the entry of Christ into history. The New Testament provides several examples of such 'types' or prefigurations. A 'typical' event is the sojourn of Jonah in the whale's belly, interpreted by Christ himself as anticipatory of his Resurrection (Matthew 12.40); and a 'typical' person is Melchizedek, who in his capacity both as 'priest of the most high God' and as 'King of Salem, which is, King of Peace', was understood to have been 'made like unto the Son of God' (Hebrews 7.1 ff.). In another instance three events were conflated—the Israelites' crossing of the Red Sea, the provision of the manna, and the rock cleft by Moses to yield water—in order to suggest the following:

> I would not that ye should be ignorant, how that all our fathers were under the cloud, and all passed through the sea; and were all baptized unto Moses in the cloud and in the sea; and did all eat the same spiritual meat; and did all drink the same spiritual drink: for they drank of that spiritual Rock that followed them: and that Rock was Christ.
>
> (1 Corinthians 10.1 ff.)

The typological implications for the sacraments of baptism and the Eucharist are obvious. Even so, however, they were greatly elaborated by later theologians, who *inter alia* also related Melchizedek to the Eucharist in that he had offered Abraham bread and wine (Genesis 14.18). By Herbert's time, such relationships were accepted as a matter of course.

It is hardly necessary to insist that typology is firmly grounded on the 'evidence' of history. So grounded, its purpose is threefold: to confirm that historical events are non-recurring and irreversible; to assert that they imply the existence of a providential design according to which the created order advances onward; and to demonstrate that they are meaningful only in so far as they are seen to relate to the advent of Christ. 'The *Old Testament*', it was summarily observed in 1640, 'contains him in the Hieroglyphicks of Sacrifices, and Types, and Ceremonies; the *New*, in legible and ordinary characters'.[2]

[1] *Practique Theories* (1629), p. 23.

[2] John Stoughton, *XI. Choice Sermons* (1640), II, 65. See the expositions by G. W. H. Lampe and K. J. Woollcombe, *Essays on Typology* (1957); A. G. Hebert, *The Throne of David* (1941); M. D. Goulder, *Type and History in Acts* (1964); Jean Daniélou, *From Shadows to Reality: Studies in the Biblical Typology of the Fathers*, trans. W. Hibberd (1960); Alan Charity, *Events and their After-Life: The Dialectics of Christian Typology in the Bible and Dante* (Cambridge, 1966); F. Michael Krouse, *Milton's Samson and the Christian Tradition* (Princeton, 1949); Helen Gardner, *The Limits of Criticism* (1956), Ch. III; *et al.*—as well as Patrides [§ 91] and Tuve [§ 219].

The Printers to the Reader[1]

The dedication of this work having been made by the Authour
to the *Divine Majestie* onely, how should we now presume to
interest any mortall man in the patronage of it? Much lesse think
we it meet to seek the recommendation of the Muses, for that
which himself was confident to have been inspired by a diviner
breath then flows from *Helicon*.[2] The world therefore shall receive
it in that naked simplicitie, with which he left it, without any
addition either of support or ornament, more than is included in
it self. We leave it free and unforestalled to every mans judgement,
and to the benefit that he shall finde by perusall. Onely for the
clearing of some passages, we have thought it not unfit to make
the common Reader privie to some few particularities of the con-
dition and disposition of the Person;

Being nobly born, and as eminently endued with gifts of the
minde, and having by industrie and happy education perfected
them to that great height of excellencie, whereof his fellowship of
Trinitie Colledge in Cambridge, and his Orator-ship in the Uni-
versitie, together with that knowledge which the Kings Court
had taken of him, could make relation farre above ordinarie.
Quitting both his deserts and all the opportunities that he had
for worldly preferment, he betook himself to the Sanctuarie and
Temple of God, choosing rather to serve at Gods Altar, then to
seek the honour of State-employments. As for those inward
enforcements to this course (for outward there was none) which
many of these ensuing verses bear witness of, they detract not

[1] The prefatory address is by Nicholas Ferrar, the leader of the com-
munity at Little Gidding, and Herbert's devoted friend ('their very
souls cleaved together most intimately' [*BO*]). According to Walton,
Herbert just before his death asked Arthur Woodnoth to deliver the
manuscript of *The Temple* to Ferrar:

> tell him, he shall find in it a picture of the many spiritual Con-
> flicts that have past betwixt God and my Soul, before I could
> subject mine to the will of *Jesus my Master*: in whose service I
> have now found perfect freedom; desire him to read it: and then,
> if he can think it may turn to the advantage of any dejected poor
> Soul, let it be made publick: if not, let him burn it: for *I and it,
> are less than the least of God's mercies* [*IW*, p. 314; cf. *FP*, p. 59].

[2] No less ambitious to christianize poetry, Milton would later also im-
plore the Holy Spirit to sustain his efforts to soar above the sacred
hill of the Greek Muses (*Paradise Lost*, I, 14–15).

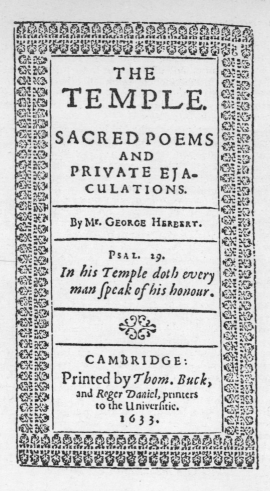

THE
TEMPLE.
SACRED POEMS
AND
PRIVATE EJA-
CULATIONS.

By Mr. GEORGE HERBERT.

PSAL. 29.

In his Temple doth every man speak of his honour.

CAMBRIDGE:
Printed by *Thom. Buck,*
and *Roger Daniel,* printers
to the Universitie.
1633.

from the freedome, but adde to the honour of this resolution in him. As God had enabled him, so he accounted him meet not onely to be called, but to be compelled to this service: Wherein his faithfull discharge was such, as may make him justly a companion to the primitive Saints, and a pattern or more for the age he lived in.

To testifie his independencie upon all others, and to quicken his diligence in this kinde, he used in his ordinarie speech, when he made mention of the blessed name of our Lord and Saviour Jesus Christ, to adde, *My Master*.

Next God, he loved that which God himself hath magnified above all things, that is, his Word:[3] so as he hath been heard to make solemne protestation, that he would not part with one leaf thereof for the whole world, if it were offered him in exchange.

His obedience and conformitie to the Church and the discipline thereof was singularly remarkable. Though he abounded in private devotions, yet went he every morning and evening with his familie to the Church; and by his example, exhortations, and encouragements drew the greater part of his parishioners to accompanie him dayly in the publick celebration of Divine Service.

As for worldly matters, his love and esteem to them was so little, as no man can more ambitiously seek, then he did earnestly endeavour the resignation of an Ecclesiasticall dignitie, which he was possessour of.[4] But God permitted not the accomplishment of this desire, having ordained him his instrument for reedifying of the Church belonging thereunto, that had layen ruinated almost twenty yeares. The reparation whereof, having been uneffectually attempted by publick collections, was in the end by his own and some few others private free-will-offerings successfully effected. With the remembrance whereof, as of an especiall good work, when a friend[5] went about to comfort him on his death-bed, he made answer, *It is a good work, if it be sprinkled with the bloud of Christ:* otherwise then in this respect he could finde nothing to glorie or comfort himself with, neither in this, nor in any other thing.

And these are but a few of many that might be said, which we have chosen to premise as a glance to some parts of the ensuing book, and for an example to the Reader. We conclude all with his own Motto, with which he used to conclude all things that might seem to tend any way to his own honour;

Lesse then the least of Gods mercies.[6]

[3] i.e. the Scriptures.
[4] Herbert had wanted to transfer his benefice at Leighton Bromswold in Huntingdonshire to Ferrar.
[5] Arthur Woodnoth (see above, note 1).
[6] The phrase—the refrain of 'The Posie' (below, p. 186)—derives from the words of Jacob after he had wrestled with God and been re-named Israel: 'I am not worthy of the least of all the mercies ... which thou hast shewed unto thy servant; for with my staff I passed over this Jordan' (Genesis 32.10 [§ 219, p. 196]). The motto was also adopted at Little Gidding [*FP*, p. 178].

The Dedication

Lord, my first fruits present themselves to thee;
Yet not mine neither: for from thee they came,
And must return. Accept of them and me,
And make us strive, who shall sing best thy name.
  Turn their eyes hither, who shall make a gain:
  Theirs, who shall hurt themselves or me, refrain.

The Church-porch

Perirrhanterium

Thou, whose sweet youth and early hopes inhance
Thy rate and price, and mark thee for a treasure;
Hearken unto a Verser, who may chance
Ryme thee to good, and make a bait of pleasure.
    A verse may finde him, who a sermon flies,   5
    And turn delight into a sacrifice.

Beware of lust: it doth pollute and foul
Whom God in Baptisme washt with his own blood.
It blots thy lesson written in thy soul;
The holy lines cannot be understood.   10
    How dare those eyes upon a Bible look,
    Much lesse towards God, whose lust is all their book?

Abstain wholly, or wed. Thy bounteous Lord
Allows thee choise of paths: take no by-wayes;
But gladly welcome what he doth afford;   15
Not grudging, that thy lust hath bounds and staies.
    Continence hath his joy: weigh both; and so
    If rottennesse have more, let Heaven go.

If God had laid all common, certainly
Man would have been th' incloser: but since now   20
God hath impal'd us, on the contrarie
Man breaks the fence, and every ground will plough.
    O what were man, might he himself misplace!
    Sure to be crosse he would shift feet and face.

Perirrhanterium: the instrument for sprinkling holy water prior to entry
    into the church proper. (In *W* the word appears atop the first of
    the two quatrains on p. 46). For the revisions to the text, consult
    FEH, pp. 6 ff.
  5. *verse* (also *rhyme*): 'persistent metaphors for divine Creation, for
    bringing order from chaos' [§ 148].
21. *impal'd us:* fenced us in. Cf. 'God do hedge us in' (450), i.e. in that
    his love 'constrains' (above, p. 20).
24. *crosse:* contrarious, perverse; but the word is always used by Her-
    bert with retroactive irony in so far as it 'prevents' (anticipates)
    its transformation by the Cross. See below, p. 171, ll. 32 ff.

Drink not the third glasse, which thou canst not tame,   25
When once it is within thee; but before
Mayst rule it, as thou list; and poure the shame,
Which it would pour on thee, upon the floore.
   It is most just to throw that on the ground,
   Which would throw me there, if I keep the round.   30

He that is drunken, may his mother kill
Bigge with his sister: he hath lost the reins,
Is outlawd by himself: all kinde of ill
Did with his liquour slide into his veins.
   The drunkard forfets Man, and doth devest   35
   All worldly right, save what he hath by beast.

Shall I, to please anothers wine-sprung minde,
Lose all mine own? God hath giv'n me a measure
Short of his canne, and bodie; must I finde
A pain in that, wherein he findes a pleasure?   40
   Stay at the third glasse: if thou lose thy hold,
   Then thou art modest, and the wine grows bold.

If reason move not Gallants, quit the room,
(All in a shipwrack shift their severall way)
Let not a common ruine thee intombe: 45
Be not a beast in courtesie; but stay,
   Stay at the third cup, or forgo the place.
   Wine above all things doth Gods stamp deface.

Yet, if thou sinne in wine or wantonnesse,
Boast not thereof; nor make thy shame thy glorie.   50
Frailtie gets pardon by submissivenesse;
But he that boasts, shuts that out of his storie.
   He makes flat warre with God, and doth defie
   With his poore clod of earth the spacious sky.

Take not his name, who made thy mouth, in vain: 55
It gets thee nothing, and hath no excuse.
Lust and wine plead a pleasure, avarice gain:
But the cheap swearer through his open sluce

---

30. *keep the round:* refill each time the bottle is passed.
35. *devest:* annul (in the legal sense).
43. *Gallants:* also a nautical term [§ 188], linking with the metaphor
    in the next line. Cf. 120.
50. Philippians 3.19: 'whose God is their belly, and whose glory is in
    their shame'.
53-4. Isaiah 45.9: 'Woe unto him that striveth with his Maker! . . .
    Shall the clay say to him that fashioned it, What makest thou?'

Lets his soul runne for nought, as little fearing.
Were I an *Epicure*, I could bate swearing.   60

When thou dost tell anothers jest, therein
Omit the oathes, which true wit cannot need:
Pick out of tales the mirth, but not the sinne.
He pares his apple, that will cleanly feed.
    Play not away the vertue of that name,   65
    Which is thy best stake, when griefs make thee tame.

The cheapest sinnes most dearely punisht are;
Because to shun them also is so cheap:
For we have wit to mark them, and to spare.
O crumble not away thy souls fair heap.   70
    If thou wilt die, the gates of hell are broad:
    Pride and full sinnes have made the way a road.

Lie not; but let thy heart be true to God,
Thy mouth to it, thy actions to them both:
Cowards tell lies, and those that fear the rod;   75
The stormie working soul spits lies and froth.
    Dare to be true. Nothing can need a ly:
    A fault, which needs it most, grows two thereby.

Flie idlenesse, which yet thou canst not flie
By dressing, mistressing, and complement.   80
If those take up thy day, the sunne will crie
Against thee: for his light was onely lent.
    God gave thy soul brave wings; put not those feathers
    Into a bed, to sleep out all ill weathers.

Art thou a Magistrate? then be severe: 85
If studious; copie fair, what time hath blurr'd;
Redeem truth from his jawes: if souldier,
Chase brave employments with a naked sword
    Throughout the world. Fool not: for all may have,
    If they dare try, a glorious life, or grave.   90

O England! full of sinne, but most of sloth;
Spit out thy flegme, and fill thy brest with glorie:
Thy Gentrie bleats, as if thy native cloth
Transfus'd a sheepishnesse into thy storie:
    Not that they all are so; but that the most   95
    Are gone to grasse, and in the pasture lost.

60. *bate:* omit (cf. 62).
66. *stake:* in the gaming sense, thereby continuing the metaphor intro-
    duced with 'Play' (65). Cf. 193-4, 227, etc.
91. *sloth:* idleness is said in *A Priest to the Temple* to be 'the great and
    nationall sin' (Ch. 32).

This losse springs chiefly from our education.
Some till their ground, but let weeds choke their sonne:
Some mark a partridge, never their childes fashion:
Some ship them over, and the thing is done.   100
    Studie this art, make it thy great designe;
    And if Gods image move thee not, let thine.

Some great estates provide, but doe not breed
A mast'ring minde; so both are lost thereby:
Or els they breed them tender, make them need   105
All that they leave: this is flat povertie.
    For he, that needs five thousand pound to live,
    Is full as poore as he, that needs but five.

The way to make thy sonne rich, is to fill
His minde with rest, before his trunk with riches: 110
For wealth without contentment, climbes a hill
To feel those tempests, which fly over ditches.
    But if thy sonne can make ten pound his measure,
    Then all thou addest may be call'd his treasure.

When thou dost purpose ought, (within thy power)   115
Be sure to doe it, though it be but small:
Constancie knits the bones, and makes us stowre,
When wanton pleasures becken us to thrall.
    Who breaks his own bond, forfeiteth himself:
    What nature made a ship, he makes a shelf.   120

Doe all things like a man, not sneakingly:
Think the king sees thee still; for his King does.
Simpring is but a lay-hypocrisie:
Give it a corner, and the clue undoes.
    Who fears to do ill, sets himself to task: 125
    Who fears to do well, sure should wear a mask.

Look to thy mouth; diseases enter there.
Thou hast two sconses, if thy stomack call;
Carve, or discourse; do not a famine fear.

---

98. *sonne:* the omnipresent pun on son/sun—inevitably directing us
    toward the Son—is well-attested (see below, *The Sonne*, p. 173, ll.
    5–6; also above, p. 12). It is emphasized in the title of Vaughan's
    'Son-dayes'.
100. *over:* abroad.
117. *stowre:* sturdy.
118. *thrall:* i.e. thraldom; cf. 'bond' (119).
120. *shelf:* reef, often the cause of shipwrecks (cf. 44).
124. *clue:* ball of thread.
128. *sconses:* forts, i.e. defences.

Who carves, is kind to two; who talks, to all.   130
  Look on meat, think it dirt, then eat a bit;
  And say withall, Earth to earth I commit.

Slight those who say amidst their sickly healths,
Thou liv'st by rule. What doth not so, but man?
Houses are built by rule, and common-wealths.   135
Entice the trusty sunne, if that you can,
  From his Ecliptick line: becken the skie.
  Who lives by rule then, keeps good companie.

Who keeps no guard upon himself, is slack,
And rots to nothing at the next great thaw.   140
Man is a shop of rules, a well truss'd pack,
Whose every parcell under-writes a law.
  Lose not thy self, nor give thy humours way:
  God gave them to thee under lock and key.

By all means use sometimes to be alone.   145
Salute thy self: see what thy soul doth wear.
Dare to look in thy chest; for 'tis thine own:
And tumble up and down what thou find'st there.
  Who cannot rest till hee good fellows finde,
  He breaks up house, turns out of doores his minde.   150

Be thriftie, but not covetous: therefore give
Thy need, thine honour, and thy friend his due.
Never was scraper brave man. Get to live;
Then live, and use it: els, it is not true
  That thou hast gotten. Surely use alone   155
  Makes money not a contemptible stone.

Never exceed thy income. Youth may make
Ev'n with the yeare: but age, if it will hit,
Shoots a bow short, and lessens still his stake,
As the day lessens, and his life with it.   160
  Thy children, kindred, friends upon thee call;
  Before thy journey fairly part with all.

Yet in thy thriving still misdoubt some evil;
Lest gaining gain on thee, and make thee dimme
To all things els. Wealth is the conjurers devil;   165
Whom when he thinks he hath, the devil hath him.
  Gold thou mayst safely touch; but if it stick
  Unto thy hands, it woundeth to the quick.

132. A phrase from the Burial Service.
137. *Ecliptick*: the apparent orbit of the sun [*OED*].
142. *under-writes*: confirms.

What skills it, if a bag of stones or gold
About thy neck do drown thee? raise thy head;   170
Take starres for money; starres not to be told
By any art, yet to be purchased.
   None is so wastefull as the scraping dame.
   She loseth three for one; her soul, rest, fame.

By no means runne in debt: take thine own measure.   175
Who cannot live on twentie pound a year,
Cannot on fourtie: he's a man of pleasure,
A kind of thing that's for it self too deere.
   The curious unthrift makes his cloth too wide,
   And spares himself, but would his taylor chide.   180

Spend not on hopes. They that by pleading clothes
Do fortunes seek, when worth and service fail,
Would have their tale beleeved for their oathes,
And are like empty vessels under sail.
   Old courtiers know this; therefore set out so,   185
   As all the day thou mayst hold out to go.

In clothes, cheap handsomnesse doth bear the bell.
Wisedome's a trimmer thing, then shop e're gave.
Say not then, This with that lace will do well;
But, This with my discretion will be brave.   190
   Much curiousnesse is a perpetuall wooing
   Nothing with labour; folly long a doing.

Play not for gain, but sport. Who playes for more,
Then he can lose with pleasure, stakes his heart;
Perhaps his wives too, and whom she hath bore: 195
Servants and churches also play their part.
   Onely a herauld, who that way doth passe,
   Findes his crackt name at length in the church-glasse.

If yet thou love game at so deere a rate,
Learn this, that hath old gamesters deerely cost: 200
Dost lose? rise up: dost winne? rise in that state.
Who strive to sit out losing hands, are lost.
   Game is a civil gunpowder, in peace
   Blowing up houses with their whole increase.

171. *Take starres:* 'provide yourselves bags which wax not old, a
    treasure in the heavens that faileth not' (Luke 12.33).
187. *doth bear the bell:* takes first place.
190. *brave:* handsome.
198. *crackt:* bankrupt [§ 243]; also, damaged [§ 188].

In conversation boldnesse now bears sway.   205
But know, that nothing can so foolish be,
As empty boldnesse: therefore first assay
To stuffe thy minde with solid braverie;
   Then march on gallant: get substantiall worth.
   Boldnesse guilds finely, and will set it forth.   210

Be sweet to all. Is thy complexion sowre?
Then keep such companie; make them thy allay:
Get a sharp wife, a servant that will lowre.
A stumbler stumbles least in rugged way.
   Command thy self in chief. He lifes warre knows,   215
   Whom all his passions follow, as he goes.

Catch not at quarrels. He that dares not speak
Plainly and home, is coward of the two.
Think not thy fame at ev'ry twitch will break:
By great deeds shew, that thou canst little do;   220
   And do them not: that shall thy wisdome be;
   And change thy temperance into braverie.

If that thy fame with ev'ry toy be pos'd,
'Tis a thinne webbe, which poysonous fancies make:
But the great souldiers honour was compos'd   225
Of thicker stuffe, which would endure a shake.
   Wisdome picks friends; civilitie playes the rest.
   A toy shunn'd cleanly passeth with the hoat.

Laugh not too much: the wittie man laughs least:
For wit is newes onely to ignorance.   230
Lesse at thine own things laugh; lest in the jest
Thy person share, and the conceit advance.
   Make not thy sport, abuses: for the fly
   That feeds on dung, is coloured thereby.

Pick out of mirth, like stones out of thy ground,   235
Profanenesse, filthinesse, abusivenesse.
These are the scumme, with which course wits abound:
The fine may spare these well, yet not go lesse.
   All things are bigge with jest: nothing that's plain,
   But may be wittie, if thou hast the vein.   240

212. *allay:* i.e. alloy.
218. *home:* used adverbially.
239-40. These lines were borrowed by Sterne in *Tristram Shandy*:
   'Everything in this world, said my father, is big with jest,—and
   has wit in it, and instruction too,—if we can but find it out' (Bk.
   V, Ch. 32 [noted in § 333]).

Wit's an unruly engine, wildly striking
Sometimes a friend, sometimes the engineer.
Hast thou the knack? pamper it not with liking:
But if thou want it, buy it not too deere.
    Many affecting wit beyond their power,   245
    Have got to be a deare fool for an houre.

A sad wise valour is the brave complexion,
That leads the van, and swallows up the cities.
The gigler is a milk-maid, whom infection,
Or a fir'd beacon frighteth from his ditties.   250
    Then he's the sport: the mirth then in him rests,
    And the sad man is cock of all his jests.

Towards great persons use respective boldnesse:
That temper gives them theirs, and yet doth take
Nothing from thine: in service, care, or coldnesse   255
Doth ratably thy fortunes marre or make.
    Feed no man in his sinnes: for adulation
    Doth make thee parcell-devil in damnation.

Envie not greatnesse: for thou mak'st thereby
Thy self the worse, and so the distance greater.   260
Be not thine own worm: yet such jealousie,
As hurts not others, but may make thee better,
    Is a good spurre. Correct thy passions spite;
    Then may the beasts draw thee to happy light.

When basenesse is exalted, do not bate   265
The place its honour, for the persons sake.
The shrine is that which thou dost venerate;
And not the beast, that bears it on his back.
    I care not though the cloth of state should be
    Not of rich arras, but mean tapestrie.   270

Thy friend put in thy bosome: wear his eies
Still in thy heart, that he may see what's there.
If cause require, thou art his sacrifice;
Thy drops of bloud must pay down all his fear:
    But love is lost; the way of friendship's gone,   275
    Though *David* had his *Jonathan*, *Christ* his *John*.

244. *want:* lack.
247. *sad:* steadfast.
253. *respective:* respectful (*W*).
256. *ratably:* proportionately.
258. *parcell-devil:* part-devil.

264. *beasts:* i.e. the passions.
267-8. In a fable by Aesop, an ass
      carrying an image assumed that
      the reverence of the bystanders
      was paid to himself [*FEH*].

Yet be not surety, if thou be a father.
Love is a personall debt. I cannot give
My childrens right, nor ought he take it: rather
Both friends should die, then hinder them to live.   280
    Fathers first enter bonds to natures ends;
    And are her sureties, ere they are a friends.

If thou be single, all thy goods and ground
Submit to love; but yet not more then all.
Give one estate, as one life. None is bound   285
To work for two, who brought himself to thrall.
    God made me one man; love makes me no more,
    Till labour come, and make my weaknesse score.

In thy discourse, if thou desire to please:
All such is courteous, usefull, new, or wittic.   290
Usefulnesse comes by labour, wit by ease;
Courtesie grows in court; news in the citie.
    Get a good stock of these, then draw the card;
    That suites him best, of whom thy speech is heard.

Entice all neatly to what they know best;   295
For so thou dost thy self and him a pleasure:
(But a proud ignorance will lose his rest,
Rather then shew his cards) steal from his treasure
    What to ask further. Doubts well rais'd do lock
    The speaker to thee, and preserve thy stock.   300

If thou be Master-gunner, spend not all
That thou canst speak, at once; but husband it,
And give men turns of speech: do not forestall
By lavishnesse thine own, and others wit,
    As if thou mad'st thy will. A civil guest   305
    Will no more talk all, then eat all the feast.

Be calm in arguing: for fiercenesse makes
Errour a fault, and truth discourtesie.
Why should I feel another mans mistakes
More, then his sicknesses or povertie?   310
    In love I should: but anger is not love,
    Nor wisdome neither: therefore gently move.

297. *rest:* in the card game of primero, the stakes kept in reserve [*OED*].
    Cf. 227.

Calmnesse is great advantage: he that lets
Another chafe, may warm him at his fire:
Mark all his wandrings, and enjoy his frets;   315
As cunning fencers suffer heat to tire.
  Truth dwels not in the clouds: the bow that's there,
  Doth often aim at, never hit the sphere.

Mark what another sayes: for many are
Full of themselves, and answer their own notion.   320
Take all into thee; then with equall care
Ballance each dramme of reason, like a potion.
  If truth be with thy friend, be with them both:
  Share in the conquest, and confesse a troth.

Be usefull where thou livest, that they may   325
Both want, and wish thy pleasing presence still.
Kindnesse, good parts, great places are the way
To compasse this. Finde out mens wants and will,
  And meet them there. All worldly joyes go lesse
  To the one joy of doing kindnesses.   330

Pitch thy behaviour low, thy projects high;
So shalt thou humble and magnanimous be:
Sink not in spirit: who aimeth at the sky,
Shoots higher much then he that means a tree.
  A grain of glorie mixt with humblenesse   335
  Cures both a fever and lethargicknesse.

Let thy minde still be bent, still plotting where,
And when, and how the businesse may be done.
Slacknesse breeds worms; but the sure traveller,
Though he alight sometimes, still goeth on.   340
  Active and stirring spirits live alone.
  Write on the others, Here lies such a one.

Slight not the smallest losse, whether it be
In love or honour: take account of all;
Shine like the sunne in every corner: see   345
Whether thy stock of credit swell, or fall.
  Who say, I care not, those I give for lost;
  And to instruct them, 'twill not quit the cost.

Scorn no mans love, though of a mean degree;
(Love is a present for a mightie king)   350
Much lesse make any one thy enemie.

317. *bow:* rainbow.
339. 'Want of exercise was thought to breed worms' [*LS*].

As gunnes destroy, so may a little sling.
  The cunning workman never doth refuse
  The meanest tool, that he may chance to use.

All forrain wisdome doth amount to this,   355
To take all that is given; whether wealth,
Or love, or language; nothing comes amisse:
A good digestion turneth all to health:
  And then as farre as fair behaviour may,
  Strike off all scores; none are so cleare as they.   360

Keep all thy native good, and naturalize
All forrain of that name; but scorn their ill:
Embrace their activenesse, not vanities.
Who follows all things, forfeiteth his will.
  If thou observest strangers in each fit,   365
  In time they'l runne thee out of all thy wit.

Affect in things about thee cleanlinesse,
That all may gladly board thee, as a flowre.
Slovens take up their stock of noisomnesse
Beforehand, and anticipate their last houre.   370
  Let thy mindes sweetnesse have his operation
  Upon thy body, clothes, and habitation.

In Almes regard thy means, and others merit.
Think heav'n a better bargain, then to give
Onely thy single market-money for it.   375
Joyn hands with God to make a man to live.
  Give to all something; to a good poore man,
  Till thou change names, and be where he began.

Man is Gods image; but a poore man is
Christs stamp to boot: both images regard.   380
God reckons for him, counts the favour his:
Write, So much giv'n to God; thou shalt be heard.
  Let thy almes go before, and keep heav'ns gate
  Open for thee; or both may come too late.

352. *a little sling:* i.e. like David's.
367-8. The original version in *W*, mercifully eliminated, reads: 'Leave
     not thine owne deere-cuntry-cleanlines / ffor this ffrench slut-
     tery . . .'!
368. *board:* approach.
369. *Slovens:* knaves.
383. Acts 10.4: 'thine alms are come up as a memorial before God'.

Restore to God his due in tithe and time: 385
A tithe purloin'd cankers the whole estate.
Sundaies observe: think when the bells do chime,
'Tis angels musick; therefore come not late.
　　God then deals blessings: If a king did so,
　　Who would not haste, nay give, to see the show?   390

Twice on the day his due is understood;
For all the week thy food so oft he gave thee.
Thy cheere is mended; bate not of the food,
Because 'tis better, and perhaps may save thee.
　　Thwart not th' Almighty God: O be not crosse.   395
　　Fast when thou wilt; but then 'tis gain, not losse.

Though private prayer be a brave designe,
Yet publick hath more promises, more love:
And love's a weight to hearts, to eies a signe.
We all are but cold suitours; let us move   400
　　Where it is warmest. Leave thy six and seven;
　　Pray with the most: for where most pray, is heaven.

When once thy foot enters the church, be bare.
God is more there, then thou: for thou art there
Onely by his permission. Then beware,   405
And make thy self all reverence and fear.
　　Kneeling ne're spoil'd silk stocking: quit thy state.
　　All equall are within the churches gate.

Resort to sermons, but to prayers most:
Praying 's the end of preaching. O be drest;   410
Stay not for th' other pin: why thou hast lost
A joy for it worth worlds. Thus hell doth jest
　　Away thy blessings, and extremely flout thee,
　　Thy clothes being fast, but thy soul loose about thee.

In time of service seal up both thine eies,   415
And send them to thine heart; that spying sinne,
They may weep out the stains by them did rise:
Those doores being shut, all by the eare comes in.
　　Who marks in church-time others symmetrie,
　　Makes all their beautie his deformitie.   420

391.　*Twice on the* [Sun]*day:* i.e. at morning and evening prayers.
401.　*six and seven:* in the gaming sense of hazarding one's fortune
　　　[*OED*].
403.　*bare:* bare-headed.
415.　*seal:* also in the sense of 'sewing up a hawk's eyelids' (a term in
　　　falconry: *FEH*)?

Let vain or busie thoughts have there no part:
Bring not thy plough, thy plots, thy pleasures thither.
Christ purg'd his temple; so must thou thy heart.
All worldly thoughts are but theeves met together
   To couzin thee. Look to thy actions well: 425
   For churches are either our heav'n or hell.

Judge not the preacher; for he is thy Judge:
If thou mislike him, thou conceiv'st him not.
God calleth preaching folly. Do not grudge
To pick out treasures from an earthen pot.   430
   The worst speak something good: if all want sense,
   God takes a text, and preacheth patience.

He that gets patience, and the blessing which
Preachers conclude with, hath not lost his pains.
He that by being at church escapes the ditch,   435
Which he might fall in by companions, gains.
   He that loves Gods abode, and to combine
   With saints on earth, shall one day with them shine.

Jest not at preachers language, or expression:
How know'st thou, but thy sinnes made him miscarrie?
Then turn thy faults and his into confession: 440
God sent him, whatsoe're he be: O tarry,
   And love him for his Master: his condition,
   Though it be ill, makes him no ill Physician.

None shall in hell such bitter pangs endure,   445
As those, who mock at Gods way of salvation.
Whom oil and balsames kill, what salve can cure?
They drink with greedinesse a full damnation.
   The Jews refused thunder; and we, folly.
   Though God do hedge us in, yet who is holy?   450

Summe up at night, what thou hast done by day;
And in the morning, what thou hast to do.
Dresse and undresse thy soul: mark the decay
And growth of it: if with thy watch, that too
   Be down, then winde up both; since we shall be   455
   Most surely judg'd, make thy accounts agree.

---

423. *purg'd his temple*: i.e. of thieves, as related in Mark 11.15 ff.
429. 1 Corinthians 1.21: 'after that in the wisdom of God the world by wisdom knew not God, it pleased God by the foolishness of preaching to save them that believe'.
430. 2 Corinthians 4.7: 'we have this treasure [the knowledge of God in Christ] in earthen vessels, that the excellency of the power may be of God, and not of us'.
449. *thunder*: i.e. through which God revealed his law at Sinai.

In brief, acquit thee bravely; play the man.
Look not on pleasures as they come, but go.
Deferre not the least vertue: lifes poore span
Make not an ell, by trifling in thy wo.   460
  If thou do ill; the joy fades, not the pains:
  If well; the pain doth fade, the joy remains.

Superliminare

Thou, whom the former precepts have
Sprinkled and taught, how to behave
Thy self in church; approach, and taste
The churches mysticall repast.

Avoid profanenesse; come not here: 5
Nothing but holy, pure, and cleare,
Or that which groneth to be so,
May at his perill further go.

460. *ell:* a measure of length—45 inches [*OED*].
461-2. The concluding epigram has had a long literary history [*FEH*, pp. 483-4],.but its normally secular content is here placed within a Christian framework. Cf. below, pp. 209–13.

Superliminare: the lintel over the entrance to the church proper.
  2. *Sprinkled:* cf. above, p. 33, note on 'Perirrhanterium'.
  4. *mysticall repast:* see above, p. 18.

The Church

The Altar

A broken A L T A R, Lord, thy servant reares,
Made of a heart, and cemented with teares:
  Whose parts are as thy hand did frame;
  No workmans tool hath touch'd the same.
     A   H E A R T   alone   5
     Is   such   a   stone,
     As   nothing   but
     Thy pow'r doth cut.
     Wherefore each part
     Of   my   hard   heart   10
     Meets in this frame,
     To praise thy name.
  That if I chance to hold my peace,
  These stones to praise thee may not cease.
O let thy blessed S A C R I F I C E be mine,   15
And sanctifie this A L T A R to be thine.

The Altar. On the tradition of 'pattern poetry', see below, pp. 209 f.
The shape of the poem recalls rather a pagan place of sacrifice—
here resolutely christianized—than the Communion Table [cf.
§ 216, pp. 141 ff.; § 204, pp. 10 ff.]. But cf. Lancelot Andrewes:
'The Holy Eucharist . . . is fitly called an *Altar*; which again is as
fitly called a *Table*, the Eucharist being considered as a *Sacrament*,
which is nothing else but a distribution and an application of the
Sacrifice to the several receivers' [§ 84, p. 497].
1 ff. The rearing of an altar is linked in Deuteronomy 27.2 ff. to Jordan
(cf. below, p. 75): 'when ye be gone over Jordan, . . . there shalt
thou built an altar unto the Lord thy God, an altar of stones'
[§ 219]. But a Christian acknowledges God 'not in tables of stone,
but in fleshy tables of the heart' (2 Corinthians 3.3).
5-6. Cf. Zechariah 7.12: 'if these [i.e. Christ's disciples] should hold
their peace, the stones would immediately cry out'.
15. *SACRIFICE:* an obvious anticipation of the poem immediately
following. So, throughout *The Temple*, poem 'prevents' poem (see
above, pp. 18 ff.).

The Sacrifice

Oh, all ye, who passe by, whose eyes and minde
To worldly things are sharp, but to me blinde;
To me, who took eyes that I might you finde:
               Was ever grief like mine?

The Princes of my people make a head   5
Against their Maker: they do wish me dead,
Who cannot wish, except I give them bread:
               Was ever grief like mine?

Without me each one, who doth now me brave,
Had to this day been an Egyptian slave.   10
They use that power against me, which I gave:
               Was ever grief like mine?

Mine own Apostle, who the bag did beare,
Though he had all I had, did not forbeare
To sell me also, and to put me there: 15
               Was ever grief, &c.

For thirtie pence he did my death devise,
Who at three hundred did the ointment prize,
Not half so sweet as my sweet sacrifice:
               Was ever grief, &c.   20

Therefore my soul melts, and my hearts deare treasure
Drops bloud (the onely beads) my words to measure:
O let this cup passe, if it be thy pleasure:
               Was ever grief, &c.

These drops being temper'd with a sinners tears,   25
A Balsome are for both the Hemispheres:
Curing all wounds, but mine; all, but my fears:
               Was ever grief, &c.

The Sacrifice is extensively indebted to the medieval Complaints of
Christ to his People which emanate from the liturgical offices of
Holy Week, notably the *Improperia* or Reproaches of Good Friday
[see § 219].
1. Cf. Lamentations of Jeremiah 1.12: 'Is it nothing to you, all ye
that pass by? behold, and see if there be any sorrow like unto my
sorrow, which is done unto me' (also Lam. 2.15, and Matthew
27.39: 'they that passed by reviled him').
13. Judas carried the 'bag' of the disciples' meagre funds (John 12.6).
Cf. above, p. 38, note on l. 171.
18. After Mary anointed Christ's feet with an expensive ointment,
Judas complained, 'Why was not this ointment sold for three
hundred pence . . .?' (John 12.3–5).

Yet my Disciples sleep: I cannot gain
One houre of watching; but their drowsie brain   30
Comforts not me, and doth my doctrine stain:
              Was ever grief like mine?

Arise, arise, they come. Look how they runne.
Alas! what haste they make to be undone!
How with their lanterns do they seek the sunne!   35
              Was ever grief, &c.

With clubs and staves they seek me, as a thief,
Who am the way of truth, the true relief;
Most true to those, who are my greatest grief:
              Was ever grief, &c.   40

Judas, dost thou betray me with a kisse?
Canst thou finde hell about my lips? and misse
Of life, just at the gates of life and blisse?
              Was ever grief, &c.

See, they lay hold on me, not with the hands   45
Of faith, but furie: yet at their commands
I suffer binding, who have loos'd their bands:
              Was ever grief, &c.

All my Disciples flie; fear puts a barre
Betwixt my friends and me. They leave the starre,   50
That brought the wise men of the East from farre.
              Was ever grief, &c.

Then from one ruler to another bound
They leade me; urging, that it was not sound
What I taught: Comments would the text confound.   55
              Was ever grief, &c.

The Priest and rulers all false witnesse seek
'Gainst him, who seeks not life, but is the meek
And readie Paschal Lambe of this great week:
              Was ever grief, &c.   60

45-6. An ironic inversion of St Paul's counsel, 'Fight the good fight of
      faith, lay hold on eternal life' (1 Timothy 6.12).
47. Ezekiel 34.27 ('they shall know that I am the Lord, when I have
      broken the bands of their yoke') conflated with Psalm 116.16 ('O
      Lord . . . thou hast loosed my bonds').
57. *Priest:* the high priest Caiaphas (Matthew 26.57 ff.).

Then they accuse me of great blasphemie,
That I did thrust into the Deitie,
Who never thought that any robberie:
          Was ever grief like mine?

Some said, that I the Temple to the floore   65
In three dayes raz'd, and raised as before.
Why, he that built the world can do much more:
          Was ever grief, &c.

Then they condemne me all with that same breath,
Which I do give them daily, unto death.   70
Thus *Adam* my first breathing rendereth:
          Was ever grief, &c.

They binde, and leade me unto *Herod*: he
Sends me to *Pilate*. This makes them agree;
But yet their friendship is my enmitie: 75
          Was ever grief, &c.

Herod and all his bands do set me light,
Who teach all hands to warre, fingers to fight,
And onely am the Lord of hosts and might:
          Was ever grief, &c.   80

Herod in judgement sits, while I do stand;
Examines me with a censorious hand:
I him obey, who all things else command:
          Was ever grief, &c.

The *Jews* accuse me with despitefulnesse;   85
And vying malice with my gentlenesse,
Pick quarrels with their onely happinesse:
          Was ever grief, &c.

I answer nothing, but with patience prove
If stonie hearts will melt with gentle love.   90
But who does hawk at eagles with a dove?
          Was ever grief, &c.

61-3. The charge against Christ was: 'thou, being a man, makest
    thyself God' (John 10.33). But 'being in the form of God', St Paul
    explained, he 'thought it not robbery to be equal with God'
    (Philippians 2.6).
65-6. In fact, of course, 'he spake of the temple of his body' (John
    2.21).

My silence rather doth augment their crie;
My dove doth back into my bosome flie,
Because the raging waters still are high: 95
        Was ever grief like mine?

Heark how they crie aloud still, *Crucifie*:
It is not fit he live a day, they crie,
Who cannot live lesse then eternally:
        Was ever grief, &c.   100

Pilate a stranger holdeth off; but they,
Mine owne deare people, cry, *Away, away,*
With noises confused frighting the day:
        Was ever grief, &c.

Yet still they shout, and crie, and stop their eares,   105
Putting my life among their sinnes and fears,
And therefore wish *my bloud on them and theirs:*
        Was ever grief, &c.

See how spite cankers things. These words aright
Used, and wished, are the whole worlds light: 110
But hony is their gall, brightnesse their night:
        Was ever grief, &c.

They choose a murderer, and all agree
In him to do themselves a courtesie:
For it was their own cause who killed me: 115
        Was ever grief, &c.

And a seditious murderer he was:
But I the Prince of peace; peace that doth passe
All understanding, more then heav'n doth glasse:
        Was ever grief, &c.   120

94-5. So Noah's dove 'returned unto him into the ark, for the waters
were on the face of the whole earth' (Genesis 8.9).
111. *hony . . . brightnesse:* traditional allusions to Christ the honey-like
manna and light-bringer [§ 219].
117. *murderer:* i.e. Barabbas (Mark 15.7 ff.).
118-9. *peace:* 'the peace of God, which passeth all understanding'
(Philippians 4.7).
119. *glasse:* cf. 'For now we see through a glass, darkly; but then face
to face' (1 Corinthians 13.12).

Why, Cesar is their onely King, not I:
He clave the stonie rock, when they were drie;
But surely not their hearts, as I well trie:
     Was ever grief like mine?

Ah! how they scourge me! yet my tendernesse   125
Doubles each lash: and yet their bitternesse
Windes up my grief to a mysteriousnesse:
     Was ever grief, &c.

They buffet me, and box me as they list,
Who grasp the earth and heaven with my fist,   130
And never yet, whom I would punish, miss'd:
     Was ever grief, &c.

Behold, they spit on me in scornfull wise,
Who by my spittle gave the blinde man eies,
Leaving his blindnesse to mine enemies: 135
     Was ever grief, &c.

My face they cover, though it be divine.
As *Moses* face was vailed, so is mine,
Lest on their double-dark souls either shine:
     Was ever grief, &c.   140

Servants and abjects flout me; they are wittie:
Now prophesie who strikes thee, is their dittie.
So they in me denie themselves all pitie:
     Was ever grief, &c.

And now I am deliver'd unto death,   145
Which each one cals for so with utmost breath,
That he before me well nigh suffereth:
     Was ever grief, &c.

121. When challenged by Pilate ('Shall I crucify your King?'), the
  hypocritical priests replied, 'We have no king but Caesar' (John
  19.15).
122. An ironic allusion to the rock cleft by Moses (Exodus 17.5 ff.,
  Numbers 20.7 ff.)—an event typologically related to the flow of
  'blood and water' from Christ's pierced side (John 19.34 [§
  219]). The connection is made explicit later (170–1).
129-31. *me . . . me . . . my . . . I:* both *W* and *B* read 'him . . . him . . .
  his . . . he'.
130. Cf. the rhetorical questions in Proverbs 30.4: 'who hath gathered
  the wind in his fists?' etc.
138. *vailed:* i.e. when speaking with the Israelites after his transfigura-
  tion on seeing God (Exodus 34.30 ff.). Typologically the event
  prefigures Christ's own transfiguration (Matthew 17.2).
141. *abjects:* degraded persons.

Weep not, deare friends, since I for both have wept
When all my tears were bloud, the while you slept: 150
Your tears for your own fortunes should be kept:
            Was ever grief like mine?

The souldiers lead me to the common hall;
There they deride me, they abuse me all:
Yet for twelve heav'nly legions I could call: 155
            Was ever grief, &c.

Then with a scarlet robe they me aray;
Which shews my bloud to be the only way,
And cordiall left to repair mans decay:
            Was ever grief, &c.   160

Then on my head a crown of thorns I wear:
For these are all the grapes *Sion* doth bear,
Though I my vine planted and watred there:
            Was ever grief, &c.

So sits the earths great curse in *Adams* fall   165
Upon my head: so I remove it all
From th' earth unto my brows, and bear the thrall:
            Was ever grief, &c.

Then with the reed they gave to me before,
They strike my head, the rock from whence all store   170
Of heav'nly blessings issue evermore:
            Was ever grief, &c.

They bow their knees to me, and cry, *Hail king:*
What ever scoffes or scornfulnesse can bring,
I am the floore, the sink, where they it fling: 175
            Was ever grief, &c.

Yet since mans scepters are as frail as reeds,
And thorny all their crowns, bloudie their weeds;
I, who am Truth, turn into truth their deeds:
            Was ever grief, &c.   180

150. *bloud:* the allusion to Luke 22.44 ('his sweat was as it were great drops of blood') carries, as always in Herbert, eucharistic connotations.
155. Cf. Matthew 26.52: 'Thinkest thou that I cannot now pray to my Father, and he shall presently give me more than twelve legions of angels?'
157. *scarlet robe:* cf. 'My coat, the type of love' (242).
163. *vine planted:* as described in Isaiah's elaborate allegory (5.1 ff.).
167. *brows:* i.e. on which rest the thorns promised to Adam after the Fall (Genesis 3.18).
170. *the rock:* so 1 Corinthians 10.4 ('that spiritual Rock ... was Christ'; see above, p. 27).

The souldiers also spit upon that face,
Which Angels did desire to have the grace,
And Prophets once to see, but found no place:
    Was ever grief like mine?

Thus trimmed forth they bring me to the rout,   185
Who *Crucifie him*, crie with one strong shout.
God holds his peace at man, and man cries out:
    Was ever grief, &c.

They leade me in once more, and putting then
Mine own clothes on, they leade me out agen.   190
Whom devils flie, thus is he toss'd of men:
    Was ever grief, &c.

And now wearie of sport, glad to ingrosse
All spite in one, counting my life their losse,
They carrie me to my most bitter crosse: 195
    Was ever grief, &c.

My crosse I bear my self, untill I faint:
Then Simon bears it for me by constraint,
The decreed burden of each mortall Saint:
    Was ever grief, &c.   200

O all ye who passe by, behold and see;
Man stole the fruit, but I must climbe the tree;
The tree of life to all, but onely me:
    Was ever grief, &c.

Lo, here I hang, charg'd with a world of sinne,   205
The greater world o' th' two; for that came in
By words, but this by sorrow I must win:
    Was ever grief, &c.

Such sorrow, as if sinfull man could feel,
Or feel his part, he would not cease to kneel   210
Till all were melted, though he were all steel:
    Was ever grief, &c.

But, *O my God, my God!* why leav'st thou me,
The sonne, in whom thou dost delight to be?
My God, my God——   215
    Never was grief like mine.

183. Cf. Luke 10.24: 'many prophets and kings have desired to see
  those things which ye see, and have not seen them'.
193. *ingrosse:* concentrate.
199. *The decreed burden:* i.e. 'If any man will come after me, let him
  deny himself, and take up his cross' (Matthew 16.24).
202. *climb the tree:* i.e. ascend the Cross.

Shame tears my soul, my bodie many a wound;
Sharp nails pierce this, but sharper that confound;
Reproches, which are free, while I am bound,
           Was ever grief like mine?   220

Now heal thy self, Physician; now come down.
Alas! I did so, when I left my crown
And fathers smile for you, to feel his frown:
           Was ever grief, &c.

In healing not my self, there doth consist   225
All that salvation, which ye now resist;
Your safetie in my sicknesse doth subsist:
           Was ever grief, &c.

Betwixt two theeves I spend my utmost breath,
As he that for some robberie suffereth.   230
Alas! what have I stollen from you? death:
           Was ever grief, &c.

A king my title is, prefixt on high;
Yet by my subjects am condemn'd to die
A servile death in servile companie: 235
           Was ever grief, &c.

They gave me vineger mingled with gall,
But more with malice: yet, when they did call,
With Manna, Angels food, I fed them all:
           Was ever grief, &c.   240

They part my garments, and by lot dispose
My coat, the type of love, which once cur'd those
Who sought for help, never malicious foes:
           Was ever grief, &c.

Nay, after death their spite shall further go;   245
For they will pierce my side, I full well know;
That as sinne came, so Sacraments might flow:
           Was ever grief, &c.

221. The proverb 'Physician heal thyself' (Luke 4.23) is conflated with
    the taunt at Golgotha, 'If thou be the Son of God, come down
    from the cross' (Matthew 27.40).
239. *Manna:* typologically, the Eucharist (see above, p. 27).
    Angels food: so Psalm 78.25.
242-3. Cf. Matthew 14.36: '[the sick] besought that they might only
    touch the hem of his garment: and as many as touched were made
    perfectly whole'.
247. The implicit parallel, entirely traditional, is between Eve's creation
    from Adam's side and the flow of sacraments from Christ's pierced
    side. Cf. note on 122.

But now I die; now all is finished.
My wo, mans weal: and now I bow my head.   250
Onely let others say, when I am dead,
                        Never was grief like mine.

The Thanksgiving

Oh King of grief! (a title strange, yet true,
    To thee of all kings onely due)
Oh King of wounds! how shall I grieve for thee,
    Who in all grief preventest me?
Shall I weep bloud? why thou hast wept such store   5
    That all thy body was one doore.
Shall I be scourged, flouted, boxed, sold?
    'Tis but to tell the tale is told.
My God, my God, why dost thou part from me?
    Was such a grief as cannot be.   10
Shall I then sing, skipping thy dolefull storie,
    And side with thy triumphant glorie?
Shall thy strokes be my stroking? thorns, my flower?
    Thy rod, my posie? crosse, my bower?
But how then shall I imitate thee, and   15
    Copie thy fair, though bloudie hand?
Surely I will revenge me on thy love,
    And trie who shall victorious prove.
If thou dost give me wealth; I will restore
    All back unto thee by the poore.   20
If thou dost give me honour; men shall see,
    The honour doth belong to thee.
I will not marry; or, if she be mine,
    She and her children shall be thine.
My bosome friend, if he blaspheme thy name,   25
    I will tear thence his love and fame.
One half of me being gone, the rest I give
    Unto some Chappell, die or live.
As for thy passion—But of that anon,
    When with the other I have done.   30

The Thanksgiving
  4. *preventest:* anticipates; surpasses. See above, p. 18.
5-6. Cf. above, p. 53, note on 150.
  6. *doore:* cf. John 10.9: 'I am the door: by me if any man enter in, he
     shall be saved'.
  9. So Matthew 27.46; cf. above, p. 54, l. 213.
 11. *skipping thy dolefull:* 'neglecting thy sad' (*W*).
 13. *thy strokes, my stroking:* an obvious play on words; also musical
     terms (cf. 39 ff.).
 20. Cf. Proverbs 19.17: 'He that hath pity upon the poor lendeth unto
     the Lord; and that which he hath given will he pay him again'.

For thy predestination I'le contrive,
    That three yeares hence, if I survive,
I'le build a spittle, or mend common wayes,
    But mend mine own without delayes.
Then I will use the works of thy creation,   35
    As if I us'd them but for fashion.
The world and I will quarrell; and the yeare
    Shall not perceive, that I am here.
My musick shall finde thee, and ev'ry string
    Shall have his attribute to sing;   40
That all together may accord in thee,
    And prove one God, one harmonie.
If thou shalt give me wit, it shall appeare,
    If thou hast giv'n it me, 'tis here.
Nay, I will reade thy book, and never move   45
    Till I have found therein thy love;
Thy art of love, which I'le turn back on thee,
    O my deare Saviour, Victorie!
Then for thy passion—I will do for that—
    Alas, my God, I know not what.   50

The Reprisall

    I have consider'd it, and finde
There is no dealing with thy mighty passion:
For though I die for thee, I am behinde;
    My sinnes deserve the condemnation.

    O make me innocent, that I   5
May give a disentangled state and free:
And yet thy wounds still my attempts defie,
    For by thy death I die for thee.

    Ah! was it not enough that thou
By thy eternal glorie didst outgo me?   10
Couldst thou not griefs sad conquests me allow,
    But in all vict'ries overthrow me?

33. *spittle:* hospital; alms-house.
44. *here:* i.e. in this book of poems.
47. *art of love:* i.e. in opposition to Ovid's *Ars amatoria.*

The Reprisall. Original title in *W: The Second Thanks-giving.* 'Reprisal'
    is used in the (military) sense of retaliation as well as in the (musical)
    sense of returning to the original subject [§ 204].

Yet by confession will I come
Into the conquest. Though I can do nought
Against thee, in thee I will overcome   15
    The man, who once against thee fought.

The Agonie

Philosophers have measur'd mountains,
Fathom'd the depths of seas, of states, and kings,
Walk'd with a staffe to heav'n, and traced fountains:
    But there are two vast, spacious things,
The which to measure it doth more behove: 5
Yet few there are that sound them; Sinne and Love.

Who would know Sinne, let him repair
Unto Mount Olivet; there shall he see
A man so wrung with pains, that all his hair,
    His skinne, his garments bloudie be.   10
Sinne is that presse and vice, which forceth pain
To hunt his cruell food through ev'ry vein.

Who knows not Love, let him assay
And taste that juice, which on the crosse a pike
Did set again abroach; then let him say   15
    If ever he did taste the like.
Love is that liquour sweet and most divine,
Which my God feels as bloude; but I, as wine.

The Sinner

Lord, how I am all ague, when I seek
    What I have treasur'd in my memorie!
    Since, if my soul make even with the week,
Each seventh note by right is due to thee.
I finde there quarries of pil'd vanities,   5

14. *the:* both *W* and *B* read 'thy'.
15. *in:* through.
15-16. The allusion is both to Jacob who had wrestled with God (cf.
above, p. 31, note 6) and to 'the new man' so often urged by St
Paul (e.g. Colossians 3.10).

The Agonie
  3. *staffe:* a rod for measuring distances and heights [*OED*]; also
known as Jacob's staff on the basis of Genesis 32.10 (quoted above,
p. 31, note 6).
11. *presse:* the wine-press, normally deployed as an image of judgement
(e.g. Revelation 14.19–20), is here applied to the Crucifixion within
the framework of the Eucharist (ll. 13 ff.).
15. *abroach:* pierce and leave running.

But shreds of holinesse, that dare not venture
To shew their face, since crosse to thy decrees:
There the circumference earth is, heav'n the centre.
In so much dregs the quintessence is small:
The spirit and good extract of my heart   10
Comes to about the many hundredth part.
Yet Lord restore thine image, heare my call:
And though my hard heart scarce to thee can grone,
Remember that thou once didst write in stone.

Good Friday

O my chief good,
How shall I measure out thy bloud?
How shall I count what thee befell,
And each grief tell?

Shall I thy woes   5
Number according to thy foes?
Or, since one starre show'd thy first breath,
Shall all thy death?

Or shall each leaf,
Which falls in Autumne, score a grief?   10
Or cannot leaves, but fruit, be signe
Of the true vine?

Then let each houre
Of my whole life one grief devoure;
That thy distresse through all may runne,   15
And be my sunne.

Or rather let
My severall sinnes their sorrows get;
That as each beast his cure doth know,
Each sinne may so.   20

Since bloud is fittest, Lord, to write
Thy sorrows in, and bloudie fight;
My heart hath store, write there, where in
One box doth lie both ink and sinne:

The Sinner
7. *crosse:* see above, p. 33, note on 24.
9. *quintessence:* scanned quíntessénce.
11. *hundredth:* both *W* and *B* read 'hundred'.
14. i.e. the 'tables of stone' delivered to Moses at Sinai (Exodus
    31.18). The contrast here as elsewhere is to the Christian's 'fleshy
    tables of the heart' (above, p. 47, note on 1).

Good Friday. Original title of ll. 21–32 in *W: The Passion.*

That when sinne spies so many foes,   25
Thy whips, thy nails, thy wounds, thy woes,
All come to lodge there, sinne may say,
No room for me, and flie away.

Sinne being gone, oh fill the place,
And keep possession with thy grace;   30
Lest sinne take courage and return,
And all the writings blot or burn.

Redemption

Having been tenant long to a rich Lord,
    Not thriving, I resolved to be bold,
    And make a suit unto him, to afford
A new small-rented lease, and cancell th' old.

In heaven at his manour I him sought: 5
    They told me there, that he was lately gone
    About some land, which he had dearly bought
Long since on earth, to take possession.

I straight return'd, and knowing his great birth,
    Sought him accordingly in great resorts;   10
    In cities, theatres, gardens, parks, and courts:
At length I heard a ragged noise and mirth

    Of theeves and murderers: there I him espied,
    Who straight, *Your suit is granted*, said, & died.

Sepulchre

O blessed bodie! Whither art thou thrown?
No lodging for thee, but a cold hard stone?
So many hearts on earth, and yet not one
           Receive thee?

Sure there is room within our hearts good store;   5
For they can lodge transgressions by the score:
Thousands of toyes dwell there, yet out of doore
           They leave thee.

Redemption. Original title in *W: The Passion* (i.e. the same as in ll.
    21–32 of the previous poem). On Herbert's parabolic teaching, see
    above, pp. 10 f.
  4. *th' old:* i.e. the old Covenant of Works, abrogated under the Cove-
    nant of Grace.

But that which shews them large, shews them unfit.
What ever sinne did this pure rock commit,   10
Which holds thee now? Who hath indited it
                        Of murder?

Where our hard hearts have took up stones to brain thee,
And missing this, most falsly did arraigne thee;
Onely these stones in quiet entertain thee,
                        And order.

And as of old, the law by heav'nly art
Was writ in stone; so thou, which also art
The letter of the word, find'st no fit heart
                        To hold thee.

Yet do we still persist as we began,   20
And so should perish, but that nothing can,
Though it be cold, hard, foul, from loving man
                        Withhold thee.

Easter

Rise heart; thy Lord is risen. Sing his praise
                        Without delayes,
Who takes thee by the hand, that thou likewise
                        With him mayst rise:
That, as his death calcined thee to dust,   5
His life may make thee gold, and much more just.

Awake, my lute, and struggle for thy part
                        With all thy art.
The crosse taught all wood to resound his name,
                        Who bore the same.   10
His streched sinews taught all strings, what key
Is best to celebrate this most high day.

Sepulchre
10. *rock:* the sepulchre's 'cold hard stone' (2), but also Christ himself
    (cf. above, p. 26).
13. John 10.31: 'Then the Jews took up stones again to stone him'.
18. *in stone:* see above, p. 59, note on 14.
Easter
 5. *calcined:* burnt to ashes; also in the alchemical sense of reducing a
    mineral to its purest form by burning off its impure substances
    [*GR*].
11-12. The sinews are stretched in order to temper them correctly but
    also to reach the high pitch which in 17th-century church music
    —as Tomkins informs us in *Musica Deo Sacra* (1668)—transcended
    by far the pitch of madrigals or chamber music [§§ 284, 301].

Consort both heart and lute, and twist a song
                Pleasant and long:
Or since all musick is but three parts vied   15
                And multiplied;
O let thy blessed Spirit bear a part,
And make up our defects with his sweet art.

I got me flowers to straw thy way;
I got me boughs off many a tree: 20
But thou wast up by break of day,
And brought'st thy sweets along with thee.

The Sunne arising in the East,
Though he give light, & th' East perfume;
If they should offer to contest   25
With thy arising, they presume.

Can there be any day but this,
Though many sunnes to shine endeavour?
We count three hundred, but we misse:
There is but one, and that one ever.   30

13. *consort:* play jointly on several instruments.
    twist: weave, as in polyphonic music.
15-18. *vied:* 'to increase in number by addition or repetition' [*OED*].
    So the Spirit is added to the heart and the lute to complete the
    three parts of the common chord.
19-20. So, during Christ's entry into Jerusalem, 'others cut down
    branches from the trees, and strawed them in the way' (Matthew
    21.8).
19-30. The 'song' promised in 13. The earlier version in *W*, also entitled
    Easter, reads:

    I had prepared many a flowre
    To stow thy way and Victorie,
    But thou wa'st up before myne houre
    Bringinge thy sweets along with thee.

    The Sunn arising in the East
    Though hee bring light & th' other sents:
    Can not make up so brave a feast
    As thy discoverie presents.

    Yet though my flours be lost, they say
    A hart can never come too late.
    Teach it to sing thy praise, this day,
    And then this day, my life shall date.

Easter wings

Lord, who createdst man in wealth and store,
Though foolishly he lost the same,
Decaying more and more,
Till he became
Most poore:
With thee
O let me rise
As larks, harmoniously,
And sing this day thy victories:
Then shall the fall further the flight in me.

My tender age in sorrow did beginne:
And still with sicknesses and shame
Thou didst so punish sinne,
That I became
Most thinne.
With thee
Let me combine,
And feel this day thy victorie:
For, if I imp my wing on thine,
Affliction shall advance the flight in me.

Easter wings. On the tradition of 'pattern poetry', see below, p. 209 f.

7. The plea to rise, as well as the poem's shape, recall Isaiah 40.31 ('they that wait upon the Lord . . . shall mount up with wings as eagles') and Malachi 4.2 ('unto you that fear my name shall the Sun of righteousness arise with healing in his wings' [§ 237]).

10. A reference to the commonplace notion of the 'fortunate' Fall of Man—'an happy fault, giuing occasion to the redemption of the elect, by Christ' (Thomas Wilson, *Theologica \Rules* [1615], II, 28–9). Cf. *Paradise Lost*, XII, 469–78.

19. *imp:* in falconry, to engraft feathers in the damaged wing of a bird so as to restore or improve its powers of flight [*OED*].

H. Baptisme (I)

As he that sees a dark and shadie grove,
    Stayes not, but looks beyond it on the skie;
    So when I view my sinnes, mine eyes remove
More backward still, and to that water flie,

Which is above the heav'ns, whose spring and rent   5
    Is in my deare Redeemers pierced side.
    O blessed streams! either ye do prevent
And stop our sinnes from growing thick and wide,

Or else give tears to drown them, as they grow.
    In you Redemption measures all my time,   10
    And spreads the plaister equall to the crime:
You taught the Book of Life my name, that so

    What ever future sinnes should me miscall,
    Your first acquaintance might discredit all.

H. Baptisme (II)

        Since, Lord, to thee
      A narrow way and little gate
Is all the passage, on my infancie
      Thou didst lay hold, and antedate
        My faith in me.   5

        O let me still
      Write thee great God, and me a childe:
Let me be soft and supple to thy will,
      Small to my self, to others milde,
        Behither ill.   10

H. Baptisme I. The earlier version in *W* begins:

    When backward on my sins I turne my eyes
    And then beyond them all my Baptisme view
    As yet Heaven beyond much thicket spyes
    I passe the shades, & fixe upon the true
    Waters above the Heavens. O sweet streams
    You doe prevent most sins . . . etc.

H. Baptisme II
2-3. Cf. Matthew 7.13–14: 'wide is the gate, and broad is the way, that leadeth to destruction . . . [but] strait is the gate, and narrow is the way, which leadeth unto life'.
10. *Behither:* short of.

                    Although by stealth
              My flesh get on; yet let her sister
My soul bid nothing, but preserve her wealth:
              The growth of flesh is but a blister;
                    Childhood is health.   15

Nature

Full of rebellion, I would die,
Or fight, or travell, or denie
That thou hast ought to do with me.
                    O tame my heart;
              It is thy highest art   5
To captivate strong holds to thee.

If thou shalt let this venome lurk,
And in suggestions fume and work,
My soul will turn to bubbles straight,
                    And thence by kinde   10
              Vanish into a winde,
Making thy workmanship deceit.

O smooth my rugged heart, and there
Engrave thy rev'rend law and fear;
Or make a new one, since the old   15
              Is saplesse grown,
              And a much fitter stone
To hide my dust, then thee to hold.

Sinne (1)

Lord, with what care hast thou begirt us round!
        Parents first season us: then schoolmasters
        Deliver us to laws; they send us bound
To rules of reason, holy messengers,

Pulpits and Sundayes, sorrow dogging sinne,   5
        Afflictions sorted, anguish of all sizes,
        Fine nets and stratagems to catch us in,
Bibles laid open, millions of surprises,

Nature
  6. Cf. 2 Corinthians 10.4: 'the weapons of our warfare are not carnal,
        but mighty through God to the pulling down of strong holds'.
  10. *by kinde:* i.e. according to their nature.
  13-14. Cf. Jeremiah 31.33: 'I will put my law in their inward parts, and
        write it in their hearts'.
  15. Cf. Ezekiel 36.26: 'A new heart also will I give you, ... and take
        away the stony heart'.
Sinne I. 6. *sorted:* i.e. assorted.

Blessings beforehand, tyes of gratefulnesse,
    The sound of glorie ringing in our eares: 10
      Without, our shame; within, our consciences;
Angels and grace, eternall hopes and fears.

    Yet all these fences and their whole aray
    One cunning bosome-sinne blows quite away.

Affliction (1)

When first thou didst entice to thee my heart,
          I thought the service brave:
So many joyes I writ down for my part,
          Besides what I might have
Out of my stock of naturall delights,   5
Augmented with thy gracious benefits.

I looked on thy furniture so fine,
          And made it fine to me:
Thy glorious houshold-stuffe did me entwine,
          And 'tice me unto thee.   10
Such starres I counted mine: both heav'n and earth
Payd me my wages in a world of mirth.

What pleasures could I want, whose King I served?
          Where joyes my fellows were.
Thus argu'd into hopes, my thoughts reserved   15
          No place for grief or fear.
Therefore my sudden soul caught at the place,
And made her youth and fiercenesse seek thy face.

At first thou gav'st me milk and sweetnesses;
          I had my wish and way: 20
My dayes were straw'd with flow'rs and happinesse;
          There was no moneth but May.
But with my yeares sorrow did twist and grow,
And made a partie unawares for wo.

My flesh began unto my soul in pain,   25
          Sicknesses cleave my bones;
Consuming agues dwell in ev'ry vein,
          And tune my breath to grones.
Sorrow was all my soul; I scarce beleeved,
Till grief did tell me roundly, that I lived.   30

Affliction I
  6. *gracious benefits:* 'graces perquisites' (*W*).
 11. *starres:* see above, p. 38, note on 171.

When I got health, thou took'st away my life,
          And more; for my friends die:
My mirth and edge was lost; a blunted knife
          Was of more use then I.
Thus thinne and lean without a fence or friend,   35
I was blown through with ev'ry storm and winde.

Whereas my birth and spirit rather took
          The way that takes the town;
Thou didst betray me to a lingring book,
          And wrap me in a gown.   40
I was entangled in the world of strife,
Before I had the power to change my life.

Yet, for I threatned oft the siege to raise,
          Not simpring all mine age,
Thou often didst with Academick praise   45
          Melt and dissolve my rage.
I took thy sweetned pill, till I came where
I could not go away, nor persevere.

Yet lest perchance I should too happie be
          In my unhappinesse,   50
Turning my purge to food, thou throwest me
          Into more sicknesses.
Thus doth thy power crosse-bias me, not making
Thine own gift good, yet me from my wayes taking.

Now I am here, what thou wilt do with me   55
          None of my books will show:
I reade, and sigh, and wish I were a tree;
          For sure then I should grow
To fruit or shade: at least some bird would trust
Her houshold to me, and I should be just.   60

Yet, though thou troublest me, I must be meek;
          In weaknesse must be stout.
Well, I will change the service, and go seek
          Some other master out.
Ah my deare God! though I am clean forgot,   65
Let me not love thee, if I love thee not.

47. *where:* the reading of *W.* The 1633 edn has 'neare;' and *B* reads
    'neere,' above which is written 'where'.
53. *crosse-bias me:* make me change my direction (*bias* is a metaphor
    from the game of bowls). See also above, p. 20.
66. Cf. Shakespeare's Sonnet 140: 'If I might teach thee wit, better it
    were, / Though not to love, yet love, to tell me so' [§ 197].

Repentance

Lord, I confesse my sinne is great;
Great is my sinne. Oh! gently treat
With thy quick flow'r, thy momentanie bloom;
                    Whose life still pressing
                    Is one undressing,   5
A steadie aiming at a tombe.

Mans age is two houres work, or three:
Each day doth round about us see.
Thus are we to delights: but we are all
                    To sorrows old,   10
                    If life be told
From what life feeleth, Adams fall.

O let thy height of mercie then
Compassionate short-breathed men.
Cut me not off for my most foul transgression: 15
                    I do confesse
                    My foolishnesse;
My God, accept of my confession.

Sweeten at length this bitter bowl,
Which thou hast pour'd into my soul;   20
Thy wormwood turn to health, windes to fair weather:
                    For if thou stay,
                    I and this day,
As we did rise, we die together.

When thou for sinne rebukest man,   25
Forthwith he waxeth wo and wan:
Bitternesse fills our bowels; all our hearts
                    Pine, and decay,
                    And drop away,
And carrie with them th' other parts.   30

Repentance
   3. *quick:* living; also, rapidly perishing [*LS*].
       momentanie: not an uncommon version of 'momentarie' (*B*).
  21. *wormwood:* cf. Jeremiah 9.15: 'I will feed them, even this people,
       with wormwood, and give them water of gall to drink'.
  22. *stay:* i.e. stay away.
  25-6. Cf. Psalm 39.11: 'When thou with rebukes dost correct man for
       iniquity, thou makest his beauty to consume away like a moth'.

But thou wilt sinne and grief destroy;
    That so the broken bones may joy,
And tune together in a well-set song,
                    Full of his praises,
                    Who dead men raises.   35
Fractures well cur'd make us more strong.

Faith

    Lord, how couldst thou so much appease
Thy wrath for sinne, as when mans sight was dimme,
And could see little, to regard his ease,
    And bring by Faith all things to him?

    Hungrie I was, and had no meat: 5
I did conceit a most delicious feast;
I had it straight, and did as truly eat,
    As ever did a welcome guest.

    There is a rare outlandish root,
Which when I could not get, I thought it here: 10
That apprehension cur'd so well my foot,
    That I can walk to heav'n well neare.

    I owed thousands and much more:
I did beleeve that I did nothing owe,
And liv'd accordingly; my creditor   15
    Beleeves so too, and lets me go.

    Faith makes me any thing, or all
That I beleeve is in the sacred storie:
And where sinne placeth me in Adams fall,
    Faith sets me higher in his glorie.   20

    If I go lower in the book,
What can be lower then the common manger?
Faith puts me there with him, who sweetly took
    Our flesh and frailtie, death and danger.

    If blisse had lien in art or strength,   25
None but the wise or strong had gained it:
Where now by Faith all arms are of a length;
    One size doth all conditions fit.

32. *bones:* for the Biblical allusion, cf. Psalm 51.8 ('that the bones which
    thou hast broken, may rejoice'); but the word also designates an
    early musical instrument, either percussion or (more rarely) wind
    [cf. § 188].

A peasant may beleeve as much
As a great Clerk, and reach the highest stature.   30
Thus dost thou make proud knowledge bend & crouch
    While grace fills up eneven nature.

When creatures had no reall light
Inherent in them, thou didst make the sunne,
Impute a lustre, and allow them bright;   35
    And in this shew, what Christ hath done.

That which before was darkned clean
With bushie groves, pricking the lookers eie,
Vanisht away, when Faith did change the scene:
    And then appear'd a glorious skie.   40

What though my bodie runne to dust?
Faith cleaves unto it, counting evr'y grain
With an exact and most particular trust,
    Reserving all for flesh again.

Prayer (1)

Prayer the Churches banquet, Angels age,
    Gods breath in man returning to his birth,
The soul in paraphrase, heart in pilgrimage,
The Christian plummet sounding heav'n and earth;

Engine against th' Almightie, sinners towre,   5
    Reversed thunder, Christ-side-piercing spear,
    The six-daies world-transposing in an houre,
A kinde of tune, which all things heare and fear;

Faith
32. The axiom was definitively phrased by St Thomas Aquinas:
    'grace does not destroy nature but perfects it' [§ 92].
37. *clean:* completely.
44. *flesh again:* i.e. during the Last Judgement.
Prayer I. For one of the reductions of this sonnet to a hymn, see below,
    p. 236, note 1.
5-6. *Engine against th' Almightie:* cf. *Artillery*, below, p. 149, l. 25 ('We
    are shooters both'). 'Earnest Prayer', said Donne, 'hath the nature
    of Importunity; Wee presse, wee importune God. . . . Prayer hath
    the nature of Impudency; Wee threaten God in Prayer. . . . And
    God suffers this Impudency, and more. Prayer hath the nature of
    Violence; In the publique Prayers of the Congregation, we besiege
    God, saies *Tertullian*, and we take God Prisoner, and bring God
    to our Conditions; and God is glad to be straitned by us in that
    siege' (*Sermons*, V, 364).

Softnesse, and peace, and joy, and love, and blisse,
    Exalted Manna, gladnesse of the best,   10
    Heaven in ordinarie, man well drest,
The milkie way, the bird of Paradise,

    Church-bels beyond the starres heard, the souls bloud,
    The land of spices; something understood.

The H. Communion

Not in rich furniture, or fine aray,
    Nor in a wedge of gold,
    Thou, who from me wast sold,
    To me dost now thy self convey;
For so thou should'st without me still have been,   5
    Leaving within me sinne:

But by the way of nourishment and strength
    Thou creep'st into my breast;
    Making thy way my rest,
    And thy small quantities my length;   10
Which spread their forces into every part,
    Meeting sinnes force and art.

Yet can these not get over to my soul,
    Leaping the wall that parts
    Our souls and fleshly hearts;   15
    But as th' outworks, they may controll
My rebel-flesh, and carrying thy name,
    Affright both sinne and shame.

---

7. *transposing:* a musical term indicating sounds reproduced at another pitch from that at which they were originally written. The image is made explicit in the next line; its centrality was recognized by Vaughan: 'Prayer is / The world in tune' ('The Morning-watch', 18–19).

10. *Manna:* typologically, the Eucharist (cf. above, p. 55, note on 239), especially as here the manna ascends to heaven—i.e. 'returning to his birth' (2).

The H. Communion. Original title of ll. 25–40 in *W: Prayer.* For another poem with the same title in *W*, see below, p. 201.

1-2. Cf. Joshua 7.21: 'I saw among the spoils a goodly Babylonish garment, and . . . a wedge of gold'. The simplicity of the Anglican communion is contrasted to the gaudiness of the Roman Catholic.

3. *from: B* reads 'for'.

15. *fleshly: B* reads 'fleshy'.

Onely thy grace, which with these elements comes,
    Knoweth the ready way,   20
    And hath the privie key,
  Op'ning the souls most subtile rooms;
While those to spirits refin'd, at doore attend
    Dispatches from their friend.

Give me my captive soul, or take   25
    My bodie also thither.
Another lift like this will make
    Them both to be together.

Before that sinne turn'd flesh to stone,
    And all our lump to leaven;   30
A fervent sigh might well have blown
    Our innocent earth to heaven.

For sure when Adam did not know
    To sinne, or sinne to smother;
He might to heav'n from Paradise go,   35
    As from one room t'another.

Thou hast restor'd us to this ease
    By this thy heav'nly bloud;
Which I can go in, when I please,
    And leave th' earth to their food.   40

Antiphon (1)

Cho. Let all the world in ev'ry corner sing,
    My God and King.

    Vers. The heav'ns are not too high,
      His praise may thither flie:
      The earth is not too low,
      His praises there may grow.   5

Cho. Let all the world in ev'ry corner sing,
    My God and King.

    Vers. The church with psalms must shout,
      No doore can keep them out:
      But above all, the heart   10
      Must bear the longest part.

23. *those:* i.e. the elements of the Eucharist.
Antiphon: 'a composition, in prose or verse, consisting of verses or
    passages sung alternately by two choirs in worship' [*OED*].

Cho. Let all the world in ev'ry corner sing,
          My God and King.

Love 1

Immortall Love, authour of this great frame,
    Sprung from that beautie which can never fade;
    How hath man parcel'd out thy glorious name,
And thrown it on that dust which thou hast made,

While mortall love doth all the title gain!   5
    Which siding with invention, they together
    Bear all the sway, possessing heart and brain,
(Thy workmanship) and give thee share in neither.

Wit fancies beautie, beautie raiseth wit:
    The world is theirs; they two play out the game,   10
    Thou standing by: and though thy glorious name
Wrought our deliverance from th' infernall pit,

    Who sings thy praise? onely a skarf or glove
    Doth warm our hands, and make them write of love.

II

Immortall Heat, O let thy greater flame
    Attract the lesser to it: let those fires,
    Which shall consume the world, first make it tame;
And kindle in our hearts such true desires,

As may consume our lusts, and make thee way.   5
    Then shall our hearts pant thee; then shall our brain
    All her invention on thine Altar lay,
And there in hymnes send back thy fire again.

Our eies shall see thee, which before saw dust;
    Dust blown by wit, till that they both were blinde: 10
    Thou shalt recover all thy goods in kinde,
Who wert disseized by usurping lust:

All knees shall bow to thee; all wits shall rise,
And praise him who did make and mend our eies.

Love I
    1. *frame:* i.e. the universe.
Love II
    6. *pant thee:* i.e. pant *after* thee, as in Psalm 42.1.
    11-12. *recover, disseized* (i.e. dispossessed): legal terms.

The Temper (I)

How should I praise thee, Lord! how should my rymes
    Gladly engrave thy love in steel,
    If what my soul doth feel sometimes,
        My soul might ever feel!

Although there were some fourtie heav'ns, or more,   5
    Sometimes I peere above them all;
    Sometimes I hardly reach a score,
        Sometimes to hell I fall.

O rack me not to such a vast extent;
    Those distances belong to thee: 10
    The world's too little for thy tent,
        A grave too big for me.

Wilt thou meet arms with man, that thou dost stretch
    A crumme of dust from heav'n to hell?
    Will great God measure with a wretch?   15
        Shall he thy stature spell?

O let me, when thy roof my soul hath hid,
    O let me roost and nestle there:
    Then of a sinner thou art rid,
        And I of hope and fear.   20

Yet take thy way; for sure thy way is best:
    Stretch or contract me thy poore debter:
    This is but tuning of my breast,
        To make the musick better.

Whether I flie with angels, fall with dust,   25
    Thy hands made both, and I am there:
    Thy power and love, my love and trust
        Make one place ev'ry where.

The Temper (II)

It cannot be. Where is that mightie joy,
    Which just now took up all my heart?
    Lord, if thou must needs use thy dart,
Save that, and me; or sin for both destroy.

The Temper I (also *The Temper II*). Original title of each poem in *W*:
    The Christian Temper.
    5. *some fourtie: W* reads 'a hundred'.
The Temper II
    4. *that:* i.e. the mighty joy.

The grosser world stands to thy word and art;   5
  But thy diviner world of grace
  Thou suddenly dost raise and race,
And ev'ry day a new Creatour art.

O fix thy chair of grace, that all my powers
  May also fix their reverence: 10
  For when thou dost depart from hence,
They grow unruly, and sit in thy bowers.

Scatter, or binde them all to bend to thee:
  Though elements change, and heaven move,
  Let not thy higher Court remove,   15
But keep a standing Majestie in me.

Jordan (1)

Who sayes that fictions onely and false hair
Become a verse? Is there in truth no beautie?
Is all good structure in a winding stair?
May no lines passe, except they do their dutie
  Not to a true, but painted chair?   5

Is it no verse, except enchanted groves
And sudden arbours shadow course-spunne lines?
Must purling streams refresh a lovers loves?
Must all be vail'd, while he that reades, divines,
  Catching the sense at two removes?   10

Shepherds are honest people; let them sing:
Riddle who list, for me, and pull for Prime:
I envie no mans nightingale or spring;
Nor let them punish me with losse of rime,
  Who plainly say, *My God, My King*.   15

7. *race:* raze.
8. Cf. 'Preservation is a Creation' etc. (quoted above, p. 17).

Jordan I. On the literal level, the title designates the river crossed by the
  Israelites as they entered the Promised Land, and of course the
  place of Christ's baptism (hence also its typological import).
  Symbolically, the title suggests purification, regeneration, conversion,
  consecration. The various strands are gathered in the Book of
  Common Prayer's orders of baptism: '[thou] didst safely lead . . .
  thy people thorow the Red Sea, figuring thereby the holy Baptisme:
  and by the Baptisme of . . . Christ, didst sanctifie the flood Jordan,
  and all other waters to the mysticall washing away of sinne' [§
  245]. See also above, p. 31, note 6.
2. *verse:* see above, p. 33, note on 5.
12. *pull for Prime:* draw for a winning hand (in the card game of
  primero, as above, p. 41, note on 297).

Employment (1)

If as a flowre doth spread and die,
 Thou wouldst extend me to some good,
Before I were by frosts extremitie
                    Nipt in the bud;

The sweetnesse and the praise were thine;   5
 But the extension and the room,
Which in thy garland I should fill, were mine
                    At thy great doom.

For as thou dost impart thy grace,
 The greater shall our glorie be.   10
The measure of our joyes is in this place,
                    The stuffe with thee.

Let me not languish then, and spend
 A life as barren to thy praise,
As is the dust, to which that life doth tend,   15
                    But with delaies.

All things are busie; onely I
 Neither bring hony with the bees,
Nor flowres to make that, nor the husbandrie
                    To water these.   20

I am no link of thy great chain,
 But all my companie is a weed.
Lord place me in thy consort; give one strain
                    To my poore reed.

The H. Scriptures 1

Oh Book! infinite sweetnesse! let my heart
    Suck ev'ry letter, and a hony gain,
    Precious for any grief in any part;
To cleare the breast, to mollifie all pain.

Employment I

21. *great chain:* the 'Great Chain of Being', the elaborate system of
    interdependent 'degrees' thought to have been arranged hierarchi-
    cally 'from the Mushrome to the Angels' (Samuel Ward, *The Life
    of Faith*, 3rd edn [1622], p. 2). Its best-known Renaissance formu-
    lations are in *Troilus and Cressida*, I, iii, 85-124, and *Paradise Lost*,
    V, 469-90 [§ 69].
23. *consort:* see above, p. 62, note on 13; cf. Milton's 'celestial consort'
    in *At a Solemn Music.*
    strain: in a musical sense; also a reference to the 'chain'.

Thou art all health, health thriving till it make   5
    A full eternitie: thou art a masse
    Of strange delights, where we may wish & take.
Ladies, look here; this is the thankfull glasse,

That mends the lookers eyes: this is the well
    That washes what it shows. Who can indeare   10
    Thy praise too much? thou art heav'ns Lidger here,
Working against the states of death and hell.

    Thou art joyes handsell: heav'n lies flat in thee,
    Subject to ev'ry mounters bended knee.

II

Oh that I knew how all thy lights combine,
    And the configurations of their glorie!
    Seeing not onely how each verse doth shine,
But all the constellations of the storie.

This verse marks that, and both do make a motion   5
    Unto a third, that ten leaves off doth lie:
    Then as dispersed herbs do watch a potion,
These three make up some Christians destinie:

Such are thy secrets, which my life makes good,
    And comments on thee: for in ev'ry thing   10
    Thy words do finde me out, & parallels bring,
And in another make me understood.

    Starres are poore books, & oftentimes do misse:
    This book of starres lights to eternall blisse.

The H. Scriptures I. See also Herbert's Latin poem *In S. Scripturas* [*LPH*, pp. 84–5].
  2. *hony gain:* cf. Psalm 119.103: 'How sweet are thy words unto my taste! yea, sweeter than honey to my mouth'.
  8. *thankfull:* grateful; also, agreeable [§ 296].
 11. *Lidger:* ledger, in the sense of ambassador or commissioner; also a pun on ledger as register [§ 204].
 13. *handsell:* a first instalment of payment; also, a gift.

The H. Scriptures II
5-6. A reiteration of the distinctly Protestant view that the best explicator of the Bible is the Bible. Cf. *A Priest to the Temple:* 'For all Truth being consonant to it self, and all being penn'd by one and the self-same Spirit, it cannot be, but that an industrious and judicious comparing of place with place must be a singular help for the right understanding of the Scriptures' (Ch. 4).
  7. A widely interpreted line [see *FEH*, p. 496] but still elusive.

Whitsunday

Listen sweet Dove unto my song,
And spread thy golden wings in me;
Hatching my tender heart so long,
Till it get wing, and flie away with thee.

Where is that fire which once descended   5
On thy Apostles? thou didst then
Keep open house, richly attended,
Feasting all comers by twelve chosen men.

Such glorious gifts thou didst bestow,
That th' earth did like a heav'n appeare;   10
The starres were coming down to know
If they might mend their wages, and serve here.

The sunne, which once did shine alone,
Hung down his head, and wisht for night,
When he beheld twelve sunnes for one   15
Going about the world, and giving light.

But since those pipes of gold, which brought
That cordiall water to our ground,
Were cut and martyr'd by the fault
Of those, who did themselves through their side wound   20

Thou shutt'st the doore, and keep'st within;
Scarce a good joy creeps through the chink:
And if the braves of conqu'ring sinne
Did not excite thee, we should wholly sink.

Lord, though we change, thou art the same;   25
The same sweet God of love and light:
Restore this day, for thy great name,
Unto his ancient and miraculous right.

Grace

My stock lies dead, and no increase
Doth my dull husbandrie improve:
O let thy graces without cease
               Drop from above!

Whitsunday. Much revised from the earlier version in *W*; ll. 13–28 are
    new.
17. *pipes of gold:* the apostles as channels of Grace.
23. *braves:* challenges, threats.
Grace 1-4. Cf. Job 14.7–9: 'there is hope of a tree, if it be cut down,
    that it will sprout again' etc.

If still the sunne should hide his face, 5
Thy house would but a dungeon prove,
Thy works nights captives: O let grace
        Drop from above!

The dew doth ev'ry morning fall;
And shall the dew out-strip thy dove? 10
The dew, for which grasse cannot call,
        Drop from above.

Death is still working like a mole,
And digs my grave at each remove:
Let grace work too, and on my soul 15
        Drop from above.

Sinne is still hammering my heart
Unto a hardnesse, void of love:
Let suppling grace, to crosse his art,
        Drop from above. 20

O come! for thou dost know the way.
Or if to me thou wilt not move,
Remove me, where I need not say,
        Drop from above.

Praise (1)

To write a verse or two, is all the praise,
        That I can raise:
    Mend my estate in any wayes,
        Thou shalt have more.

I go to Church; help me to wings, and I 5
        Will thither flie;
    Or, if I mount unto the skie,
        I will do more.

Man is all weaknesse; there is no such thing
        As Prince or King: 10
    His arm is short; yet with a sling
        He may do more.

Praise I
11. *sling:* i.e. David's against Goliath.

An herb destill'd, and drunk, may dwell next doore,
   On the same floore,
  To a brave soul: Exalt the poore,   15
   They can do more.

O raise me then! poore bees, that work all day,
   Sting my delay,
  Who have a work, as well as they,
   And much, much more.   20

Affliction (II)

   Kill me not ev'ry day,
Thou Lord of life; since thy one death for me
 Is more then all my deaths can be,
   Though I in broken pay
Die over each houre of Methusalems stay.   5

   If all mens tears were let
Into one common sewer, sea, and brine;
 What were they all, compar'd to thine?
   Wherein if they were set,
They would discolour thy most bloudy sweat.   10

   Thou art my grief alone,
Thou Lord conceal it not: and as thou art
 All my delight, so all my smart:
   Thy crosse took up in one,
By way of imprest, all my future mone.   15

Mattens

   I cannot ope mine eyes,
 But thou art ready there to catch
 My morning-soul and sacrifice:
Then we must needs for that day make a match.

   My God, what is a heart?   5
 Silver, or gold, or precious stone,
 Or starre, or rainbow, or a part
Of all these things, or all of them in one?

13–15. The soul resides in the heart, 'next doore' to the stomach.
Affliction II
 4. *in broken pay:* in instalments.
 5. Methuselah lived 969 years (Genesis 5.27).
 10. *discolour:* remove the colour from.
 15. *imprest:* payment in advance.

My God, what is a heart,
That thou shouldst it so eye, and wooe,   10
Powring upon it all thy art,
As if that thou hadst nothing els to do?

Indeed mans whole estate
Amounts (and richly) to serve thee:
He did not heav'n and earth create,   15
Yet studies them, not him by whom they be.

Teach me thy love to know;
That this new light, which now I see,
May both the work and workman show:
Then by a sunne-beam I will climbe to thee.   20

Sinne (II)

O that I could a sinne once see!
We paint the devil foul, yet he
Hath some good in him, all agree.
Sinne is flat opposite to th' Almighty, seeing
It wants the good of *vertue*, and of *being*.   5

But God more care of us hath had:
If apparitions make us sad,
By sight of sinne we should grow mad.
Yet as in sleep we see foul death, and live:
So devils are our sinnes in perspective.   10

Even-song

Blest be the God of love,
Who gave me eyes, and light, and power this day,
Both to be busie, and to play.
But much more blest be God above,

Who gave me sight alone,   5
Which to himself he did denie:
For when he sees my waies, I dy:
But I have got his sonne, and he hath none.

Sinne II
4-5. One of the great commonplaces of Christian theology. Cf. Donne's
lengthy exposition of the sense in which 'evill is nothing, sin is
nothing; that is, it hath no reality, it is no created substance, it is
but a privation, as a shadow is ...' (*Sermons*, VI, 238-40).

Even-song. For the poem with the same title in *W*, see below, p. 203.
8. *sonne*: as above, p. 36, note on 98.

What have I brought thee home
For this thy love? have I discharg'd the debt,   10
Which this dayes favour did beget?
I ranne; but all I brought, was fome.

Thy diet, care, and cost
Do end in bubbles, balls of winde;
Of winde to thee whom I have crost,   15
But balls of wilde-fire to my troubled minde.

Yet still thou goest on.
And now with darknesse closest wearie eyes,
Saying to man, *It doth suffice:*
Henceforth repose; your work is done.   20

Thus in thy Ebony box
Thou dost inclose us, till the day
Put our amendment in our way,
And give new wheels to our disorder'd clocks.

I muse, which shows more love,   25
The day or night: that is the gale, this th' harbour;
That is the walk, and this the arbour;
Or that the garden, this the grove.

My God, thou art all love.
Not one poore minute scapes thy breast,   30
But brings a favour from above;
And in this love, more then in bed, I rest.

Church-monuments

While that my soul repairs to her devotion,
Here I intombe my flesh, that it betimes
May take acquaintance of this heap of dust;
To which the blast of deaths incessant motion,
Fed with the exhalation of our crimes,   5
Drives all at last. Therefore I gladly trust

My bodie to this school, that it may learn
To spell his elements, and finde his birth
Written in dustie heraldrie and lines;
Which dissolution sure doth best discern,   10
Comparing dust with dust, and earth with earth.
These laugh at Jeat, and Marble put for signes,

21-22. Poisonous liquids enclosed in a box of ebony were thought to be
    rendered harmless [§ 296].

Church-monuments
12. *these:* i.e. dust and earth.

To sever the good fellowship of dust,
And spoil the meeting. What shall point out them,
When they shall bow, and kneel, and fall down flat   15
To kisse those heaps, which now they have in trust?
Deare flesh, while I do pray, learn here thy stemme
And true descent; that when thou shalt grow fat,

And wanton in thy cravings, thou mayest know,
That flesh is but the glasse, which holds the dust   20
That measures all our time; which also shall
Be crumbled into dust. Mark here below
How tame these ashes are, how free from lust,
That thou mayst fit thy self against thy fall.

Church-musick

Sweetest of sweets, I thank you: when displeasure
    Did through my bodie wound my minde,
You took me thence, and in your house of pleasure
    A daintie lodging me assign'd.

Now I in you without a bodie move,   5
    Rising and falling with your wings:
We both together sweetly live and love,
    Yet say sometimes, *God help poore Kings*.

Comfort, 'Ile die; for if you poste from me,
    Sure I shall do so, and much more: 10
But if I travell in your companie,
    You know the way to heavens doore.

Church-lock and key

I know it is my sinne, which locks thine eares,
    And bindes thy hands,
Out-crying my requests, drowning my tears;
Or else the chilnesse of my faint demands.

Church-musick
8. *God help poore Kings* could be read in the light of Shakespeare's
Sonnet 29: 'thy sweet love remember'd such wealth brings / That
then I scorn to change my state with kings'. But the allusion might
be to the well-known lament in *Richard II* ('let us sit upon the
ground / And tell sad stories of the death of kings': III, ii, 144 ff.)
which begins 'of *comfort* no man speak' (so Herbert in l. 9 [§ 197].

Church-lock and key. Original title in *W* (before it was much revised):
Prayer.

But as cold hands are angrie with the fire,   5
              And mend it still;
So I do lay the want of my desire,
Not on my sinnes, or coldnesse, but thy will.

Yet heare, O God, only for his blouds sake
              Which pleads for me: 10
For though sinnes plead too, yet like stones they make
His blouds sweet current much more loud to be.

The Church-floore

Mark you the floore? that square & speckled stone,
            Which looks so firm and strong,
                Is *Patience*:

And th' other black and grave, wherewith each one
            Is checker'd all along,   5
                Humilitie:

The gentle rising, which on either hand
            Leads to the Quire above,
                Is *Confidence*:

But the sweet cement, which in one sure band   10
            Ties the whole frame, is *Love*
              And *Charitie*.

        Hither sometimes Sinne steals, and stains
        The marbles neat and curious veins:
But all is cleansed when the marble weeps.   15
        Sometimes Death, puffing at the doore,
        Blows all the dust about the floore:
But while he thinks to spoil the room, he sweeps.
        Blest be the *Architect*, whose art
        Could build so strong in a weak heart.   20

The Windows

Lord, how can man preach thy eternall word?
            He is a brittle crazie glasse:
Yet in thy temple thou dost him afford
            This glorious and transcendent place,
            To be a window, through thy grace.   5

The Church-floore
10. *one sure band:* 'charity, which is the bond of perfectness' (Colossians 3.14).
14. *neat and curious:* delicate and beautifully wrought.

But when thou dost anneal in glasse thy storie,
    Making thy life to shine within
The holy Preachers; then the light and glorie
    More rev'rend grows, & more doth win:
    Which else shows watrish, bleak, & thin.   10

Doctrine and life, colours and light, in one
    When they combine and mingle, bring
A strong regard and aw: but speech alone
    Doth vanish like a flaring thing,
    And in the eare, not conscience ring.   15

Trinitie Sunday

Lord, who hast form'd me out of mud,
    And hast redeem'd me through thy bloud,
    And sanctifi'd me to do good;

Purge all my sinnes done heretofore:
    For I confesse my heavie score,   5
    And I will strive to sinne no more.

Enrich my heart, mouth, hands in me,
    With faith, with hope, with charitie;
    That I may runne, rise, rest with thee.

Content

Peace mutt'ring thoughts, and do not grudge to keep
    Within the walls of your own breast:
Who cannot on his own bed sweetly sleep,
    Can on anothers hardly rest.

Gad not abroad at ev'ry quest and call   5
    Of an untrained hope or passion.
To court each place or fortune that doth fall,
    Is wantonnesse in contemplation.

Mark how the fire in flints doth quiet lie,
    Content and warm t' it self alone: 10
But when it would appeare to others eye,
    Without a knock it never shone.

The Windows
    6. *anneal in glasse:* burn in colours upon glass; enamel by encaustic
    process [*OED*].

Trinitie Sunday. Followed in *W* by a second poem with the same title
    (below, p. 203).

Give me the pliant minde, whose gentle measure
      Complies and suits with all estates;
Which can let loose to a crown, and yet with pleasure   15
      Take up within a cloisters gates.

This soul doth span the world, and hang content
      From either pole unto the centre:
Where in each room of the well-furnisht tent
      He lies warm, and without adventure.   20

The brags of life are but a nine dayes wonder;
      And after death the fumes that spring
From private bodies, make as big a thunder,
      As those which rise from a huge King.

Onely thy Chronicle is lost; and yet   25
      Better by worms be all once spent,
Then to have hellish moths still gnaw and fret
      Thy name in books, which may not rent:

When all thy deeds, whose brunt thou feel'st alone,
      Are chaw'd by others pens and tongue;   30
And as their wit is, their digestion,
      Thy nourisht fame is weak or strong.

Then cease discoursing soul, till thine own ground,
      Do not thy self or friends importune.
He that by seeking hath himself once found,   35
      Hath ever found a happie fortune.

The Quidditie

My God, a verse is not a crown,
No point of honour, or gay suit,
No hawk, or banquet, or renown,
Nor a good sword, nor yet a lute:

Content
15. *let loose to:* aim at (a term in archery).
16. *Take up* [residence] etc.: the Emperor Charles V had abdicated in
    1556 for a cloister.
24. *huge King:* the corpse of the corpulent William the Conqueror is
    reported to have given off an intolerable odour [*FEH*].
28. *rent:* i.e. rend, tear.
33. *discoursing:* busily thinking.
The Quidditie. Original title in *W: Poetry*. The title, properly 'the real
    nature or essence of a thing', came to mean subtlety in argument,
    quirk, quibble [*OED*; § 243].
  1. *verse:* see above, p. 33, note on 5.

It cannot vault, or dance, or play;   5
It never was in *France* or *Spain*;
Nor can it entertain the day
With a great stable or demain:

It is no office, art, or news,
Nor the Exchange, or busie Hall;   10
But it is that which while I use
I am with thee, and *Most take all.*

Humilitie

I saw the Vertues sitting hand in hand
In sev'rall ranks upon an azure throne,
Where all the beasts and fowls by their command
Presented tokens of submission.
Humilitie, who sat the lowest there   5
          To execute their call,
When by the beasts the presents tendred were,
          Gave them about to all.

The angrie Lion did present his paw,
Which by consent was giv'n to Mansuetude.   10
The fearfull Hare her eares, which by their law
Humilitie did reach to Fortitude,
'The jealous Turkie brought his corall-chain;
          That went to Temperance.
On Justice was bestow'd the Foxes brain,   15
          Kill'd in the way by chance.

At length the Crow bringing the Peacocks plume,
(For he would not) as they beheld the grace
Of that brave gift, each one began to fume,
And challenge it, as proper to his place,   20
Till they fell out: which when the beasts espied,
          They leapt upon the throne;
And if the Fox had liv'd to rule their side,
          They had depos'd each one.

8. *a great:* both *W* and *B* read 'my great'.
12. *Most take all:* a worldly proverb ('most' used in the sense of 'the
    most powerful'), here christianized [§ 303]. Cf. above, p. 35, note
    on 66.

Humilitie
  3. *beasts:* man's natural passions (as above, p. 40, ll. 263–4).
10. *Mansuetude:* gentleness.
13. *corall-chain:* i.e. the turkey's red wattle.

Humilitie, who held the plume, at this   25
Did weep so fast, that the tears trickling down
Spoil'd all the train: then saying, *Here it is*
For which ye wrangle, made them turn their frown
Against the beasts: so joyntly bandying,
                    They drive them soon away;   30
And then amerc'd them, double gifts to bring
                At the next Session-day.

Frailtie

Lord, in my silence how do I despise
                What upon trust
Is styled *honour*, *riches*, or *fair eyes;*
                But is *fair dust!*
        I surname them *guilded clay*,   5
            Deare earth, fine grasse or *hay;*
In all, I think my foot doth ever tread
                Upon their head.

But when I view abroad both Regiments;
                The worlds, and thine: 10
Thine clad with simplenesse, and sad events;
                The other fine,
        Full of glorie and gay weeds
            Brave language, braver deeds:
That which was dust before, doth quickly rise,   15
                And prick mine eyes.

O brook not this, lest if what even now
                My foot did tread,
Affront those joyes, wherewith thou didst endow,
                And long since wed   20
        My poore soul, ev'n sick of love:
It may a Babel prove
Commodious to conquer heav'n and thee
                Planted in me.

29. *bandying:* banding together.
31. *amerc'd:* fined.

Frailtie
11. *sad:* serious.
16. *And prick:* 'Troubling' (*W*).

Constancie

       Who is the honest man?
He that doth still and strongly good pursue,
To God, his neighbour, and himself most true:
       Whom neither force nor fawning can
Unpinne, or wrench from giving all their due.   5

       Whose honestie is not
So loose or easie, that a ruffling winde
Can blow away, or glittering look it blinde:
       Who rides his sure and even trot,
While the world now rides by, now lags behinde.   10

       Who, when great trials come,
Nor seeks, nor shunnes them; but doth calmly stay,
Till he the thing and the example weigh:
       All being brought into a summe,
What place or person calls for, he doth pay.   15

       Whom none can work or wooe
To use in any thing a trick or sleight;
For above all things he abhorres deceit:
       His words and works and fashion too
All of a piece, and all are cleare and straight.   20

       Who never melts or thaws
At close tentations: when the day is done,
His goodnesse sets not, but in dark can runne:
       The sunne to others writeth laws,
And is their vertue; Vertue is his Sunne.   25

       Who, when he is to treat
With sick folks, women, those whom passions sway,
Allows for that, and keeps his constant way:
       Whom others faults do not defeat;
But though men fail him, yet his part doth play.   30

       Whom nothing can procure,
When the wide world runnes bias, from his will
To writhe his limbes, and share, not mend the ill.
       This is the Mark-man, safe and sure,
Who still is right, and prayes to be so still.   35

Constancie
22. *tentations:* i.e. temptations.
24-5. *sunne:* as above, p. 36, note on 98.
32. *his:* i.e. the bowler's (*bias* is a metaphor from the game, as above,
    p. 67, l. 53).

Affliction (III)

My heart did heave, and there came forth, *O God!*
By that I knew that thou wast in the grief,
To guide and govern it to my relief,
    Making a scepter of the rod:
      Hadst thou not had thy part,   5
Sure the unruly sigh had broke my heart.

But since thy breath gave me both life and shape,
Thou knowst my tallies; and when there's assign'd
So much breath to a sigh, what's then behinde?
    Or if some yeares with it escape,   10
      The sigh then onely is
A gale to bring me sooner to my blisse.

Thy life on earth was grief, and thou art still
Constant unto it, making it to be
A point of honour, now to grieve in me,   15
    And in thy members suffer ill.
      They who lament one crosse,
Thou dying dayly, praise thee to thy losse.

The Starre

Bright spark, shot from a brighter place,
    Where beams surround my Saviours face,
      Canst thou be any where
        So well as there?

Yet, if thou wilt from thence depart,   5
    Take a bad lodging in my heart;
      For thou canst make a debter,
        And make it better.

First with thy fire-work burn to dust
    Folly, and worse then folly, lust: 10
      Then with thy light refine,
        And make it shine:

So disengag'd from sinne and sicknesse,
    Touch it with thy celestiall quicknesse,
      That it may hang and move   15
        After thy love.

Affliction III
  8. *tallies:* accounts; also, deals (in the gaming sense).
 10. 'A sigh was thought to shorten man's life' [*LS*].

Then with our trinitie of light,
  Motion, and heat, let's take our flight
    Unto the place where thou
      Before didst bow.   20

Get me a standing there, and place
  Among the beams, which crown the face
    Of him, who dy'd to part
      Sinne and my heart:

That so among the rest I may   25
  Glitter, and curle, and winde as they:
    That winding is their fashion
      Of adoration.

Sure thou wilt joy, by gaining me
  To flie home like a laden bee
    Unto that hive of beams   30
      And garland-streams.

Sunday

    O day most calm, most bright,
The fruit of this, the next worlds bud,
Th' indorsement of supreme delight,
Writ by a friend, and with his bloud;
The couch of time, cares balm and bay: 5
The week were dark, but for thy light:
    Thy torch doth show the way.

    The other dayes and thou
Make up one man; whose face thou art,
Knocking at heaven with thy brow: 10
The worky-daies are the back-part;
The burden of the week lies there,
Making the whole to stoup and bow,
    Till thy release appeare.

    Man had straight forward gone   15
To endlesse death: but thou dost pull
And turn us round to look on one,
Whom, if we were not very dull,
We could not choose but look on still;
Since there is no place so alone,   20
    The which he doth not fill.

Sunday. On the title's pun, see above, p. 36, note on 98.
6-7. Cf. Psalm 119.105: 'Thy word is a lamp unto my feet, and a light
  unto my path'.

Sundaies the pillars are,
On which heav'ns palace arched lies:
The other dayes fill up the spare
And hollow room with vanities.   25
They are the fruitfull beds and borders
In Gods rich garden: that is bare,
      Which parts their ranks and orders.

The Sundaies of mans life,
Thredded together on times string,   30
Make bracelets to adorn the wife
Of the eternall glorious King.
On Sunday heavens gate stands ope;
Blessings are plentifull and rife,
      More plentifull then hope.   35

This day my Saviour rose,
And did inclose this light for his:
That, as each beast his manger knows,
Man might not of his fodder misse.
Christ hath took in this piece of ground,   40
And made a garden there for those
      Who want herbs for their wound.

The rest of our Creation
Our great Redeemer did remove
With the same shake, which at his passion   45
Did th' earth and all things with it move.
As Samson bore the doores away,
Christs hands, though nail'd, wrought our salvation,
      And did unhinge that day.

The brightnesse of that day   50
We sullied by our foul offence:
Wherefore that robe we cast away,
Having a new at his expence,

27-8. *that is bare, | Which parts:* 'Parted with alleys or with grass' (*W*).
45-6. At the death of Jesus, 'the earth did quake, and the rocks rent'
    (Matthew 27.51). Nature's reaction was usually interpreted as 'an
    undoubted signe' of God's wrath, 'a doleful Sermon' addressed to
    sinful humanity (John Mayer, *A Treasury of Ecclesiasticall Ex-
    positions* [1622], p. 336, and Robert Allen, *The Doctrine of the
    Gospel* [1606], II, 192).
47-9. The allusion is to Samson's removal of the gates of Gaza (Judges
    16.3). The typological commonplace was expanded in Herbert's
    Latin poem on the Passion to include Samson's shattering of the
    Philistine temple: 'with the cross / You move the whole [earth]
    to and fro / As Sampson moved the pillars long ago' [*LPH*, p. 77].
49. *that day:* i.e. the day of his Crucifixion, or the old Sabbath, or both.
52-3. Cf. Revelation 7.14: 'These are they which came out of great
    tribulation, and have washed their robes, and made them white
    in the blood of the Lamb'.

Whose drops of bloud paid the full price,
That was requir'd to make us gay,
    And fit for Paradise.   55

    Thou art a day of mirth:
And where the week-dayes trail on ground,
Thy flight is higher, as thy birth.
O let me take thee at the bound,   60
Leaping with thee from sev'n to sev'n,
Till that we both, being toss'd from earth,
    Flie hand in hand to heav'n!

Avarice

Money, thou bane of blisse, & source of wo,
    Whence com'st thou, that thou art so fresh and fine?
    I know thy parentage is base and low:
Man found thee poore and dirtie in a mine.

Surely thou didst so little contribute   5
    To this great kingdome, which thou now hast got,
    That he was fain, when thou wert destitute,
To digge thee out of thy dark cave and grot:

Then forcing thee, by fire he made thee bright:
    Nay, thou hast got the face of man; for we   10
    Have with our stamp and seal transferr'd our right:
Thou art the man, and man but drosse to thee.

    Man calleth thee his wealth, who made thee rich;
    And while he digs out thee, falls in the ditch.

Ana- $\left\{ \begin{matrix} \text{M A R Y} \\ \text{A R M Y} \end{matrix} \right\}$ *gram*

How well her name an *Army* doth present,
In whom the *Lord of Hosts* did pitch his tent!

55. *gay* (also *mirth* in 57): see above, p. 21.

Avarice

10. *the face of man:* i.e. the king's face stamped on coins (as in Donne's
    'The Canonization', l. 7).

Anagram. The only change in the arrangement of the poems in *B* and
    in the 1st edition of 1633 is the removal of this poem from its
    former place after *Church-musick* (above, p. 83) to this point
    [cf. § 254].

  2. *pitch his tent:* cf. John 1.14: 'the Word was made flesh and dwelt
    [literally 'pitched his tent'] among us' [§ 287].

To all Angels and Saints

Oh glorious spirits, who after all your bands
See the smooth face of God, without a frown
        Or strict commands;
Where ev'ry one is king, and hath his crown,
If not upon his head, yet in his hands: 5

Not out of envie or maliciousnesse
Do I forbear to crave your speciall aid:
        I would addresse
My vows to thee most gladly, blessed Maid,
And Mother of my God, in my distresse.   10

Thou art the holy mine, whence came the gold,
The great restorative for all decay
        In young and old;
Thou art the cabinet where the jewell lay:
Chiefly to thee would I my soul unfold: 15

But now (alas!) I dare not; for our King,
Whom we do all joyntly adore and praise,
        Bids no such thing:
And where his pleasure no injunction layes,
('Tis your own case) ye never move a wing.   20

All worship is prerogative, and a flower
Of his rich crown, from whom lyes no appeal
        At the last houre:
Therefore we dare not from his garland steal,
To make a posie for inferiour power.   25

Although then others court you, if ye know
What's done on earth, we shall not fare the worse,
        Who do not so;
Since we are ever ready to disburse,
If any one our Masters hand can show.   30

To all Angels and Saints
  1. *bands:* ranks; or possibly *bonds*, i.e. 'fetters of sin' [*FEH*].
  4-5. Cf. the vision of the twenty-four elders whose golden crowns are
     cast before God's throne (Revelation 4.4 ff.).
  12. *restorative:* gold was thought to have medicinal powers.
  16 ff. A tactful censure of Mariolatry, especially the Roman Catholic
     tendency to regard the Virgin as co-redemptrix with Christ.

Employment (11)

He that is weary, let him sit.
    My soul would stirre
And trade in courtesies and wit,
    Quitting the furre
To cold complexions needing it.   5

Man is no starre, but a quick coal
    Of mortall fire:
Who blows it not, nor doth controll
    A faint desire,
Lets his own ashes choke his soul.   10

When th' elements did for place contest
    With him, whose will
Ordain'd the highest to be best;
    The earth sat still,
And by the others is opprest.   15

Life is a businesse, not good cheer;
    Ever in warres.
The sunne still shineth there or here,
    Whereas the starres
Watch an advantage to appeare.   20

Oh that I were an Orenge-tree,
    That busie plant!
Then should I ever laden be,
    And never want
Some fruit for him that dressed me.   25

But we are still too young or old;
    The man is gone,
Before we do our wares unfold:
    So we freeze on,
Untill the grave increase our cold.   30

Employment II
5. *complexions:* habits or constitutions, thought to have been determined by the four 'humours' corresponding to the four elements (below, note on 11).
6. *quick coal:* 'live coal' (Isaiah 6.6).
11. *elements:* earth (the least active, l. 14), water, air and fire (*the highest*, l. 13).
22. *busie:* because it bears blossom and fruit at the same time.
27. *man:* 'Man' (*W* and *B*).

Deniall

When my devotions could not pierce
          Thy silent eares;
Then was my heart broken, as was my verse:
          My breast was full of fears
                    And disorder: 5

My bent thoughts, like a brittle bow,
          Did flie asunder:
Each took his way; some would to pleasures go,
          Some to the warres and thunder
                    Of alarms.   10

As good go any where, they say,
          As to benumme
Both knees and heart, in crying night and day,
          Come, come, my God, O come,
                    But no hearing.   15

O that thou shouldst give dust a tongue
          To crie to thee,
And then not heare it crying! all day long
          My heart was in my knee,
                    But no hearing.   20

Therefore my soul lay out of sight,
          Untun'd, unstrung:
My feeble spirit, unable to look right,
          Like a nipt blossome, hung
                    Discontented.   25

O cheer and tune my heartlesse breast,
          Deferre no time;
That so thy favours granting my request,
          They and my minde may chime,
                    And mend my ryme.   30

Christmas

All after pleasures as I rid one day,
          My horse and I, both tir'd, bodie and minde,
          With full crie of affections, quite astray;
I took up in the next inne I could finde.

Deniall
  3. *verse:* as above, p. 33, note on 5.
  5. *disorder:* unrhymed (so are all the concluding lines of each stanza
      except the last). [cf. §§ 148, 188, 213].

Christmas. Original title in *W: Christmas-Day.*
  1. *rid:* rode.

There when I came, whom found I but my deare,   5
   My dearest Lord, expecting till the grief
   Of pleasures brought me to him, readie there
To be all passengers most sweet relief?

O Thou, whose glorious, yet contracted light,
   Wrapt in nights mantle, stole into a manger;   10
   Since my dark soul and brutish is thy right,
To Man of all beasts be not thou a stranger:

   Furnish & deck my soul, that thou mayst have
   A better lodging, then a rack, or grave.

The shepherds sing; and shall I silent be?   15
     My God, no hymne for thee?
My soul's a shepherd too; a flock it feeds
     Of thoughts, and words, and deeds.
The pasture is thy word: the streams, thy grace
     Enriching all the place.   20
Shepherd and flock shall sing, and all my powers
     Out-sing the day-light houres.
Then we will chide the sunne for letting night
     Take up his place and right:
We sing one common Lord; wherefore he should   25
     Himself the candle hold.
I will go searching, till I finde a sunne
     Shall stay, till we have done;
A willing shiner, that shall shine as gladly,
     As frost-nipt sunnes look sadly.   30
Then we will sing, and shine all our own day,
     And one another pay:
His beams shall cheer my breast, and both so twine,
'Till ev'n his beams sing, and my musick shine.

Ungratefulnesse

Lord, with what bountie and rare clemencie
     Hast thou redeem'd us from the grave!
         If thou hadst let us runne,
     Gladly had man ador'd the sunne,
         And thought his god most brave;   5
Where now we shall be better gods then he.

14. *a rack:* a heck to hold fodder. The word also anticipates the Passion.
15 ff. Set to music by Vaughan Williams in *Hodie: A Christmas Cantata*
   (1953).
Ungratefulnesse
  6. *better gods then he:* cf. Matthew 13.43: 'Then shall the righteous
    shine forth as the sun in the kingdom of their Father'.

Thou hast but two rare cabinets full of treasure,
  The *Trinitie*, and *Incarnation*:
   Thou hast unlockt them both,
  And made them jewels to betroth   10
   The work of thy creation
Unto thy self in everlasting pleasure.

The statelier cabinet is the *Trinitie*,
  Whose sparkling light accesse denies:
   Therefore thou dost not show   15
  This fully to us, till death blow
   The dust into our eyes:
For by that powder thou wilt make us see.

But all thy sweets are packt up in the other;
  Thy mercies thither flock and flow: 20
   That as the first affrights,
  This may allure us with delights;
   Because this box we know;
For we have all of us just such another.

But man is close, reserv'd, and dark to thee: 25
  When thou demandest but a heart,
   He cavils instantly.
  In his poore cabinet of bone
   Sinnes have their box apart,
Defrauding thee, who gavest two for one.   30

Sighs and Grones

    O do not use me
After my sinnes! look not on my desert,
But on thy glorie! then thou wilt reform
And not refuse me: for thou onely art
The mightie God, but I a sillie worm;   5
    O do not bruise me!

14. *sparkling light accesse denies:* so Milton's God is 'Dark with excessive
  bright' (*Paradise Lost*, III, 380).
18. 'A common treatment of a horse or dog with bad eyes was to blow
  powder into them to clear the film' [*FEH*].
19. *sweets:* perfumes.
23. *this box:* i.e. the Incarnation.
30. *two:* the 'two rare cabinets' (7).
  one: i.e. 'a heart' (26).

Sighs and Grones
1-2. Cf. Psalm 103.10: 'He hath not dealt with us after our sins'.

O do not urge me!
For what account can thy ill steward make?
I have abus'd thy stock, destroy'd thy woods,
Suckt all thy magazens: my head did ake,　　　　10
Till it found out how to consume thy goods:
　　　　　O do not scourge me!

O do not blinde me!
I have deserv'd that an Egyptian night
Should thicken all my powers; because my lust　　15
Hath still sow'd fig-leaves to exclude thy light:
But I am frailtie, and already dust;
　　　　　O do not grinde me!

O do not fill me
With the turn'd viall of thy bitter wrath!　　20
For thou hast other vessels full of bloud,
A part whereof my Saviour empti'd hath,
Ev'n unto death: since he di'd for my good,
　　　　　O do not kill me!

But O reprieve me!　　25
For thou hast *life* and *death* at thy command;
Thou art both *Judge* and *Saviour, feast* and *rod,*
Cordiall and *Corrosive*: put not thy hand
Into the bitter box; but O my God,
　　　　　My God, relieve me!　　30

The World

Love built a stately house; where *Fortune* came,
And spinning phansies, she was heard to say,
That her fine cobwebs did support the frame,
Whereas they were supported by the same:
But *Wisdome* quickly swept them all away.　　5

Then *Pleasure* came, who liking not the fashion,
Began to make *Balcones, Terraces,*
Till she had weakned all by alteration:
But rev'rend *laws,* and many a *proclamation*
Reformed all at length with menaces.　　10

10. *magazens:* storehouses.
14. *Egyptian night:* cf. the plague of 'thick darkness in all the land of Egypt' (Exodus 10.22).
16. *fig-leaves:* used by Adam and Eve to cover their nakedness after the Fall (Genesis 3.7).
20. *turn'd viall:* cf. the 'seven golden vials full of the wrath of God' (Revelation 15.7).

The World
7. *Balcones:* trisyllabic, scanned balcónes.

Then enter'd *Sinne*, and with that Sycomore,
Whose leaves first sheltred man from drought & dew,
Working and winding slily evermore,
The inward walls and Sommers cleft and tore:
But *Grace* shor'd these, and cut that as it grew.   15

Then *Sinne* combin'd with *Death* in a firm band
To rase the building to the very floore:
Which they effected, none could them withstand.
But *Love* and *Grace* took *Glorie* by the hand,
And built a braver Palace then before.   20

Coloss. 3.3

Our life is hid with Christ in God

My words & thoughts do both expresse this notion,
That   *Life* hath with the sun a double motion.
The   first   *Is* straight, and our diurnall friend,
The   other   *Hid* and doth obliquely bend.
One life is wrapt *In* flesh, and tends to earth.   5
The other winds towards *Him*, whose happie birth
Taught me to live here so, *That* still one eye
Should aim and shoot at that which *Is* on high:
Quitting   with   daily   labour   all   *My* pleasure,
To   gain   at   harvest   an   eternall   *Treasure*.   10

Vanitie (1)

          The fleet Astronomer can bore,
And thred the spheres with his quick-piercing minde:
He views their stations, walks from doore to doore,
          Surveys, as if he had design'd
To make a purchase there: he sees their dances,   5
          And knoweth long before,
Both their full-ey'd aspects, and secret glances.

11. *Sycomore:* sycamore, which by a mistaken etymology was said to be
    a species of fig-tree (cf. *fig-leaves* in the previous poem, l. 16).
    [§ 232].
14. *Sommers:* supporting beams.
15. *that:* i.e. the sycamore.
17. *rase:* 'raze' (*W* and *B*).
20. *braver Palace:* cf. above, p. 63, note on 10.
Coloss. 3.3. The full verse reads: 'For ye are dead, and your life is hid
    with Christ in God'.
 4. *obliquely bend:* i.e. like the motto across the poem.
Vanitie I
 2. *spheres:* the concentric hollow globes thought to revolve about the
    earth carrying with them the heavenly bodies.
 7. *aspects:* positions in relation to bodies on earth.

    The nimble Diver with his side
Cuts through the working waves, that he may fetch
His dearely-earned pearl, which God did hide   10
     On purpose from the ventrous wretch;
That he might save his life, and also hers,
      Who with excessive pride
Her own destruction and his danger wears.

    The subtil Chymick can devest   15
And strip the creature naked, till he finde
The callow principles within their nest:
     There he imparts to them his minde,
Admitted to their bed-chamber, before
      They appeare trim and drest   20
To ordinarie suitours at the doore.

    What hath not man sought out and found,
But his deare God? who yet his glorious law
Embosomes in us, mellowing the ground
     With showres and frosts, with love & aw,   25
So that we need not say, Where's this command?
      Poore man, thou searchest round
To finde out *death*, but missest *life* at hand.

Lent

Welcome deare feast of Lent: who loves not thee,
He loves not Temperance, or Authoritie,
     But is compos'd of passion.
The Scriptures bid us *fast*; the Church sayes, *now*:
Give to thy Mother, what thou wouldst allow   5
     To ev'ry Corporation.

The humble soul compos'd of love and fear
Begins at home, and layes the burden there,
     When doctrines disagree.
He says, in things which use hath justly got,   10
I am a scandall to the Church, and not
     The Church is so to me.

15. *Chymick:* i.e. chemist.
17. *callow:* without feathers, suggesting principles in their essence, not
  as they *appeare trim and drest* (20).
23. *his glorious law:* as above, p. 65, note on 13–14.

Lent. Walton reports Herbert's reminder to his parishioners 'that by the
  Lent-fast, we imitate and commemorate our Saviours humiliation
  in fasting Forty days' [*IW*, p. 300]. Fasting as prescribed by
  Authoritie (l. 2) is set forth in *A Priest to the Temple* (Ch. 10).
11. *scandall:* stumbling-block, offence.

True Christians should be glad of an occasion
To use their temperance, seeking no evasion,
   When good is seasonable;   15
Unlesse Authoritie, which should increase
The obligation in us, make it lesse,
   And Power it self disable.

Besides the cleannesse of sweet abstinence,
Quick thoughts and motions at a small expense, 20
   A face not fearing light:
Whereas in fulnesse there are sluttish fumes,
Sowre exhalations, and dishonest rheumes,
   Revenging the delight.

Then those same pendant profits, which the spring 25
And Easter intimate, enlarge the thing,
   And goodnesse of the deed.
Neither ought other mens abuse of Lent
Spoil the good use; lest by that argument
   We forfeit all our Creed.   30

It's true, we cannot reach Christs forti'th day;
Yet to go part of that religious way,
   Is better then to rest:
We cannot reach our Saviours puritie;
Yet are we bid, *Be holy ev'n as he.*   35
   In both let's do our best.

Who goeth in the way which Christ hath gone,
Is much more sure to meet with him, then one
   That travelleth by-wayes:
Perhaps my God, though he be farre before,   40
May turn, and take me by the hand, and more
   May strengthen my decayes.

Yet Lord instruct us to improve our fast
By starving sinne and taking such repast,
   As may our faults controll: 45
That ev'ry man may revell at his doore,
Not in his parlour; banquetting the poore,
   And among those his soul.

24. *Revenging:* 'exacting appropriate punishment for' [*FEH*].
25. *pendant:* suspended like fruits before they are gathered.
35. *Be holy:* cf. Matthew 5.48: 'be ... perfect, even as your Father
which is in heaven is perfect'.

Vertue

Sweet day, so cool, so calm, so bright,
The bridall of the earth and skie:
The dew shall weep thy fall to night;
        For thou must die.

Sweet rose, whose hue angrie and brave   5
Bids the rash gazer wipe his eye:
Thy root is ever in its grave,
        And thou must die.

Sweet spring, full of sweet dayes and roses,
A box where sweets compacted lie;   10
My musick shows ye have your closes,
        And all must die.

Onely a sweet and vertuous soul,
Like season'd timber, never gives;
But though the whole world turn to coal,   15
        Then chiefly lives.

The Pearl. Matth. 13

I know the wayes of learning; both the head
And pipes that feed the presse, and make it runne;
What reason hath from nature borrowed,
Or of it self, a good huswife, spunne
In laws and policie; what the starres conspire,   5
What willing nature speaks, what forc'd by fire;
Both th' old discoveries, and the new-found seas,
The stock and surplus, cause and historie:
All these stand open, or I have the keyes:
        Yet I love thee.   10

Vertue

10. *box* [of] *sweets:* box of perfumes; also, a music box [§ 283]. Coleridge in quoting the poem's first three stanzas in *Biographia Literaria* (Ch. 19), amended *box* to *nest.*
11. *closes:* also in the technical sense of 'cadences'.
14. *timber:* an allusion to the Cross? [§ 197].
15. *turn to coal:* i.e. to cinder, during the final conflagration; but *coal* could also be intended in the sense of 'glowing coal' [§ 250]. The stanza appears to have influenced Yeats in *A Friend's Illness* [§ 322]:

    Why should I be dismayed
    Though flame had burned the whole
    World, as it were a coal,
    Now I have seen it weighed
    Against a soul?

The Pearl. Matthew 13.45 reads: 'the kingdom of heaven is like unto a

I know the wayes of honour, what maintains
The quick returns of courtesie and wit:
In vies of favours whether partie gains,
When glorie swells the heart, and moldeth it
To all expressions both of hand and eye,   15
Which on the world a true-love-knot may tie,
And bear the bundle, wheresoe'er it goes:
How many drammes of spirit there must be
To sell my life unto my friends or foes:
            Yet I love thee.   20

I know the wayes of pleasure, the sweet strains,
The lullings and the relishes of it;
The propositions of hot bloud and brains;
What mirth and musick mean; what love and wit
Have done these twentie hundred yeares, and more: 25
I know the projects of unbridled store:
My stuffe is flesh, not brasse; my senses live,
And grumble oft, that they have more in me
Then he that curbs them being but one to five:
            Yet I love thee.   30

I know all these, and have them in my hand:
Therefore not sealed, but with open eyes
I flie to thee, and fully understand
Both the main sale, and the commodities;
And at what rate and price I have thy love;   35
With all the circumstances that may move:
Yet through the labyrinths, not my groveling wit,
But thy silk twist let down from heav'n to me,
Did both conduct and teach me, how by it
            To climbe to thee.   40

      merchant-man seeking goodly pearls: who, when he had found one
      pearl of great price, went and sold all that he had, and bought it'.
      On Herbert's parabolic teaching, see above, pp. 10 f.
21-3. *strains, lullings, relishes:* musical terms suggesting tones, melodies,
      embellishments.
      propositions: the term *proposta* designates the leading part, or
      subject, of a fugue [cf. § 284].
32.   *sealed:* 'seeled' (*W*). Cf. above, p. 44, note on 415.
38.   *silk twist:* symbolic of faith [§ 276]? Cf. the cord by which Ariadne
      led Theseus out of the Labyrinth; but especially the familiar notion
      of the *scala coeli* allegorized by its interpreters from Jacob's ladder
      (Genesis 28.10–15) as much as from Homer's golden chain/rope
      let down from heav'n by Zeus (*Iliad*, VIII, 19–27). Both ladder and
      rope were thought 'to set forth Gods prouidence' (Andrew Willet,
      Hexapla in Genesin [1608], p. 302) but also the Incarnation: 'The
      Cross of Christ is the Jacobs ladder by which we Ascend into the
      Highest Heavens' (Traherne, *Centuries*, I, 60). Cf. § 220.

Affliction (IV)

Broken in pieces all asunder,
      Lord, hunt me not,
      A thing forgot,
Once a poore creature, now a wonder,
      A wonder tortur'd in the space   5
      Betwixt this world and that of grace.

My thoughts are all a case of knives,
      Wounding my heart
      With scatter'd smart,
As watring pots give flowers their lives.   10
      Nothing their furie can controll,
      While they do wound and prick my soul.

All my attendants are at strife,
      Quitting their place
      Unto my face: 15
Nothing performs the task of life:
      The elements are let loose to fight,
      And while I live, tric out their right.

Oh help, my God! let not their plot
      Kill them and me,   20
      And also thee,
Who art my life: dissolve the knot,
      As the sunne scatters by his light
      All the rebellions of the night.

Then shall those powers, which work for grief,   25
      Enter thy pay,
      And day by day
Labour thy praise, and my relief;
      With care and courage building me,
      Till I reach heav'n, and much more thee.   30

Affliction IV. Original title in *W: Tentation* (i.e. Temptation).
  4. *now a wonder*: cf. Psalm 71.7: 'I am as a wonder unto many; but
    thou art my strong refuge'.
  12. *prick*: 'pink' (*W* and *B*), a fencing term.
  17. *elements*: as above, p. 95, note on 11.

Man

My God, I heard this day,
That none doth build a stately habitation,
       But he that means to dwell therein.
       What house more stately hath there been,
Or can be, then is Man? to whose creation   5
       All things are in decay.

       For Man is ev'ry thing,
And more: He is a tree, yet bears no fruit;
       A beast, yet is, or should be more:
       Reason and speech we onely bring.   10
Parrats may thank us, if they are not mute,
       They go upon the score.

       Man is all symmetrie,
Full of proportions, one limbe to another,
       And all to all the world besides: 15
       Each part may call the farthest, brother:
For head with foot hath private amitie,
       And both with moons and tides.

       Nothing hath got so farre,
But Man hath caught and kept it, as his prey.   20
       His eyes dismount the highest starre:
       He is in little all the sphere:
Herbs gladly cure our flesh; because that they
       Finde their acquaintance there.

Man
  5. *to:* compared to.
  7. *Man is ev'ry thing:* i.e. not only a microcosm (see note on 13–18)
     but 'the tye, bond, knot, joynt, packet or bundle of all the Creatures'
     (Oswaldus Crollius, in *Philosophy Reformed* [1653], p. 55). Cf.
     above, p. 76, note on 21.
  8. *no fruit:* so *B* and the 1633 edn; but *W* reads 'more fruit'.
 12. *go upon the score:* are in our debt.
13-18. The widely disseminated belief was thus reiterated by Thomas
     Heywood among others:

Man is a ligament,
And folding up in a small continent,
Some part of all things which before were made;
For in this Microcosme are stor'd and layd
Connexiuely, as things made up and bound,
Corporeall things with incorporeall.

       (*The Hierarchy of the Blessed Angells* [1635], p. 338).

17-18. According to one version of this commonplace, 'God hath dis-
     posed the parts of the world, as the *members* of the body, and hath
     so tyed them together in mutuall and reciprocall offices, that no
     part of the whole universe can say to another, *I have no need of*

> For us the windes do blow,   25
> The earth doth rest, heav'n move, and fountains flow.
>   Nothing we see, but means our good,
>   As our *delight*, or as our *treasure*:
> The whole is, either our cupboard of *food*,
>   Or cabinet of *pleasure*.   30

>   The starres have us to bed;
> Night draws the curtain, which the sunne withdraws;
>   Musick and light attend our head.
>   All things unto our *flesh* are kinde
> In their *descent* and *being*; to our *minde*   35
>   In their *ascent* and *cause*.

>   Each thing is full of dutie:
> Waters united are our navigation;
>   Distinguished, our habitation;
>   Below, our drink; above, our meat;
> Both are our cleanlinesse. Hath one such beautie?   40
>   Then how are all things neat?

>   More servants wait on Man,
> Then he'l take notice of: in ev'ry path
>   He treads down that which doth befriend him,
>   When sicknesse makes him pale and wan.   45
> Oh mightie love! Man is one world, and hath
>   Another to attend him.

>   Since then, my God, thou hast
> So brave a Palace built; O dwell in it,
>   That it may dwell with thee at last!   50
>   Till then, afford us so much wit;
> That, as the world serves us, we may serve thee,
>   And both thy servants be.

thee' (Henry Valentine, *Four Sea-Sermons* [1635], p. 9). The related fable of the belly as told by Livy (II, xxxii, 9–12) was variously adapted by Shakespeare (*Coriolanus*, I, i, 101 ff.) and Milton (*Of Reformation*, in Columbia edn, III, 47-9).

25-6. Herbert's Ptolemaic universe is as earth-centred as Traherne's: 'For Me the World created was by Lov; / For Me the Skies, the Seas, the Sun, do mov; / The Earth for Me doth stable stand ...' ('Hosanna', 61 ff.). But Herbert uses *rest* with an irony which *The Pulley* (below, p. 166) makes explicit.

39. *Distinguished:* separated from the land during the creation (Genesis 1.9–10).

40. *our meat:* because rain is needed to produce our food. The eucharistic overtones are inescapable.

47-8. Cf. *A Priest to the Temple:* '[Thou] made us Lords of all thy creatures; giving us one world in our selves, and another to serve us' [*FEH*, p. 288].

Antiphon (II)

Chor.   Praised be the God of love,
        Men.   Here below,
        Angels. And here above:
Cho.   Who hath dealt his mercies so,
        Ang.   To his friend,   5
        Men.   And to his foe;

Cho.   That both grace and glorie tend
        Ang.   Us of old,
        Men.   And us in th'end.
Cho.   The greatest shepherd of the fold   10
        Ang.   Us did make,
        Men.   For us was sold.

Cho.   He our foes in pieces brake;
        Ang.   Him we touch;
        Men.   And him we take.
Cho.   Wherefore since that he is such,   15
        Ang.   We adore,
        Men.   And we do crouch.

Cho.   Lord, thy praises should be more.
        Men.   We have none,
        Ang.   And we no store.   20
Cho.   Praised be the God alone,
        Who hath made of two folds one.

Unkindnesse

Lord, make me coy and tender to offend:
In friendship, first I think, if that agree,
        Which I intend,
    Unto my friends intent and end.
I would not use a friend, as I use Thee.   5

If any touch my friend, or his good name;
It is my honour and my love to free
        His blasted fame
    From the least spot or thought of blame.
I could not use a friend, as I use Thee.   10

Antiphon II. Original title in *W*: *Ode.* See also above, p. 72.
15. *we take:* i.e. in the Eucharist.
18. *crouch:* bow low in reverence [*OED*].

Unkindnesse. The title implies both lack of compassion and unnatural-
   ness [§ 204].
  1. *coy:* reserved.

My friend may spit upon my curious floore:
Would he have gold? I lend it instantly;
          But let the poore,
     And thou within them starve at doore.
I cannot use a friend, as I use Thee.   15

When that my friend pretendeth to a place,
I quit my interest, and leave it free:
          But when thy grace
      Sues for my heart, I thee displace,
Nor would I use a friend, as I use Thee.   20

Yet can a friend what thou hast done fulfill?
O write in brasse, *My God upon a tree*
          His bloud did spill
      Onely to purchase my good-will:
Yet use I not my foes, as I use thee.   25

Life

I made a posie, while the day ran by:
Here will I smell my remnants out, and tie
          My life within this band.
But time did becken to the flowers, and they
By noon most cunningly did steal away,
          And wither'd in my hand.   5

My hand was next to them, and then my heart:
I took, without more thinking, in good part
          'Times gentle admonition:
Who did so sweetly deaths sad taste convey,
Making my minde to smell my fatall day;   10
          Yet sugring the suspicion.

Farewell deare flowers, sweetly your time ye spent,
Fit, while ye liv'd, for smell or ornament,
          And after death for cures.   15
I follow straight without complaints or grief,
Since if my sent be good, I care not, if
          It be as short as yours.

16. *pretendeth:* aspires.

Life
1. *posie:* bouquet; also, motto or poetry (as below, p. 186).
15. Cf. Donne: 'herbes, and roots, by dying lose not all, / But they,
    yea Ashes too, are medicinall' ('The First Anniversary', 403-4).

Submission

But that thou art my wisdome, Lord,
    And both mine eyes are thine,
My minde would be extreamly stirr'd
    For missing my designe.

Were it not better to bestow   5
    Some place and power on me?
Then should thy praises with me grow,
    And share in my degree.

But when I thus dispute and grieve,
    I do resume my sight,   10
And pilfring what I once did give,
    Disseize thee of thy right.

How know I, if thou shouldst me raise,
    That I should then raise thee?
Perhaps great places and thy praise   15
    Do not so well agree.

Wherefore unto my gift I stand;
    I will no more advise:
Onely do thou lend me a hand,
    Since thou hast both mine eyes.   20

Justice (1)

    I cannot skill of these thy wayes.
Lord, thou didst make me, yet thou woundest me;
Lord, thou dost wound me, yet thou dost relieve me:
Lord, thou relievest, yet I die by thee:
Lord, thou dost kill me, yet thou dost reprieve me.   5

    But when I mark my life and praise,
    Thy justice me most fitly payes:
For, *I do praise thee, yet I praise thee not:*
My prayers mean thee, yet my prayers stray:
I would do well, yet sinne the hand hath got: 10
My soul doth love thee, yet it loves delay.
    I cannot skill of these my wayes.

Submission
5-6. Cf. *A Priest to the Temple:* 'Ambition, or untimely desire of pro-
motion to an higher state, or place, . . . is a common temptation to
men' (Ch. 9).
12. *Disseize:* dispossess (a legal term).

Justice I
10. *the hand:* i.e. the upper hand.

Charms and Knots

Who reade a chapter when they rise,
Shall ne're be troubled with ill eyes.

A poore mans rod, when thou dost ride,
Is both a weapon and a guide.

Who shuts his hand, hath lost his gold: 5
Who opens it, hath it twice told.

Who goes to bed and doth not pray,
Maketh two nights to ev'ry day.

Who by aspersions throw a stone
At th' head of others, hit their own.   10

Who looks on ground with humble eyes,
Findes himself there, and seeks to rise.

When th' hair is sweet through pride or lust,
The powder doth forget the dust.

Take one from ten, and what remains?   15
Ten still, if sermons go for gains.

In shallow waters heav'n doth show;
But who drinks on, to hell may go.

Affliction (v)

My God, I read this day,
That planted Paradise was not so firm,
As was and is thy floting Ark; whose stay
And anchor thou art onely, to confirm
     And strengthen it in ev'ry age,   5
     When waves do rise, and tempests rage.

Charms and Knots. Two couplets in *W* were considerably revised (see
   notes on 3–4, 17–18), and three were eliminated. On Herbert's
   fondness for proverbs and his influence by wisdom literature
   generally, see above, p. 9.
3–4. Cf. *W:* 'A poore mans rod if thou wilt hire / Thy horse shal never
   fall or tire'.
9–10. Cf. *A Priest to the Temple:* 'he that throws a stone at another,
   hits himselfe' (Ch. 28).
17–18. Cf. *W:* 'In small draughts Heav'n does shine & dwell: / Who
   dives on further may find Hell'.

Affliction V
  3. *Ark:* i.e. the ark of Noah; but also, typologically, the Church.

At first we liv'd in pleasure;
Thine own delights thou didst to us impart:
When we grew wanton, thou didst use displeasure
To make us thine: yet that we might not part,   10
    As we at first did board with thee,
    Now thou wouldst taste our miserie.

There is but joy and grief;
If either will convert us, we are thine:
Some Angels us'd the first; if our relief   15
Take up the second, then thy double line
    And sev'rall baits in either kinde
    Furnish thy table to thy minde.

Affliction then is ours;
We are the trees, whom shaking fastens more,   20
While blustring windes destroy the wanton bowres,
And ruffle all their curious knots and store.
    My God, so temper joy and wo,
    That thy bright beams may tame thy bow.

Mortification

How soon doth man decay!
When clothes are taken from a chest of sweets
    To swaddle infants, whose young breath
    Scarce knows the way;
Those clouts are little winding sheets,   5
Which do consigne and send them unto death.

When boyes go first to bed,
They step into their voluntarie graves,
    Sleep bindes them fast; onely their breath
    Makes them not dead: 10
Successive nights, like rolling waves,
Convey them quickly, who are bound for death.

17. *baits:* 'used in the old sense of food, along with overtones of a
    fisherman's lure' [§ 191]. Other eucharistic words are more ex-
    plicit: *board* (11), *taste* (12), etc. Cf. above, p. 18.
22. *curious knots:* intricately-designed flower-beds.
24. *bow:* i.e. divine punishment (as in Isaiah 41.2, etc.); but also 'rain-
    bow' which after Noah's Flood appeared as 'a token of a covenant'
    between God and the elect (Genesis 9.13).

Mortification
 2. *sweets:* perfumes.
 5. *clouts:* swaddling clothes.

When youth is frank and free,
And calls for musick, while his veins do swell,
All day exchanging mirth and breath 15
In companie;
That musick summons to the knell,
Which shall befriend him at the house of death.

When man grows staid and wise,
Getting a house and home, where he may move 20
Within the circle of his breath,
Schooling his eyes;
That dumbe inclosure maketh love
Unto the coffin, that attends his death.

When age grows low and weak,
Marking his grave, and thawing ev'ry yeare, 25
Till all do melt, and drown his breath
When he would speak;
A chair or litter shows the biere,
Which shall convey him to the house of death. 30

Man, ere he is aware,
Hath put together a solemnitie,
And drest his herse, while he has breath
As yet to spare:
Yet Lord, instruct us so to die, 35
That all these dyings may be life in death.

Decay

Sweet were the dayes, when thou didst lodge with Lot,
Struggle with Jacob, sit with Gideon,
Advise with Abraham, when thy power could not
Encounter Moses strong complaints and mone:
Thy words were then, *Let me alone.* 5

17. *the knell:* the passing-bell, rung not only after death but while someone was dying.
18. *house:* 'houre' (*W*).
24. *attends:* awaits.
33. *herse:* bier, not funeral carriage.
Decay
2. *Struggle with Jacob:* cf. above, p. 31, note. 6. The other Biblical references are to Genesis 19.1 ff. (on Lot), Judges 6.11 ff. (Gideon), and Genesis 18.22 ff. (Abraham).
5. So Exodus 32.10: 'let me alone, that my wrath may wax hot against them'.

One might have sought and found thee presently
At some fair oak, or bush, or cave, or well:
Is my God this way? No, they would reply:
He is to Sinai gone, as we heard tell:
      List, ye may heare great Aarons bell.   10

But now thou dost thy self immure and close
In some one corner of a feeble heart:
Where yet both Sinne and Satan, thy old foes,
Do pinch and straiten thee, and use much art
      To gain thy thirds and little part.   15

I see the world grows old, when as the heat
Of thy great love once spread, as in an urn
Doth closet up it self, and still retreat,
Cold sinne still forcing it, till it return,
      And calling Justice, all things burn.   20

Miserie

    Lord, let the Angels praise thy name.
Man is a foolish thing, a foolish thing,
    Folly and Sinne play all his game.
His house still burns, and yet he still doth sing,
      Man is but grasse,   5
      He knows it, fill the glasse.

    How canst thou brook his foolishnesse?
Why he'l not lose a cup of drink for thee:
    Bid him but temper his excesse;
Not he: he knows, where he can better be,   10
      As he will swear,
      Then to serve thee in fear.

    What strange pollutions doth he wed,
And make his own? as if none knew, but he.
    No man shall beat into his head,   15
That thou within his curtains drawn canst see:
      They are of cloth,
      Where never yet came moth.

7. God appeared to Gideon near an *oak* (Judges 6.11) and to Moses in a
burning *bush* (Exodus 3.2), spoke to Elijah in a *cave* (1 Kings 19.9),
and had Abraham's servant meet Rebekah by a *well* (Genesis
24.11).
10. *great Aarons bell:* see below, p. 179, note on 1–4.
12. Cf. Luke 17.21: 'the kingdom of God is within you'.
15. *thirds:* a legal term, 'the third of the personal property of a de-
ceased husband allowed to his widow' [OED].

Miserie. Original title in *W: The Publican.*
  5. Isaiah 40.6: 'all flesh is grass'.

    The best of men, turn but thy hand
For one poore minute, stumble at a pinne: 20
    They would not have their actions scann'd,
Nor any sorrow tell them that they sinne,
            Though it be small,
            And measure not their fall.

    They quarrell thee, and would give over   25
The bargain made to serve thee: but thy love
    Holds them unto it, and doth cover
Their follies with the wing of thy milde Dove,
            Not suff'ring those
            Who would, to be thy foes.   30

    My God, Man cannot praise thy name:
Thou art all brightnesse, perfect puritie;
    The sunne holds down his head for shame,
Dead with eclipses, when we speak of thee:
            How shall infection   35
            Presume on thy perfection?

    As dirtie hands foul all they touch,
And those things most, which are most pure and fine:
    So our clay hearts, ev'n when we crouch
To sing thy praises, make them lesse divine.   40
            Yet either this,
            Or none thy portion is.

    Man cannot serve thee; let him go,
And serve the swine: there, there is his delight:
    He doth not like this vertue, no;   45
Give him his dirt to wallow in all night:
            These Preachers make
            His head to shoot and ake.

    Oh foolish man! where are thine eyes?
How hast thou lost them in a croud of cares?
    Thou pull'st the rug, and wilt not rise,   50
No not to purchase the whole pack of starres:
            There let them shine,
            Thou must go sleep, or dine.

    The bird that sees a daintie bowre   55
Made in the tree, where she was wont to sit,
    Wonders and sings, but not his power
Who made the arbour: this exceeds her wit.
            But Man doth know
            The spring, whence all things flow: 60

39. *crouch:* as above, p. 108, note on 18.
51. *pull'st the rug:* 'lyest warme' (*W*).

And yet as though he knew it not,
His knowledge winks, and lets his humours reigne;
    They make his life a constant blot,
And all the bloud of God to run in vain.
                    Ah wretch! what verse   65
                    Can thy strange wayes rehearse?

    Indeed at first Man was a treasure,
A box of jewels, shop of rarities,
    A ring, whose posie was, *My pleasure:*
He was a garden in a Paradise: 70
                    Glorie and grace
                    Did crown his heart and face.

    But sinne hath fool'd him. Now he is
A lump of flesh, without a foot or wing
    To raise him to the glimpse of blisse: 75
A sick toss'd vessel, dashing on each thing;
                    Nay, his own shelf:
                    My God, I mean my self.

Jordan (II)

When first my lines of heav'nly joyes made mention,
Such was their lustre, they did so excell,
That I sought out quaint words, and trim invention;
My thoughts began to burnish, sprout, and swell,
Curling with metaphors a plain intention,   5
Decking the sense, as if it were to sell.

Thousands of notions in my brain did runne,
Off'ring their service, if I were not sped:
I often blotted what I had begunne;
This was not quick enough, and that was dead.   10

69. *posie:* motto, verse (as below, p. 186).
77. *shelf:* reef (as above, p. 36, note on 120).
Jordan II. Original title in *W: Invention* (cf. l. 3). On the title's import see
    the headnote to *Jordan I*, above, p. 75; and on the poem as 'sacred
    parody': below, p. 211.
  5. *Curling with metaphors:* so Traherne was to promise

    No curling Metaphors that gild the Sence,
    Nor Pictures here, nor painted Eloquence;
    No florid Streams of Superficial Gems,
    But real Crowns and Thrones and Diadems!
                    ('The Author to the Critical Peruser', 11-14)
 10. *quick:* lively.

Nothing could seem too rich to clothe the sunne,
Much lesse those joyes which trample on his head.

As flames do work and winde, when they ascend,
So did I weave my self into the sense.
But while I bustled, I might heare a friend   15
Whisper, *How wide is all this long pretence!*
There is in love a sweetnesse readie penn'd:
Copie out onely that, and save expense.

Prayer (II)

   Of what an easie quick accesse,
My blessed Lord, art thou! how suddenly
   May our requests thine eare invade!
To shew that state dislikes not easinesse,
If I but lift mine eyes, my suit is made: 5
Thou canst no more not heare, then thou canst die.

   Of what supreme almightie power
Is thy great arm which spans the east and west,
   And tucks the centre to the sphere!
By it do all things live their measur'd houre: 10
We cannot ask the thing, which is not there,
Blaming the shallownesse of our request.

   Of what unmeasurable love
Art thou possest, who, when thou couldst not die,
   Wert fain to take our flesh and curse,   15
And for our sakes in person sinne reprove,
That by destroying that which ty'd thy purse,
Thou mightst make sure for liberalitie!

   Since then these three wait on thy throne,
Ease, Power, and *Love*; I value prayer so,   20
   That were I to leave all but one,
Wealth, fame, endowments, vertues, all should go;
I and deare prayer would together dwell,
And quickly gain, for each inch lost, an ell.

11. *sunne:* both sun and Son (as above, p. 36, note on 98).
Prayer II
  9. Perhaps an allusion to the commonplace notion of God as a circle
    whose centre is everywhere, and circumference nowhere.
    sphere: the outermost limit of the universe.
15. *curse:* 'Christ hath redeemed us from the curse of the law, being
    made a curse for us' (Galatians 3.13).
24. *ell:* as above, p. 46, note on 460.

Obedience

My God, if writings may
Convey a Lordship any way
Whither the buyer and the seller please;
Let it not thee displease,
If this poore paper do as much as they.   5

On it my heart doth bleed
As many lines as there doth need
To passe it self and all it hath to thee.
To which I do agree,
And here present it as my speciall deed.   10

If that hereafter Pleasure
Cavill, and claim her part and measure,
As if this passed with a reservation,
Or some such words in fashion;
I here exclude the wrangler from thy treasure.   15

O let thy sacred will
All thy delight in me fulfill!
Let me not think an action mine own way,
But as thy love shall sway,
Resigning up the rudder to thy skill.   20

Lord, what is man to thee,
That thou shouldst minde a rotten tree?
Yet since thou canst not choose but see my actions;
So great are thy perfections,
Thou mayest as well my actions guide, as see.   25

Besides, thy death and bloud
Show'd a strange love to all our good:
Thy sorrows were in earnest; no faint proffer,
Or superficiall offer
Of what we might not take, or be withstood.   30

Wherefore I all forgo:
To one word onely I say, No:
Where in the deed there was an intimation
Of a *gift* or *donation*,
Lord, let it now by way of *purchase* go.   35

Obedience
2. *Convey:* the first of the poem's numerous legal terms.
8. *passe:* convey legally.
13. *reservation:* clause reserving rights in property conveyed to another.
16. *will:* intention; also, a legal document [§ 204].

He that will passe his land,
As I have mine, may set his hand
And heart unto this deed, when he hath read;
And make the purchase spread
To both our goods, if he to it will stand.   40

How happie were my part,
If some kinde man would thrust his heart
Into these lines; till in heav'ns court of rolls
They were by winged souls
Entred for both, farre above their desert!   45

Conscience

Peace pratler, do not lowre:
Not a fair look, but thou dost call it foul:
Not a sweet dish, but thou dost call it sowre:
Musick to thee doth howl.
By listening to thy chatting fears   5
I have both lost mine eyes and eares.

Pratler, no more, I say:
My thoughts must work, but like a noiseless sphere;
Harmonious peace must rock them all the day:
No room for pratlers there.   10
If thou persistest, I will tell thee,
That I have physick to expell thee.

And the receit shall be
My Saviours bloud: when ever at his board
I do but taste it, straight it cleanseth me,   15
And leaves thee not a word;
No, not a tooth or nail to scratch,
And at my actions carp, or catch.

Yet if thou talkest still,
Besides my physick, know there's some for thee: 20
Some wood and nails to make a staffe or bill
For those that trouble me:
The bloudie crosse of my deare Lord
Is both my physick and my sword.

41-3. Responding to this invitation by his 'dear friend', Vaughan wrote:
'Here I joyn hands, and thrust my stubborn heart / Into thy
Deed' ('The Match', 7–8 [§ 332]).
43. *court of rolls:* custodian of legal documents.
Conscience
14. *board:* i.e. Holy Communion.
21. *bill:* halberd.

Sion

Lord, with what glorie wast thou serv'd of old,
When Solomons temple stood and flourished!
    Where most things were of purest gold;
    The wood was all embellished
With flowers and carvings, mysticall and rare: 5
All show'd the builders, crav'd the seers care.

Yet all this glorie, all this pomp and state
Did not affect thee much, was not thy aim;
    Something there was, that sow'd debate:
    Wherefore thou quitt'st thy ancient claim: 10
And now thy Architecture meets with sinne;
For all thy frame and fabrick is within.

There thou art struggling with a peevish heart,
Which sometimes crosseth thee, thou sometimes it:
    The fight is hard on either part.   15
    Great God doth fight, he doth submit.
All Solomons sea of brasse and world of stone
Is not so deare to thee as one good grone.

And truly brasse and stones are heavie things,
Tombes for the dead, not temples fit for thee: 20
    But grones are quick, and full of wings,
    And all their motions upward be;
And ever as they mount, like larks they sing;
The note is sad, yet musick for a king.

Home

Come Lord, my head doth burn, my heart is sick,
    While thou dost ever, ever stay:
Thy long deferrings wound me to the quick,
    My spirit gaspeth night and day.
        O shew thy self to me,   5
        Or take me up to thee!

Sion
  2. *Solomons temple:* see above, pp. 15–17.
      flourished: cf. 'flourish' in the sense of a fanfare. So other words
      also carry musical overtones, e.g. *embellished* (4), which involves
      melodic decoration, and *pomp* (7) or ceremonious music [§ 204].
  24. *musick for a king:* the phrase is probably a deliberate allusion to
      'The King's Music', the official title of the *secular* musical estab-
      lishment at court.

Home
  2. *stay:* stay away (as in 7, 31, 67, 76).

How canst thou stay, considering the pace
    The bloud did make, which thou didst waste?
When I behold it trickling down thy face,
    I never saw thing make such haste.   10
        O show thy self to me,
        Or take me up to thee!

When man was lost, thy pitie lookt about
    To see what help in th' earth or skie:
But there was none; at least no help without: 15
    The help did in thy bosome lie.
        O show thy, &c.

There lay thy sonne: and must he leave that nest,
    That hive of sweetnesse, to remove   20
Thraldome from those, who would not at a feast
    Leave one poore apple for thy love?
        O show thy, &c.

He did, he came: O my Redeemer deare,   25
    After all this canst thou be strange?
So many yeares baptiz'd, and not appeare?
    As if thy love could fail or change.
        O show thy, &c.   29

Yet if thou stayest still, why must I stay?
    My God, what is this world to me?
This world of wo? hence all ye clouds, away,
    Away; I must get up and see.
        O show thy, &c.   35

What is this weary world; this meat and drink,
    That chains us by the teeth so fast?
What is this woman-kinde, which I can wink
    Into a blacknesse and distaste?   40
        O show thy, &c.

With one small sigh thou gav'st me th' other day
    I blasted all the joyes about me:
And scouling on them as they pin'd away,
    Now come again, said I, and flout me.   45
        O show thy, &c.

13-15. Cf. Isaiah 59.16: '[God] wondered that there was no intercessor'.
19. The change from addressing the Son (6 ff.) to addressing the Father
is trinitarian theology in action.
22. Cf. *A Priest to the Temple*: 'for an apple once we lost our God, and
still lose him for no more' [*FEH*, p. 288].

Nothing but drought and dearth, but bush and brake,
    Which way so-e're I look, I see.   50
Some may dream merrily, but when they wake,
    They dresse themselves and come to thee.
        O show thy self to me,
        Or take me up to thee!

We talk of harvests; there are no such things,   55
    But when we leave our corn and hay:
There is no fruitfull yeare, but that which brings
    The last and lov'd, though dreadfull day.
        O show thy, &c.

Oh loose this frame, this knot of man untie!   61
    That my free soul may use her wing,
Which now is pinion'd with mortalitie,
    As an intangled, hamper'd thing.
        O show thy, &c.   65

What have I left, that I should stay and grone?
    The most of me to heav'n is fled:
My thoughts and joyes are all packt up and gone,
    And for their old acquaintance plead.   70
        O show thy, &c.

Come dearest Lord, passe not this holy season,
    My flesh and bones and joynts do pray:
And ev'n my verse, when by the ryme and reason   75
    The word is, *Stay*, sayes ever, *Come*.
        O show thy, &c.

The British Church

I joy, deare Mother, when I view
Thy perfect lineaments, and hue
        Both sweet and bright.

76. *The word is, Stay:* i.e. in order to rhyme with *pray* (74). The sub-
    stituted word *Come* joins with the poem's title to complete the
    meaning.

The British Church. A far less militant poem than its counterpart in
    Latin (quoted in part above, p. 21), it invites comparison with
    Donne's sonnet 'Show me deare Christ, thy spouse'. The argument
    involves 'the middle way between superstition and slovenliness'
    (*A Priest to the Temple*, Ch. 13).

Beautie in thee takes up her place,
And dates her letters from thy face,   5
   When she doth write.

A fine aspect in fit aray,
Neither too mean, nor yet too gay,
   Shows who is best.

Outlandish looks may not compare: 10
For all they either painted are,
   Or else undrest.

She on the hills, which wantonly
Allureth all in hope to be
   By her preferr'd,   15

Hath kiss'd so long her painted shrines,
That ev'n her face by kissing shines,
   For her reward.

She in the valley is so shie
Of dressing, that her hair doth lie   20
   About her eares:

While she avoids her neighbours pride,
She wholly goes on th' other side,
   And nothing wears.

But dearest Mother, (what those misse)   25
The mean thy praise and glorie is,
   And long may be.

Blessed be God, whose love it was
To double-moat thee with his grace,
   And none but thee.   30

The Quip

The merrie world did on a day
With his train-bands and mates agree
To meet together, where I lay,
And all in sport to geere at me.

5. *dates her letters:* Lady Day (the Annunciation) still officially marked
  the beginning of the new year [*JHS*].
13. *She on the hills:* Roman Catholicism.
19. *She in the valley:* Genevan Calvinism.
26. *The mean:* the *via media*, 'the middle way'.

The Quip. The title means both 'sharp remark' and 'verbal equivocation'
  [*OED*].
2. *train-bands:* 'trained bands', the citizen soldiery.

First, Beautie crept into a rose,   5
Which when I pluckt not, Sir, said she,
Tell me, I pray, Whose hands are those?
But thou shalt answer, Lord, for me.

Then Money came, and chinking still,
What tune is this, poore man? said he: 10
I heard in Musick you had skill.
But thou shalt answer, Lord, for me.

Then came brave Glorie puffing by
In silks that whistled, who but he?
He scarce allow'd me half an eie.   15
But thou shalt answer, Lord, for me.

Then came quick Wit and Conversation,
And he would needs a comfort be,
And, to be short, make an oration.
But thou shalt answer, Lord, for me.   20

Yet when the houre of thy designe
To answer these fine things shall come;
Speak not at large, say, I am thine:
And then they have their answer home.

Vanitie (II)

Poore silly soul, whose hope and head lies low;
Whose flat delights on earth do creep and grow;
To whom the starres shine not so fair, as eyes;
Nor solid work, as false embroyderies;
Heark and beware, lest what you now do measure   5
And write for sweet, prove a most sowre displeasure.

O heare betimes, lest thy relenting
                    May come too late!
To purchase heaven for repenting,
                    Is no hard rate.   10
If souls be made of earthly mold,
                    Let them love gold;
                    If born on high,
Let them unto their kindred flie:
For they can never be at rest,   15
                    Till they regain their ancient nest.
Then silly soul take heed; for earthly joy
Is but a bubble, and makes thee a boy.

8. Quoted from Psalm 38.15 in the Book of Common Prayer (cf. 12,
   16, 20).
17. *Wit and Conversation:* regarded as one entity.
24. *home:* used adverbially.

The Dawning

Awake sad heart, whom sorrow ever drowns;
   Take up thine eyes, which feed on earth;
Unfold thy forehead gather'd into frowns:
   Thy Saviour comes, and with him mirth:
      Awake, awake;   5
And with a thankfull heart his comforts take.
   But thou dost still lament, and pine, and crie;
   And feel his death, but not his victorie.

Arise sad heart; if thou dost not withstand,
   Christs resurrection thine may be: 10
Do not by hanging down break from the hand,
   Which as it riseth, raiseth thee:
      Arise, arise;
And with his buriall-linen drie thine eyes:
   Christ left his grave-clothes, that we might, when grief   15
   Draws tears, or bloud, not want an handkerchief.

JESU

J E S U is in my heart, his sacred name
Is deeply carved there: but th'other week
A great affliction broke the little frame,
Ev'n all to pieces: which I went to seek:
And first I found the corner, where was *J*,   5
After, where *E S*, and next where *U* was graved.
When I had got these parcels, instantly
I sat me down to spell them, and perceived
That to my broken heart he was *I ease you,*
      And to my whole is *J E S U*.   10

Businesse

      Canst be idle? canst thou play,
      Foolish soul who sinn'd to day?

Rivers run, and springs each one
Know their home, and get them gone:
Hast thou tears, or hast thou none?   5

The Dawning—i.e. of Easter Day. Cf. *Easter* (p. 61) and *Easter-wings*
  (p. 63).
16. *handkerchief:* used not in the modern but in the Biblical sense of
  miraculous means of healing. Cf. Acts 19.11–12: 'God wrought
  special miracles by the hands of Paul: so that from his body were
  brought unto the sick handkerchiefs or aprons, and the diseases
  departed from them' [§ 216].

If, poore soul, thou hast no tears;
Would thou hadst no faults or fears!
Who hath these, those ill forbears.

Windes still work: it is their plot,
Be the season cold, or hot: 10
Hast thou sighs, or hast thou not?

If thou hast no signs or grones,
Would thou hadst no flesh and bones!
Lesser pains scape greater ones.

    But if yet thou idle be,   15
    Foolish soul, Who di'd for thee?

Who did leave his Fathers throne,
To assume thy flesh and bone;
Had he life, or had he none?

If he had not liv'd for thee,   20
Thou hadst di'd most wretchedly;
And two deaths had been thy fee.

He so farre thy good did plot,
That his own self he forgot.
Did he die, or did he not?   25

If he had not di'd for thee,
Thou hadst liv'd in miserie.
Two lives worse then ten deaths be.

    And hath any space of breath
    'Twixt his sinnes and Saviours death?   30

He that loseth gold, though drosse,
Tells to all he meets, his crosse:
He that sinnes, hath he no losse?

He that findes a silver vein,
Thinks on it, and thinks again,   35
Brings thy Saviours death no gain?

    Who in heart not ever kneels,
    Neither sinne nor Saviour feels.

Businesse
22. *two deaths:* the natural one of the body, and the eternal one beyond
    the Last Judgement (Revelation 21.8). Cf. § 242.
    fee: allotted portion, reward.
28. *Two lives:* one here, the other hereafter, but alike in misery.

Dialogue

Sweetest Saviour, if my soul
    Were but worth the having,
Quickly should I then controll
    Any thought of waving.
But when all my care and pains   5
Cannot give the name of gains
To thy wretch so full of stains;
What delights or hope remains?

What (childe) is the ballance thine,
    Thine the poise and measure?   10
If I say, Thou shalt be mine;
    Finger not my treasure.
What the gains in having thee
Do amount to, onely he,
Who for man was sold, can see;   15
That transferr'd th' accounts to me.

But as I can see no merit,
    Leading to this favour:
So the way to fit me for it,
    Is beyond my savour.   20
As the reason then is thine;
So the way is none of mine:
I disclaim the whole designe:
Sinne disclaims and I resigne.

That is all, if that I could   25
    Get without repining;
And my clay my creature would
    Follow my resigning.
That as I did freely part
With my glorie and desert,   30
Left all joyes to feel all smart— —
    Ah! no more: thou break'st my heart.

Dulnesse

Why do I languish thus, drooping and dull,
    As if I were all earth?
O give me quicknesse, that I may with mirth
    Praise thee brim-full!

Dialogue
  4. *waving:* declining the offer, waiving.
 20. *savour:* perception, understanding. Cf. below, p. 180, headnote.
 22. Cf. 'Jesus saith unto him, I am the way . . .' (John 14.6).
 30. *desert:* pronounced and often written 'desart'.

The wanton lover in a curious strain   5
      Can praise his fairest fair;
And with quaint metaphors her curled hair
      Curl o're again.

Thou art my lovelinesse, my life, my light,
      Beautie alone to me: 10
Thy bloudy death and undeserv'd, makes thee
      Pure red and white.

When all perfections as but one appeare,
      That those thy form doth show,
The very dust, where thou dost tread and go,   15
      Makes beauties here;

Where are my lines then? my approaches? views?
      Where are my window-songs?
Lovers are still pretending, & ev'n wrongs
      Sharpen their Muse: 20

But I am lost in flesh, whose sugred lyes
      Still mock me, and grow bold:
Sure thou didst put a minde there, if I could
      Finde where it lies.

Lord, cleare thy gift, that with a constant wit   25
      I may but look towards thee:
Look onely; for to *love* thee, who can be,
      What angel fit?

Love-joy

As on a window late I cast mine eye,
I saw a vine drop grapes with *J* and *C*
Anneal'd on every bunch. One standing by
Ask'd what it meant. I (who am never loth
To spend my judgement) said, It seem'd to me   5
To be the bodie and the letters both
Of *Joy* and *Charitie*. Sir, you have not miss'd,
The man reply'd; It figures *JESUS CHRIST*.

Dulnesse
12. *Pure red and white:* a bold appropriation of the language of secular
    poets, but in the light of the Song of Solomon 5.10 ('My beloved is
    white and ruddy').
18. *Window-songs:* i.e. serenades.
19. *pretending:* wooing.
25. *cleare:* discharge the promise of.

Love-joy
  3. *Anneal'd:* enamelled by encaustic process (as above, p. 85, note
    on 6); also (?) 'aneled' or anointed in baptism [§ 265].

Providence

O sacred Providence, who from end to end
Strongly and sweetly movest! shall I write,
And not of thee, through whom my fingers bend
To hold my quill? shall they not do thee right?

Of all the creatures both in sea and land   5
Onely to Man thou hast made known thy wayes,
And put the penne alone into his hand,
And made him Secretarie of thy praise.

Beasts fain would sing; birds dittie to their notes;
Trees would be tuning on their native lute   10
To thy renown: but all their hands and throats
Are brought to Man, while they are lame and mute.

Man is the worlds high Priest: he doth present
The sacrifice for all; while they below
Unto the service mutter an assent,   15
Such as springs use that fall, and windes that blow.

He that to praise and laud thee doth refrain,
Doth not refrain unto himself alone,
But robs a thousand who would praise thee fain,
And doth commit a world of sinne in one.   20

The beasts say, Eat me: but, if beasts must teach,
The tongue is yours to eat, but mine to praise.
The trees say, Pull me: but the hand you stretch,
Is mine to write, as it is yours to raise.

Wherefore, most sacred Spirit, I here present   25
For me and all my fellows praise to thee:
And just it is that I should pay the rent,
Because the benefit accrues to me.

We all acknowledge both thy power and love
To be exact, transcendent, and divine;   30
Who dost so strongly and so sweetly move,
While all things have their will, yet none but thine.

Providence. A celebration of 'the wonderful providence and thrift of the
   great householder of the world' (*A Priest to the Temple*, Ch. 10).
   The major Biblical analogues are Psalm 104 and Job 38.
1-2. Cf. Wisdom of Solomon 8.1: 'Wisdom reacheth from one end to
   another mightily: and sweetly doth she order all things' [§ 282].
   Cf. 31, 38-9.

For either thy *command*, or thy *permission*
Lay hands on all: they are thy *right* and *left*.
The first puts on with speed and expedition;   35
The other curbs sinnes stealing pace and theft.

Nothing escapes them both; all must appeare,
And be dispos'd, and dress'd, and tun'd by thee,
Who sweetly temper'st all. If we could heare
Thy skill and art, what musick would it be!   40

Thou art in small things great, not small in any:
Thy even praise can neither rise, nor fall.
Thou art in all things one, in each thing many:
For thou art infinite in one and all.

Tempests are calm to thee; they know thy hand,   45
And hold it fast, as children do their fathers,
Which crie and follow. Thou hast made poore sand
Check the proud sea, ev'n when it swells and gathers.

Thy cupboard serves the world: the meat is set,
Where all may reach: no beast but knows his feed.   50
Birds teach us hawking; fishes have their net:
The great prey on the lesse, they on some weed.

Nothing ingendred doth prevent his meat:
Flies have their table spread, ere they appeare.
Some creatures have in winter what to eat;   55
Others do sleep, and envie not their cheer.

How finely dost thou times and seasons spin,
And make a twist checker'd with night and day!
Which as it lengthens windes, and windes us in,
As bouls go on, but turning all the way.   60

Each creature hath a wisdome for his good.
The pigeons feed their tender off-spring, crying,
When they are callow; but withdraw their food
When they are fledge, that need may teach them flying.

33. *permission:* an undogmatic affirmation of the permissive theory of
    evil so emphatically upheld in *Paradise Lost* (I, 211 ff.).
39. *temper'st:* bring into harmony, tune.
48. *proud sea:* cf. 'proud waves' (Job 38.11).
51. *their net:* i.e. their open mouths.
53. *prevent:* anticipate.

Bees work for man; and yet they never bruise   65
Their masters flower, but leave it, having done,
As fair as ever, and as fit to use;
So both the flower doth stay, and hony run.

Sheep eat the grasse, and dung the ground for more:
Trees after bearing drop their leaves for soil: 70
Springs vent their streams, and by expense get store:
Clouds cool by heat, and baths by cooling boil.

Who hath the vertue to expresse the rare
And curious vertues both of herbs and stones?
Is there an herb for that? O that thy care,   75
Would show a root, that gives expressions!

And if an herb hath power, what have the starres?
A rose, besides his beautie, is a cure.
Doubtlesse our plagues and plentie, peace and warres
Are there much surer then our art is sure.   80

Thou hast hid metals: man may take them thence;
But at his perill: when he digs the place,
He makes a grave; as if the thing had sense,
And threatned man, that he should fill the space.

Ev'n poysons praise thee. Should a thing be lost?   85
Should creatures want for want of heed their due?
Since where are poysons, antidots are most:
The help stands close, and keeps the fear in view.

The sea, which seems to stop the traveller,
Is by a ship the speedier passage made.   90
The windes, who think they rule the mariner,
Are rul'd by him, and taught to serve his trade.

And as thy house is full, so I adore
Thy curious art in marshalling thy goods.
The hills with health abound; the vales with store;   95
The South with marble; North with furres & woods.

Hard things are glorious; easie things good cheap.
The common all men have; that which is rare,
Men therefore seek to have, and care to keep.
The healthy frosts with summer-fruits compare.   100

72. *baths:* hot springs.
73. *expresse:* describe; also, squeeze out [*JHS*].
78. Roses are said in *A Priest to the Temple* to be 'home-bred medicines' (Ch. 23). Cf. below, p. 183, note on 18.
85. *poysons praise thee:* i.e. because of their medicinal powers.

Light without winde is glasse: warm without weight
Is wooll and furres: cool without closenesse, shade:
Speed without pains, a horse: tall without height,
A servile hawk: low without losse, a spade.

All countreys have enough to serve their need: 105
If they seek fine things, thou dost make them run
For their offence; and then dost turn their speed
To be commerce and trade from sunne to sunne.

Nothing wears clothes, but Man; nothing doth need
But he to wear them. Nothing useth fire,   110
But Man alone, to show his heav'nly breed:
And onely he hath fuell in desire.

When th' earth was dry, thou mad'st a sea of wet:
When that lay gather'd, thou didst broach the mountains:
When yet some places could no moisture get,   115
The windes grew gard'ners, and the clouds good fountains.

Rain, do not hurt my flowers; but gently spend
Your hony drops: presse not to smell them here:
When they are ripe, their odour will ascend,
And at your lodging with their thanks appeare.   120

How harsh are thorns to pears! and yet they make
A better hedge, and need lesse reparation.
How smooth are silks compared with a stake,
Or with a stone! yet make no good foundation.

Sometimes thou dost divide thy gifts to man,   125
Sometimes unite. The Indian nut alone
Is clothing, meat and trencher, drink and kan,
Boat, cable, sail and needle, all in one.

Most herbs that grow in brooks, are hot and dry.
Cold fruits warm kernells help against the winde.   130
The lemmons juice and rinde cure mutually.
The whey of milk doth loose, the milk doth binde.

Thy creatures leap not, but expresse a feast,
Where all the guests sit close, and nothing wants.

116. *grew:* i.e. grew into.
121. *to:* compared to.
126. *Indian nut:* coconut.
133-6. Proponents of the Chain of Being (above, p. 76, note on 21,
     and p. 106, note on 7) claimed that there is 'no where any leap or

Frogs marry fish and flesh; bats, bird and beast;   135
Sponges, non-sense and sense; mines, th' earth & plants.

To show thou art not bound, as if thy lot
Were worse then ours; sometimes thou shiftest hands.
Most things move th' under-jaw; the Crocodile not.
Most things sleep lying; th' Elephant leans or stands.   140

But who hath praise enough? nay who hath any?
None can expresse thy works, but he that knows them:
And none can know thy works, which are so many,
And so complete, but onely he that owes them.

All things that are, though they have sev'rall wayes,   145
Yet in their being joyn with one advise
To honour thee: and so I give thee praise
In all my other hymnes, but in this twice.

Each thing that is, although in use and name
It go for one, hath many wayes in store   150
To honour thee; and so each hymne thy fame
Extolleth many wayes, yet this one more.

Hope

I gave to Hope a watch of mine: but he
          An anchor gave to me.
Then an old prayer-book I did present:
          And he an optick sent.
With that I gave a viall full of tears: 5
          But he a few green eares:
Ah Loyterer! I'le no more, no more I'le bring:
          I did expect a ring.

gap', 'no *vaccum*, or vacuity in the world' (John Randol, *A Sermon*
[1624], p. 3, and Charles Herle, *Contemplations* [1631], p. 499).
Characteristically, Herbert transmutes the commonplace into an
eucharistic *feast*.
135. *marry:* connect.   144. *owes:* owns.   146. *advise:* judgement.
148. *twice:* i.e. as poet, and as 'the worlds high Priest' (13, 25 f.).
Hope
2. Cf. the 'hope we have as an anchor of the soul' (Hebrews 6.19).
   Walton reports that Donne, shortly before his death, 'caused many
   Seals to be made, and in them to be ingraven the figure of *Christ
   crucified* on an *Anchor*, which is the emblem of hope' [*IW*, p. 274].
   The poem in Latin which accompanied the seals, elicited from
   Herbert a few verses [printed with their English version in *FEH*,
   pp. 438–9].
4. *optick:* telescope; also, eye-glass.
8. *ring:* i.e., of Christ the Bridegroom.

Sinnes round

Sorrie I am, my God, sorrie I am,
That my offences course it in a ring.
My thoughts are working like a busie flame,
Untill their cockatrice they hatch and bring:
And when they once have perfected their draughts,   5
My words take fire from my inflamed thoughts.

My words take fire from my inflamed thoughts,
Which spit it forth like the Sicilian hill.
They vent the wares, and passe them with their faults,
And by their breathing ventilate the ill.   10
But words suffice not, where are lewd intentions:
My hands do joyn to finish the inventions.

My hands do joyn to finish the inventions:
And so my sinnes ascend three stories high,
As Babel grew, before there were dissentions.   15
Yet ill deeds loyter not: for they supplie
New thoughts of sinning: wherefore, to my shame,
Sorrie I am, my God, sorrie I am.

Time

Meeting with Time, slack thing, said I,
Thy sithe is dull; whet it for shame.
No marvell Sir, he did replie,
If it at length deserve some blame:
    But where one man would have me grinde it,   5
    Twentie for one too sharp do finde it.

Perhaps some such of old did passe,
Who above all things lov'd this life;
To whom thy sithe a hatchet was,
Which now is but a pruning-knife.   10
    Christs coming hath made man thy debter,
    Since by thy cutting he grows better.

Sinnes round
    4. *cockatrice:* a mythical creature hatched by a serpent from a cock's
       egg, and thought to kill by its breath (cf. 10).
    8. *Sicilian hill:* Mount Etna, the workshop of the Cyclops' destructive
       wares [§ 204].
    9. *vent:* discharge ('spit forth'); also, sell.

And in his blessing thou art blest:
For where thou onely wert before
An executioner at best;   15
Thou art a gard'ner now, and more,
   An usher to convey our souls
    Beyond the utmost starres and poles.

And this is that makes life so long,
While it detains us from our God.   20
Ev'n pleasures here increase the wrong,
And length of dayes lengthen the rod.
   Who wants the place, where God doth dwell,
    Partakes already half of hell.

Of what strange length must that needs be,   25
Which ev'n eternitie excludes!
Thus farre Time heard me patiently:
Then chafing said, This man deludes:
   What do I here before his doore?
    He doth not crave lesse time, but more.   30

Gratefulnesse

Thou that hast giv'n so much to me,
Give one thing more, a gratefull heart.
See how thy beggar works on thee
          By art.

He makes thy gifts occasion more,   5
And sayes, If he in this be crost,
All thou hast giv'n him heretofore
          Is lost.

But thou didst reckon, when at first
Thy word our hearts and hands did crave,   10
What it would come to at the worst
          To save.

Perpetuall knockings at thy doore,
Tears sullying thy transparent rooms,
Gift upon gift, much would have more,   15
          And comes.

Time
13 ff. See *Death*, below, p. 189.
23. *wants:* lacks.

This not withstanding, thou wentst on,
And didst allow us all our noise:
Nay thou hast made a sigh and grone
            Thy joyes.   20

Not that thou hast not still above
Much better tunes, then grones can make;
But that these countrey-aires thy love
            Did take.

Wherefore I crie, and crie again;   25
And in no quiet canst thou be,
Till I a thankfull heart obtain
            Of thee:

Not thankfull, when it pleaseth me;
As if thy blessings had spare dayes: 30
But such a heart, whose pulse may be
            Thy praise.

Peace

Sweet Peace, where dost thou dwell? I humbly crave,
          Let me once know.
    I sought thee in a secret cave,
          And ask'd, if Peace were there.
A hollow winde did seem to answer, No: 5
          Go seek elsewhere.

I did; and going did a rainbow note:
          Surely, thought I,
    This is the lace of Peaces coat:
          I will search out the matter.   10
But while I lookt, the clouds immediately
          Did break and scatter.

Then went I to a garden, and did spy
          A gallant flower,
    The crown Imperiall: Sure, said I,   15
          Peace at the root must dwell.
But when I digg'd, I saw a worm devoure
          What show'd so well.

Gratefulnesse
24. *take:* captivate.

At length I met a rev'rend good old man,
    Whom when for Peace   20
  I did demand; he thus began:
    There was a Prince of old
At Salem dwelt, who liv'd with good increase
    Of flock and fold.

He sweetly liv'd; yet sweetnesse did not save 25
    His life from foes.
  But after death out of his grave
    There sprang twelve stalks of wheat:
Which many wondring at, got some of those
    To plant and set.   30

It prosper'd strangely, and did soon disperse
    Through all the earth:
  For they that taste it do rehearse,
    That vertue lies therein,
A secret vertue bringing peace and mirth 35
    By flight of sinne.

Take of this grain, which in my garden grows,
    And grows for you;
  Make bread of it: and that repose
    And peace which ev'ry where 40
With so much earnestnesse you do pursue,
    Is onely there.

Confession

    O what a cunning guest
Is this same grief! within my heart I made
  Closets; and in them many a chest;
  And like a master in my trade,
In those chests, boxes; in each box, a till: 5
Yet grief knows all, and enters when he will.

    No scrue, no piercer can
Into a piece of timber work and winde,
  As Gods afflictions into man,
  When he a torture hath design'd. 10
They are too subtill for the subt'llest hearts;
And fall, like rheumes, upon the tendrest parts.

Peace
22. *a Prince of old:* on Melchizedek as an eucharistic type of Christ, see
 above, p. 26.
28. *twelve stalks:* the apostles.

We are the earth; and they,
Like moles within us, heave, and cast about:
    And till they foot and clutch their prey,   15
    They never cool, much lesse give out.
No smith can make such locks, but they have keyes:
Closets are halls to them; and hearts, high-wayes.

    Onely an open breast
Doth shut them out, so that they cannot enter;   20
    Or, if they enter, cannot rest,
    But quickly seek some new adventure.
Smooth open hearts no fastning have; but fiction
Doth give a hold and handle to affliction.

    Wherefore my faults and sinnes,   25
Lord, I acknowledge; take thy plagues away:
    For since confession pardon winnes,
    I challenge here the brightest day,
The clearest diamond: let them do their best,
They shall be thick and cloudie to my breast.   30

Giddinesse

Oh, what a thing is man! how farre from power,
    From setled peace and rest!
He is some twentie sev'rall men at least
    Each sev'rall houre.

One while he counts of heav'n, as of his treasure: 5
    But then a thought creeps in,
And calls him coward, who for fear of sinne
    Will lose a pleasure.

Now he will fight it out, and to the warres;
    Now eat his bread in peace,   10
And snudge in quiet: now he scorns increase;
    Now all day spares.

He builds a house, which quickly down must go,
    As if a whirlwinde blew
And crusht the building: and it's partly true,   15
    His minde is so.

Confession
15. *foot:* seize with the talons (of a bird of prey).
19. *open breast:* i.e. confession.
30. *to:* compared to.
Giddinesse
11. *snudge:* remain snug and quiet; also, be stingy [*OED*].

O what a sight were Man, if his attires
      Did alter with his minde;
And like a Dolphins skinne, his clothes combin'd
      With his desires!   20

Surely if each one saw anothers heart,
      There would be no commerce,
No sale or bargain passe: all would disperse,
      And live apart.

Lord, mend or rather make us: one creation   25
      Will not suffice our turn:
Except thou make us dayly, we shall spurn
      Our own salvation.

The bunch of grapes

Joy, I did lock thee up: but some bad man
      Hath let thee out again:
And now, me thinks, I am where I began
      Sev'n yeares ago: one vogue and vein,
      One aire of thoughts usurps my brain.   5
I did toward Canaan draw; but now I am
Brought back to the Red sea, the sea of shame.

For as the Jews of old by Gods command
      Travell'd, and saw no town:
So now each Christian hath his journeys spann'd: 10
      Their storie pennes and sets us down.
A single deed is small renown.
Gods works are wide, and let in future times;
His ancient justice overflows our crimes.

---

25 ff. On 'continued creation'—i.e. the world's preservation—see above, p. 17.

The bunch of grapes. The narrator enacts in his life the wanderings of the Israelites from *the Red sea* (l. 7) to the Promised Land (*Canaan*, 6). The sojourn, itself replete with 'types' (see above, p. 26), encompasses the prefiguration of Christ 'the true vine' (John 15.1) in both the 'cluster of grapes' at Eshcol (Numbers 13.23) and Noah's vineyard (Genesis 9.20).

4. *vogue:* general course or tendency [*OED*].

10. *spann'd:* measured out.

13-14. The lines articulate the rationale of typology (*let in* should be read more or less in the sense of 'prefiguring').

Then have we too our guardian fires and clouds;   15
          Our Scripture-dew drops fast:
We have our sands and serpents, tents and shrowds;
          Alas! our murmurings come not last.
          But where's the cluster? where's the taste
Of mine inheritance? Lord, if I must borrow,   20
Let me as well take up their joy, as sorrow.

But can he want the grape, who hath the wine?
          I have their fruit and more.
Blessed be God, who prosper'd *Noahs* vine,
          And made it bring forth grapes good store.   25
          But much more him I must adore,
Who of the laws sowre juice sweet wine did make,
Ev'n God himself, being pressed for my sake.

Love unknown

Deare Friend, sit down, the tale is long and sad:
And in my faintings I presume your love
Will more complie, then help. A Lord I had,
And have, of whom some grounds which may improve,
I hold for two lives, and both lives in me.   5
To him I brought a dish of fruit one day,
And in the middle plac'd my heart. But he
          (I sigh to say)
Lookt on a servant, who did know his eye
Better then you know me, or (which is one)   10
Then I my self. The servant instantly
Quitting the fruit, seiz'd on my heart alone,
And threw it in a font, wherein did fall
A stream of bloud, which issu'd from the side
Of a great rock: I well remember all,   15
And have good cause: there it was dipt and di'd,
And washt, and wrung: the very wringing yet
Enforceth tears. *Your heart was foul, I fear.*
Indeed 'tis true. I did and do commit

15. Cf. 'the Lord went before them by day in a pillar of cloud, to lead
    them the way; and by night in a pillar of fire, to give them light'
    (Exodus 13.21).
16. Cf. 'when the dew fell upon the camp in the night, the manna fell
    upon it' (Numbers 11.9).
17. *shrowds:* temporary shelters.
28. *pressed:* cf. above, p. 58, note on 11.
Love unknown. The major Biblical analogue is Psalm 51 ('Have mercy
    upon me, O God . . . Create in me a clean heart' etc.).
11 ff. One of the poem's major eucharistic images; cf. 40 ff.
15. *rock:* on the typology of the Mosaic rock, see above, p. 26.

Many a fault more then my lease will bear;　　　　　　20
Yet still askt pardon, and was not deni'd.
But you shall heare. After my heart was well,
And clean and fair, as I one even-tide
　　　　　　(I sigh to tell)
Walkt by my self abroad, I saw a large　　　　　　25
And spacious fornace flaming, and thereon
A boyling caldron, round about whose verge
Was in great letters set *AFFLICTION.*
The greatnesse shew'd the owner. So I went
To fetch a sacrifice out of my fold,　　　　　　30
Thinking with that, which I did thus present,
To warm his love, which I did fear grew cold.
But as my heart did tender it, the man
Who was to take it from me, slipt his hand,
And threw my heart into the scalding pan;　　　　　　35
My heart, that brought it (do you understand?)
The offerers heart. *Your heart was hard, I fear.*
Indeed 'tis true. I found a callous matter
Began to spread and to expatiate there:
But with a richer drug then scalding water,　　　　　　40
I bath'd it often, ev'n with holy bloud,
Which at a board, while many drunk bare wine,
A friend did steal into my cup for good,
Ev'n taken inwardly, and most divine
To supple hardnesses. But at the length　　　　　　45
Out of the caldron getting, soon I fled
Unto my house, where to repair the strength
Which I had lost, I hasted to my bed.
But when I thought to sleep out all these faults
　　　　　　(I sigh to speak)　　　　　　50
I found that some had stuff'd the bed with thoughts,
I would say *thorns.* Deare, could my heart not break,
When with my pleasures ev'n my rest was gone?
Full well I understood, who had been there:
For I had giv'n the key to none, but one:　　　　　　55
It must be he. *Your heart was dull, I fear.*
Indeed a slack and sleepie state of minde
Did oft possesse me, so that when I pray'd,
Though my lips went, my heart did stay behinde.
But all my scores were by another paid,　　　　　　60
Who took the debt upon him. *Truly, Friend,*
For ought I heare, your Master shows to you
More favour then you wot of. Mark the end.
The Font did onely, what was old, renew:
The Caldron suppled, what was grown too hard:　　　　　　65
The Thorns did quicken, what was grown too dull:

---

42. *board:* i.e. Holy Communion (as above, p. 119, note on 14).

All did but strive to mend, what you had marr'd.
Wherefore be cheer'd, and praise him to the full
Each day, each houre, each moment of the week,
Who fain would have to be, new, tender, quick.   70

Mans medley

   Heark, how the birds do sing,
    And woods do ring.
All creatures have their joy: and man hath his.
   Yet if we rightly measure,
    Mans joy and pleasure   5
Rather hereafter, then in present, is.

   To this life things of sense
    Make their pretence:
In th' other Angels have a right by birth:
   Man ties them both alone,   10
    And makes them one,
With th' one hand touching heav'n, with th' other earth.

   In soul he mounts and flies,
    In flesh he dies.
He wears a stuffe whose thread is course and round,   15
   But trimm'd with curious lace,
    And should take place
After the trimming, not the stuffe and ground.

   Not, that he may not here
    Taste of the cheer,   20
But as birds drink, and straight lift up their head,
   So must he sip and think
    Of better drink
He may attain to, after he is dead.

   But as his joyes are double;   25
    So is his trouble.
He hath two winters, other things but one:
   Both frosts and thoughts do nip,
    And bite his lip;
And he of all things fears two deaths alone.   30

Mans medley. 'Medley'—not used originally in a pejorative sense—
  means combination or mixture; also, 'a cloth woven with wools of
  different colours or shades' [*OED*].
10. *Man ties them:* see above, p. 106, note on 7.
18. *After:* according to.
  ground: 'cloth used as a basis for embroidery or decoration' [*OED*].
27. *two winters:* i.e. the physical ('frosts') and the spiritual ('thoughts').
30. *two deaths:* as above, p. 126, note on 22.

> Yet ev'n the greatest griefs
> May be reliefs,
> Could he but take them right, and in their wayes.
> Happie is he, whose heart
> Hath found the art   35
> To turn his double pains to double praise.

The Storm

> If us the windes and waters here below
> Do flie and flow,
> My sighs and tears as busie were above;
> Sure they would move
> And much affect thee, as tempestuous times   5
> Amaze poore mortals, and object their crimes.

> Starres have their storms, ev'n in a high degree,
> As well as we.
> A throbbing conscience spurred by remorse
> Hath a strange force: 10
> It quits the earth, and mounting more and more,
> Dares to assault, and besiege thy doore.

> There it stands knocking, to thy musicks wrong,
> And drowns the song.
> Glorie and honour are set by till it   15
> An answer get.
> Poets have wrong'd poore storms: such dayes are best;
> They purge the aire without, within the breast.

Paradise

> I blesse thee, Lord, because I G R O W
> Among thy trees, which in a   R O W
> To thee both fruit and order   O W.

> What open force, or hidden C H A R M
> Can blast my fruit, or bring me H A R M,   5
> While the inclosure is thine A R M?

> Inclose me still for fear I S T A R T.
> Be to me rather sharp and T A R T,
> Then let me want thy hand & A R T.

The Storm
  6. *object:* place before the mind, accuse [*OED*].
  7. *storms:* i.e. meteor-showers.

Paradise. On the apparently naïve rhyme scheme, see above, pp. 12–13.
  Visually, the poem enacts the pruning of the trees.

When thou dost greater judgements S P A R E,   10
And with thy knife but prune and P A R E,
Ev'n fruitfull trees more fruitfull A R E.

Such sharpnes shows the sweetest F R E N D:
Such cuttings rather heal than R E N D:
And such beginnings touch their E N D.   15

The Method

                    Poore heart, lament.
For since thy God refuseth still,
There is some rub, some discontent,
                    Which cools his will.

                    Thy Father *could*   5
Quickly effect, what thou dost move;
For he is *Power*: and sure he *would*;
                    For he is *Love*.

                    Go search this thing,
Tumble thy breast, and turn thy book.   10
If thou hadst lost a glove or ring,
                    Wouldst thou not look?

                    What do I see
Written above there? *Yesterday*   15
I did behave me carelesly,
                    When I did pray.

                    And should Gods eare
To such indifferents chained be,
Who do not their own motions heare?
                    Is God lesse free?   20

                    But stay! what's there?
Late when I would have something done,
I had a motion to forbear,
                    Yet I went on.

                    And should Gods eare,   25
Which needs not man, be ty'd to those
Who heare not him, but quickly heare
                    His utter foes?

15. *END:* in the sense of finality but also of purpose [§ 216].
The Method
  3. *rub:* impediment (a metaphor from bowls).
 10. *turn thy book:* i.e. search through the register of your life.

>   Then once more pray:
> Down with thy knees, up with thy voice.
> Seek pardon first, and God will say,
>   *Glad heart rejoyce.*

30

Divinitie

As men, for fear the starres should sleep and nod,
    And trip at night, have spheres suppli'd;
As if a starre were duller then a clod,
    Which knows his way without a guide:

Just so the other heav'n they also serve,   5
    Divinities transcendent skie:
Which with the edge of wit they cut and carve.
    Reason triumphs, and faith lies by.

Could not that wisdome, which first broacht the wine,
    Have thicken'd it with definitions?   10
And jagg'd his seamlesse coat, had that been fine,
    With curious questions and divisions?

But all the doctrine, which he taught and gave,
    Was cleare as heav'n, from whence it came.
At least those beams of truth, which onely save,   15
    Surpasse in brightnesse any flame.

Love God, and love your neighbour. Watch and pray.
    Do as ye would be done unto.
O dark instructions; ev'n as dark as day!
    Who can these Gordian knots undo?   20

But he doth bid us take his bloud for wine.
    Bid what he please; yet I am sure,
To take and taste what he doth there designe,
    Is all that saves, and not obscure.

Then burn thy Epicycles, foolish man;   25
    Break all thy spheres, and save thy head.
Faith needs no staff of flesh, but stoutly can
    To heav'n alone both go, and leade.

Divinitie
2. *spheres:* as above, *Vanitie I,* p. 100, note on 2.
3. *clod:* clodhopper.
9. *broacht:* cf. 'abroach', above, p. 58, note on 15.
    wine: the eucharistic allusion is made explicit later (21).
11. *seamlesse coat:* 'the type of love' (as above, p. 55, l. 242).
21. Cf. above, p. 58, l. 18.
25. *Epicycles:* the smaller circles described by each planet, their centres moving along a greater circle [*OED*].
27. *staff:* cf. above, p. 58, note on 3.

Ephes. 4.30

Grieve not the Holy Spirit, &c.

And art thou grieved, sweet and sacred Dove,
   When I am sowre,
   And crosse thy love?
Grieved for me? the God of strength and power
   Griev'd for a worm, which when I tread, 5
   I passe away and leave it dead?

Then weep mine eyes, the God of love doth grieve:
   Weep foolish heart,
   And weeping live:
For death is drie as dust. Yet if ye part, 10
   End as the night, whose sable hue
   Your sinnes expresse; melt into dew.

When sawcie mirth shall knock or call at doore,
   Cry out, Get hence,
   Or cry no more. 15
Almightie God doth grieve, he puts on sense:
   I sinne not to my grief alone,
   But to my Gods too; he doth grone.

Oh take thy lute, and tune it to a strain,
   Which may with thee 20
   All day complain.
There can be no discord but in ceasing be.
   Marbles can weep; and surely strings
   More bowels have, then such hard things.

Lord, I adjudge my self to tears and grief, 25
   Ev'n endlesse tears
   Without relief.
If a cleare spring for me no time forbears,
   But runnes, although I be not drie;
   I am no Crystall, what shall I? 30

Yet if I wail not still, since still to wail
   Nature denies;
   And flesh would fail,
If my deserts were masters of mine eyes:
   Lord, pardon, for thy sonne makes good 35
   My want of tears with store of bloud.

Ephes. 4.30. The full verse reads: 'grieve not the holy Spirit of God,
 whereby ye are sealed unto the day of redemption'.
 3. *crosse:* cf. above, p. 34, note on 24.
10. *part:* die.
22. *discord:* i.e. as opposed to 'consort' (above, p. 62, note on 13).
35. The change from addressing the Holy Spirit (1 ff.) to addressing
 the Father is trinitarian theology in action. Cf. p. 121, note on 19.

The Familie

What doth this noise of thoughts within my heart
   As if they had a part?
What do these loud complaints and pulling fears,
  As if there were no rule or eares?

But, Lord, the house and familie are thine,   5
   Though some of them repine.
Turn out these wranglers, which defile thy seat:
  For where thou dwellest all is neat.

First Peace and Silence all disputes controll,
   Then Order plaies the soul;   10
And giving all things their set forms and houres,
  Makes of wilde woods sweet walks and bowres.

Humble Obedience neare the doore doth stand,
   Expecting a command:
Then whom in waiting nothing seems more slow, 15
  Nothing more quick when she doth go.

Joyes oft are there, and griefs as oft as joyes;
   But griefs without a noise:
Yet speak they louder, then distemper'd fears.
  What is so shrill as silent tears?   20

This is thy house, with these it doth abound:
   And where these are not found,
Perhaps thou com'st sometimes, and for a day;
  But not to make a constant stay.

The Size

   Content thee, greedie heart.
Modest and moderate joyes to those, that have
Title to more hereafter when they part,
   Are passing brave.
  Let th' upper springs into the low   5
  Descend and fall, and thou dost flow.

   What though some have a fraught
Of cloves and nutmegs, and in cinamon sail;
If thou hast wherewithall to spice a draught,
   When griefs prevail;   10
  And for the future time art heir
  To th' Isle of spices? Is't not fair?

The Familie
10. *plaies:* tunes.
The Size—i.e. status or state.

    To be in both worlds full
Is more then God was, who was hungrie here.
Wouldst thou his laws of fasting disanull?   15
        Enact good cheer?
    Lay out thy joy, yet hope to save it?
    Wouldst thou both eat thy cake, and have it?

    Great joyes are all at once;
But little do reserve themselves for more: 20
Those have their hopes; these what they have renounce,
        And live on score:
    Those are at home; these journey still,
    And meet the rest on Sions hill.

    Thy Saviour sentenc'd joy,   25
And in the flesh condemn'd it as unfit,
At least in lump: for such doth oft destroy;
        Whereas a bit
    Doth tice us on to hopes of more,
    And for the present health restore.   30

    A Christians state and case
Is not a corpulent, but a thinne and spare,
Yet active strength: whose long and bonie face
        Content and care
    Do seem to equally divide,   35
    Like a pretender, not a bride.

    Wherefore sit down, good heart;
Grasp not at much, for fear thou losest all.
If comforts fell according to desert,
    They would great frosts and snows destroy: 40
    For we should count, Since the last joy.

    Then close again the seam,
Which thou hast open'd: do not spread thy robe
In hope of great things. Call to minde thy dream,
        An earthly globe,   45
    On whose meridian was engraven.
    These seas are tears, and heav'n the haven.

22. *score:* credit.
36. *pretender:* wooer, suitor (cf. above, p. 128, note on 19).
46. *meridian:* 'a graduated ring of brass in which an artificial globe is
    suspended' [*OED*].

Artillerie

As I one ev'ning sat before my cell,
Me thoughts a starre did shoot into my lap.
I rose, and shook my clothes, as knowing well,
That from small fires comes oft no small mishap.
  When suddenly I heard one say,   5
   Do as thou usest, disobey,
   Expell good motions from thy breast,
Which have the face of fire, but end in rest.

I, who had heard of musick in the spheres,
But not of speech in starres, began to muse: 10
But turning to my God, whose ministers
The starres and all things are; If I refuse,
   Dread Lord, said I, so oft my good;
   Then I refuse not ev'n with bloud
   To wash away my stubborn thought: 15
For I will do, or suffer what I ought.

But I have also starres and shooters too,
Born where thy servants both artilleries use.
My tears and prayers night and day do wooe,
And work up to thee; yet thou dost refuse.   20
   Not, but I am (I must say still)
   Much more oblig'd to do thy will,
   Then thou to grant mine: but because
Thy promise now hath ev'n set thee thy laws.

Then we are shooters both, and thou dost deigne   25
To enter combate with us, and contest
With thine own clay. But I would parley fain:
Shunne not my arrows, and behold my breast.
   Yet if thou shunnest, I am thine:
   I must be so, if I am mine.   30
   There is no articling with thee:
I am but finite, yet thine infinitely.

Artillerie. The poem is an extension of St Paul's military metaphors
 (e.g. Ephesians 6.13 ff.: 'take unto you the whole armour of God',
 etc.); but 'the weapons of our warfare', as he so often insisted, 'are
 not carnal' (quoted above, p. 65, note on 6).
11-12. Cf. Psalm 104.4: '[He] maketh his angels spirits; his ministers
 a flaming fire'.
17. *shooters:* shooting stars (but in the ordinary sense in l. 25).
25. *shooters both:* cf. above, p. 70, note on 5-6.
29-30. The lines anticipate the argument in *Clasping of Hands*, below,
 p. 164.

Church-rents and schismes

Brave rose, (alas!) where art thou? in the chair
Where thou didst lately so triumph and shine,
A worm doth sit, whose many feet and hair
Are the more foul, the more thou wert divine.
This, this hath done it, this did bite the root   5
And bottome of the leaves: which when the winde
Did once perceive, it blew them under foot,
Where rude unhallow'd steps do crush and grinde
    Their beauteous glories. Onely shreds of thee,
    And those all bitten, in thy chair I see.   10

Why doth my Mother blush? is she the rose,
And shows it so? Indeed Christs precious bloud
Gave you a colour once; which when your foes
Thought to let out, the bleeding did you good,
And made you look much fresher then before.   15
But when debates and fretting jealousies
Did worm and work within you more and more,
Your colour faded, and calamities
    Turned your ruddie into pale and bleak:
    Your health and beautie both began to break.   20

Then did your sev'rall parts unloose and start:
Which when your neighbours saw, like a north-winde,
They rushed in, and cast them in the dirt
Where Pagans tread. O Mother deare and kinde,
Where shall I get me eyes enough to weep,   25
As many eyes as starres? since it is night,
And much of Asia and Europe fast asleep,
And ev'n all Africk; would at least I might
    With these two poore ones lick up all the dew,
    Which falls by night, and poure it out for you!   30

Justice (II)

O dreadfull Justice, what a fright and terrour
        Wast thou of old,

Church-rents and ['or' in *B*] *schismes*
  1. *rose:* i.e. the Church, figured as 'the rose of Sharon' (Song of
     Solomon 2.1), in her *chair* of authority.
  21. *start:* explode. Milton's use of the word is followed by: 'As when a
     spark / Lights on a heap of nitrous Powder' etc. (*Paradise Lost*,
     IV, 813 ff.).
  22. *a north-winde:* Scotland's Presbyterians? [*GHP*].
  29-30. The allusion is to the manna, a type of the Eucharist (above, p.
     55, note on 239).

Justice II
  2. *of old:* i.e. during the old dispensation of the Law, now abrogated
     under the Covenant of Grace.

When sinne and errour
Did show and shape thy looks to me,
And through their glasse discolour thee!   5
He that did but look up, was proud and bold.

The dishes of thy ballance seem'd to gape,
Like two great pits;
The beam and scape
Did like some tort'ring engine show: 10
Thy hand above did burn and glow,
Danting the stoutest hearts, the proudest wits.

But now that Christs pure vail presents the sight,
I see no fears:
Thy hand is white,   15
Thy scales like buckets, which attend
And interchangeably descend,
Lifting to heaven from this well of tears.

For where before thou still didst call on me,
Now I still touch   20
And harp on thee.
Gods promises have made thee mine;
Why should I justice now decline?
Against me there is none, but for me much.

The Pilgrimage

I travell'd on, seeing the hill, where lay
My expectation.
A long it was and weary way.
The gloomy cave of Desperation
I left on th' one, and on the other side   5
The rock of Pride.

And so I came to Phansies medow strow'd
With many a flower:
Fair would I here have made abode,
But I was quicken'd by my houre.   10
So to Cares cops I came, and there got through
With much ado.

9. *scape:* the upright shaft of the balance.
13. *Christs pure vail:* 'that is to say, his flesh' (Hebrews 10.20), in opposition to the multicoloured veil of the old dispensation in Solomon's Temple (2 Chronicles 3.14).

The Pilgrimage
7. *Phansies:* the first letter is capitalized only in *B* (as in 11: *Cares*, and 13: *Passion*).
10. *my houre:* cf. 'my houre, / My inch of life' (below, p. 153, ll. 17–18).

That led me to the wilde of Passion, which
        Some call the wold;
   A wasted place, but sometimes rich.   15
    Here I was robb'd of all my gold,
Save one good Angell, which a friend had ti'd
        Close to my side.

At length I got unto the gladsome hill,
        Where lay my hope,   20
   Where lay my heart; and climbing still,
    When I had gain'd the brow and top,
A lake of brackish waters on the ground
        Was all I found.

With that abash'd and struck with many a sting   25
        Of swarming fears,
   I fell, and cry'd, Alas my King;
    Can both the way and end be tears?
Yet taking heart I rose, and then perceiv'd
        I was deceiv'd: 30

My hill was further: so I flung away,
        Yet heard a crie
   Just as I went, *None goes that way*
    And lives: If that be all, said I,
After so foul a journey death is fair,   35
        And but a chair.

The Holdfast

I threatned to observe the strict decree
   Of my deare God with all my power & might.
   But I was told by one, it could not be;
Yet I might trust in God to be my light.

Then will I trust, said I, in him alone.   5
   Nay, ev'n to trust in him, was also his:
   We must confesse, that nothing is our own.
Then I confesse that he my succour is:

14. *wold:* open country, moorland. *B* reads 'would'; and the editions
    after 1656: 'world'.
17. *Angell:* i.e. guardian angel; also, gold coin.
29. *rose:* an 'unconscious' recollection of the Church's 'rose' (above,
    p. 150, l. 1), reinforced by the reference to *chair* (36).
36. *chair:* literally a sedan-chair, a comfortable mode of transport (cf.
    above, p. 113, l. 29).

The Holdfast. Cf. Psalm 73.27 in the Book of Common Prayer: 'it is
    good for me to hold me fast by God' [*FEH*].

But to have nought is ours, not to confesse
    That we have nought. I stood amaz'd at this,   10
     Much troubled, till I heard a friend expresse,
That all things were more ours by being his.
    What Adam had, and forfeited for all,
    Christ keepeth now, who cannot fail or fall.

Complaining

       Do not beguile my heart,
         Because thou art
My power and wisdome. Put me not to shame,
         Because I am
    Thy clay that weeps, thy dust that calls.   5

       Thou art the Lord of glorie:
         The deed and storie
Are both thy due: but I a silly flie,
         That live or die
    According as the weather falls.   10

       Art thou all justice, Lord?
         Shows not thy word
More attributes? Am I all throat or eye,
         To weep or crie?
    Have I no parts but those of grief?   15

       Let not thy wrathfull power
         Afflict my houre,
My inch of life: or let thy gracious power
         Contract my houre,
    That I may climbe and finde relief.   20

The Discharge

Busie enquiring heart, what wouldst thou know?
        Why dost thou prie,
And turn, and leer, and with a licorous eye
        Look high and low;
    And in thy lookings stretch and grow?   5

13-14. Cf. 1 Corinthians 15.22: 'as in Adam all die, even so in Christ
shall all be made alive'.
The Discharge—i.e. in the legal sense of releasing from an obligation.
  3. *licorous:* 'lickerous', i.e. lecherous, wanton.

Hast thou not made thy counts, and summ'd up all?
                    Did not thy heart
Give up the whole, and with the whole depart?
                    Let what will fall:
          That which is past who can recall?   10

Thy life is Gods, thy time to come is gone,
                    And is his right.
He is thy night at noon: he is at night
                    Thy noon alone.
          The crop is his, for he hath sown.   15

And well it was for thee, when this befell,
                    That God did make
Thy businesse his, and in thy life partake:
                    For thou canst tell,
          If it be his once, all is well.   20

Onely the present is thy part and fee.
                    And happy thou,
If, though thou didst not beat thy future brow,
                    Thou couldst well see
          What present things requir'd of thee.   25

They ask enough; why shouldst thou further go?
                    Raise not the muddle
Of future depths, but drink the cleare and good.
                    Dig not for wo
          In times to come; for it will grow.   30

Man and the present fit: if he provide,
                    He breaks the square.
This houre is mine: if for the next I care,
                    I grow too wide,
          And do encroach upon deaths side.   35

For death each houre environs and surrounds.
                    He that would know
And care for future chances, cannot go
                    Unto those grounds,
          But through a Church-yard which them bounds.   40

Things present shrink and die: but they that spend
                    Their thoughts and sense
On future grief, do not remove it thence,
                    But it extend,
          And draw the bottome out an end.   45

6. *counts:* i.e. accounts.
31. *provide:* be provident (of the future).
45. *draw the bottome out an end:* unravel a skein of thread to the end.

God chains the dog till night: wilt loose the chain,
    And wake thy sorrow?
Wilt thou forestall it, and now grieve to morrow,
    And then again
        Grieve over freshly all thy pain?   50

Either grief will not come: or if it must,
    Do not forecast.
And while it cometh, it is almost past.
        Awuy distrust;
        My God hath promis'd, he is just.   55

Praise (II)

King of Glorie, King of Peace,
    I will love thee;
And that love may never cease,
    I will move thee.

Thou has granted my request,   5
    Thou hast heard me:
Thou didst note my working breast,
    Thou hast spar'd me.

Wherefore with my utmost art
    I will sing thee,   10
And the cream of all my heart
    I will bring thee.

Though my sinnes against me cried,
    Thou didst cleare me;
And alone, when they replied,   15
    Thou didst heare me.

Sev'n whole dayes, not one in seven,
    I will praise thee.
In my heart, though not in heaven,
    I can raise thee.   20

Thou grew'st soft and moist with tears,
    Thou relentedst:
And when Justice call'd for fears,
    Thou dissentedst.

Small it is, in this poore sort   25
    To enroll thee:
Ev'n eternitie is too short
    To extoll thee.

Praise II. The principal Biblical analogue is Psalm 116.
1. The line is repeated in *L'Envoy* (below, p. 200).
26. *enroll:* record with honour, celebrate.

An Offering

Come, bring thy gift. If blessings were as slow
As mens returns, what would become of fools?
What hast thou there? a heart? but is it pure?
Search well and see; for hearts have many holes.
Yet one pure heart is nothing to bestow: 5
In Christ two natures met to be thy cure.

O that within us hearts had propagation,
Since many gifts do challenge many hearts!
Yet one, if good, may title to a number;
And single things grow fruitfull by deserts.   10
In publick judgements one may be a nation,
And fence a plague, while others sleep and slumber.

But all I fear is lest thy heart displease,
As neither good, nor one: so oft divisions
Thy lusts have made, and not thy lusts alone;   15
Thy passions also have their set partitions.
These parcell out thy heart: recover these,
And thou mayst offer many gifts in one.

There is a balsome, or indeed a bloud,
Dropping from heav'n, which doth both cleanse and close   20
All sorts of wounds; of such strange force it is.
Seek out this All-heal, and seek no repose,
Untill thou finde and use it to thy good:
Then bring thy gift, and let thy hymne be this;

       Since my sadnesse   25
       Into gladnesse
Lord thou dost convert,
       O accept
       What thou hast kept,
As thy due desert.   30

       Had I many,
       Had I any,
(For this heart is none)
       All were thine
       And none of mine: 35
Surely thine alone.

An Offering
11-12. *one may be a nation, | And fence a plague:* i.e. one may represent
    a nation and divert a pestilence on himself—as David did (1
    Chronicles 21.17), or Christ.
22. *All-heal:* balsam for all wounds.

                    Yet thy favour
                    May give savour
To this poore oblation;
                    And it raise   40
                    To be thy praise,
And be my salvation.

Longing

                    With sick and famisht eyes,
With doubling knees and weary bones,
                    To thee my cries,
                    To thee my grones,
To thee my sighs, my tears ascend: 5
                    No end?

                    My throat, my soul is hoarse;
My heart is wither'd like a ground
                    Which thou dost curse.
                    My thoughts turn round,   10
And make me giddie; Lord, I fall,
                    Yet call.

                    From thee all pitie flows.
Mothers are kinde, because thou art,
                    And dost dispose   15
                    To them a part:
Their infants, them; and they suck thee
                    More free.

                    Bowels of pitie, heare!
Lord of my soul, love of my minde,   20
                    Bow down thine eare!
                    Let not the winde
Scatter my words, and in the same
                    Thy name!

                    Look on my sorrows round!   25
Mark well my furnace! O what flames,
                    What heats abound!
                    What griefs, what shames!
Consider, Lord; Lord, bow thine eare,
                    And heare!   30

Longing. Set to music by Purcell.
  9. Cf. the sentence on Adam after the Fall: 'cursed is the ground for
     thy sake' (Genesis 3.17).
 21. So Psalm 86.1: 'Bow down thine ear, O Lord, hear me'.

                Lord Jesu, thou didst bow
Thy dying head upon the tree:
                O be not now
                More dead to me!
Lord heare! *Shall he that made the eare,*   35
                Not heare?

                Behold, thy dust doth stirre,
It moves, it creeps, it aims at thee:
                Wilt thou deferre
                To succour me,   40
Thy pile of dust, wherein each crumme
                Sayes, Come?

                To thee help appertains.
Hast thou left all things to their course,
                And laid the reins   45
                Upon the horse?
Is all lockt? hath a sinners plea
                No key?

                Indeed the world's thy book,
Where all things have their leafe assign'd: 50
                Yet a meek look
                Hath interlin'd.
Thy board is full, yet humble guests
                Finde nests.

                Thou tarriest, while I die,   55
And fall to nothing: thou dost reigne,
                And rule on high,
                While I remain
In bitter grief: yet am I stil'd
                Thy childe.   60

                Lord, didst thou leave thy throne,
Not to relieve? how can it be,
                That thou art grown
                Thus hard to me?
Were sinne alive, good cause there were   65
                To bear.

35-6. So Psalm 94.9: 'He that planted the ear, shall he not hear?'
52. *interlin'd:* come between the lines.
53. *board:* i.e. Holy Communion (as above, p. 119, note on 14).

But now both sinne is dead,
And all thy promises live and bide.
That wants his head;
These speak and chide,   70
And in thy bosome poure my tears,
As theirs.

Lord J E S U, heare my heart,
Which hath been broken now so long,
That ev'ry part   75
Hath got a tongue!
Thy beggars grow; rid them away
To day.

My love, my sweetnesse, heare!
By these thy feet, at which my heart   80
Lies all the ycare,
Pluck out thy dart,
And heal my troubled breast which cryes,
Which dyes.

The Bag

Away despair; my gracious Lord doth heare.
Though windes and waves assault my keel,
He doth preserve it: he doth steer,
Ev'n when the boat seems most to reel.
Storms are the triumph of his art: 5
Well may he close his eyes, but not his heart.

Hast thou not heard, that my Lord JESUS di'd?
Then let me tell thee a strange storie.
The God of power, as he did ride
In his majestick robes of glorie,   10
Resolv'd to light; and so one day
He did descend, undressing all the way.

The starres his tire of light and rings obtain'd,
The cloud his bow, the fire his spear,
The sky his azure mantle gain'd.   15
And when they ask'd, what he would wear;
He smil'd and said as he did go,
He had new clothes a making here below.

The Bag. 'A *saccus* was both a purse [cf. l. 32] and a bag for straining
   wine through' [§ 219]. The eucharistic implications are reinforced
   by the typological connections of *the blow upon his side* (l. 29; see
   above, p. 52, note on 122).
6. *close his eyes:* as he did on the *boat* (4) during the storm on the Sea
   of Galilee (Matthew 8.24).
13. *tire:* head-dress.   14. *fire:* lightning.

When he was come, as travellers are wont,
  He did repair unto an inne.   20
  Both then, and after, many a brunt
  He did endure to cancell sinne:
  And having giv'n the rest before,
Here he gave up his life to pay our score.

But as he was returning, there came one   25
  That ran upon him with a spear.
  He, who came hither all alone,
  Bringing nor man, nor arms, nor fear,
  Receiv'd the blow upon his side,
And straight he turn'd, and to his brethren cry'd, 30

If ye have any thing to send or write,
  (I have no bag, but here is room)
  Unto my fathers hands and sight
  (Beleeve me) it shall safely come.
  That I shall minde, what you impart;   35
Look, you may put it very neare my heart.

Or if hereafter any of my friends
  Will use me in this kinde, the doore
  Shall still be open; what he sends
  I will present, and somewhat more,   40
  Not to his hurt. Sighs will convey
Any thing to me. Heark despair, away.

The Jews

  Poore nation, whose sweet sap, and juice
Our cyens have purloin'd, and left you drie:
Whose streams we got by the Apostles sluce,
And use in baptisme, while ye pine and die:
Who by not keeping once, became a debter; 5
  And now by keeping lose the letter:

  Oh that my prayers! mine, alas!
Oh that some Angel might a trumpet sound;

---

38. *doore:* see above, p. 56, note on 6.
The Jews
 2. *cyens:* i.e. 'scions', slips for grafting.
 5. *debter:* i.e. sinner, in the light of Adam's primal disobedience.
  While Christians are 'delivered from the law' and serve 'not in the
  oldness of the letter' (Romans 7.6), every Jew remains 'a debtor to
  do the whole law' (Galatians 5.3). Cf. § 243.
8-10. The conversion of the Jews was traditionally expected to be one

At which the Church falling upon her face
Should crie so loud, untill the trump were drown'd,   10
And by that crie of her deare Lord obtain,
      That your sweet sap might come again!

The Collar

    I struck the board, and cry'd, No more.
            I will abroad.
    What? shall I ever sigh and pine?
My lines and life are free; free as the rode,
    Loose as the winde, as large as store.   5
        Shall I be still in suit?
Have I no harvest but a thorn
To let me bloud, and not restore
What I have lost with cordiall fruit?
          Sure there was wine   10
Before my sighs did drie it: there was corn
    Before my tears did drown it.
    Is the yeare onely lost to me?
      Have I no bayes to crown it?
No flowers, no garlands gay? all blasted?   15
        All wasted?
Not so, my heart: but there is fruit,
      And thou hast hands.
Recover all thy sigh-blown age
On double pleasures: leave thy cold dispute   20
Of what is fit, and not forsake thy cage,
        Thy rope of sands,

of the 'signs' heralding the Last Judgement.
12. Cf. above, *Grace*, p. 78, note on 1–4.
The Collar. The title refers not to the modern clerical collar but to the
    common figurative expression 'to slip the collar'. It may even be a
    nautical term: Sir Henry Manwayring's *The Sea-mans Dictionary*
    (1644) defines it as 'that rope about the main-mast-head, which is
    [sometimes] called . . . a garland, and is there placed to save the
    shrouds from galling' [§ 271]. A pun may be intended in collar/
    choler; a less likely one, in collar/caller [§§ 285, 231].
        The poem's circumference appears to include allusions to the
    disobedience of Adam and Eve (esp. ll. 17–18) as well as to the
    Passion (see above, p. 19 [§ 286]).
  1. *board:* the literal meaning does not preclude an allusion to the Holy
    Communion, anticipated by several other poems (e.g. above, p.
    141, note on 42).
21. *not forsake thy cage: B* reads 'not. Forsake thy cage'
22. *rope of sands:* as Thomas Adams explained (*c.* 1625), 'Sand is not
    fit, one would thinke, to binde an unruly beast, they call it *Irritum
    laborum*, proverbially, a rope of sand: yet is this the cordage and
    ligature to shackle the roaring monster' [§ 258].

Which pettie thoughts have made, and made to thee
    Good cable, to enforce and draw,
        And be thy law,
While thou didst wink and wouldst not see.   25
        Away; take heed:
        I will abroad.
Call in thy deaths head there: tie up thy fears.
        He that forbears
    To suit and serve his need,   30
        Deserves his load.
But as I rav'd and grew more fierce and wilde
        At every word,
Me thoughts I heard one calling, *Child*:
        And I reply'd, *My Lord*.   35

The Glimpse

      Whither away delight?
Thou cam'st but now; wilt thou so soon depart,
    And give me up to night?
For many weeks of lingring pain and smart
But one half houre of comfort for my heart?   5

      Me thinks delight should have
More skill in musick, and keep better time.
    Wert thou a winde or wave,
They quickly go and come with lesser crime:
Flowers look about, and die not in their prime.   10

      Thy short abode and stay
Feeds not, but addes to the desire of meat.
    Lime begg'd of old (they say)
A neighbour spring to cool his inward heat;
Which by the springs accesse grew much more great.   15

      In hope of thee my heart
Pickt here and there a crumme, and would not die;
    But constant to his part
When as my fears foretold this, did replie,
A slender thread a gentle guest will tie.   20

      Yet if the heart that wept
Must let thee go, return when it doth knock.
    Although thy heap be kept
For future times, the droppings of the stock
May oft break forth, and never break the lock.   25

The Glimpse
13. *Lime:* quicklime.

If I have more to spinne,
The wheel shall go, so that thy stay be short.
            Thou knowst how grief and sinne
Disturb the work. O make me not their sport,
Who by thy coming may be made a court!   30

Assurance

            O spitefull bitter thought!
Bitterly spitefull thought! Couldst thou invent
So high a torture? Is such poyson bought?
Doubtlesse, but in the way of punishment,
            When wit contrives to meet with thee,   5
            No such rank poyson can there be.

            Thou said'st but even now,
That all was not so fair, as I conceiv'd,
Betwixt my God and me; that I allow
And coin large hopes; but, that I was deceiv'd: 10
            Either the league was broke, or neare it;
            And, that I had great cause to fear it.

            And what to this? what more
Could poyson, if it had a tongue, expresse?
What is thy aim? wouldst thou unlock the doore   15
To cold despairs, and gnawing pensivenesse?
            Wouldst thou raise devils? I see, I know,
            I writ thy purpose long ago.

            But I will to my Father,
Who heard thee say it. O most gracious Lord,   20
If all the hope and comfort that I gather,
Were from my self, I had not half a word,
            Not half a letter to oppose
            What is objected by my foes.

            But thou art my desert: 25
And in this league, which now my foes invade,
Thou art not onely to perform thy part,
But also mine; as when the league was made
            Thou didst at once thy self indite,
            And hold my hand, while I did write.   30

            Wherefore if thou canst fail,
Then can thy truth and I: but while rocks stand,
And rivers stirre, thou canst not shrink or quail:
Yea, when both rocks and all things shall disband,
            Then shalt thou be my rock and tower,   35
            And make their ruine praise thy power.

27. *stay:* staying away.

Now foolish thought go on,

Spin out thy thread, and make thereof a coat
To hide thy shame: for thou hast cast a bone
Which bounds on thee, and will not down thy throat: 40

What for it self love once began,
Now love and truth will end in man.

The Call

Come, my Way, my Truth, my Life:
Such a Way, as gives us breath:
Such a Truth, as ends all strife:
And such a Life, as killeth death.

Come, my Light, my Feast, my Strength: 5
Such a Light, as shows a feast:
Such a Feast, as mends in length:
Such a Strength, as makes his guest.

Come, my Joy, my Love, my Heart:
Such a Joy, as none can move: 10
Such a Love, as none can part:
Such a Heart, as joyes in love.

Clasping of hands

Lord, thou art mine, and I am thine,
If mine I am: and thine much more,
Then I or ought, or can be mine.
Yet to be thine, doth me restore;
So that again I now am mine,   5
And with advantage mine the more.
Since this being mine, brings with it thine,
And thou with me dost thee restore.

If I without thee would be mine,
I neither should be mine nor thine.   10

Lord, I am thine, and thou art mine:
So mine thou art, that something more
I may presume thee mine, then thine.
For thou didst suffer to restore

Assurance
39. *bone:* i.e. bone of contention.
39-40. Cf. above, p. 111, ll. 9-10.
The Call
  7. *mends in length:* improves as it continues.

Not thee, but me, and to be mine: 15
And with advantage mine the more,
Since thou in death wast none of thine,
Yet then as mine didst me restore.
  O be mine still! still make me thine!
  Or rather make no Thine and Mine! 20

Praise (III)

  Lord, I will mean and speak thy praise,
    Thy praise alone.
My busie heart shall spin it all my dayes:
  And when it stops for want of store,
Then will I wring it with a sigh or grone, 5
  That thou mayst yet have more.

  When thou dost favour any action,
    It runnes, it flies:
All things concurre to give it a perfection.
  That which had but two legs before, 10
When thou dost blesse, hath twelve: one wheel doth rise
  To twentie then, or more.

  But when thou dost on businesse blow,
    It hangs, it clogs:
Not all the teams of Albion in a row 15
  Can hale or draw it out of doore.
Legs are but stumps, and Pharaohs wheel but logs,
  And struggling hinders more.

  Thousands of things do thee employ
    In ruling all 20
This spacious globe: Angels must have their joy,
  Devils their rod, the sea his shore,
The windes their stint: and yet when I did call,
  Thou heardst my call, and more.

  I have not lost one single tear: 25
    But when mine eyes
Did weep to heav'n, they found a bottle there
  (As we have boxes for the poore)
Readie to take them in; yet of a size
  That would contain much more. 30

Praise III
17. *Pharaohs wheel:* removed by God as the Israelites were crossing the
  Red Sea (Exodus 14.25).
23. *stint:* limit.
27. *bottle:* cf. Psalm 56.8: 'put thou my tears in thy bottle'.

But after thou hadst slipt a drop
                From thy right eye,
(Which there did hang like streamers neare the top
    Of some fair church to show the sore
And bloudie battell which thou once didst trie)   35
            The glasse was full and more.

Wherefore I sing. Yet since my heart,
                Though press'd, runnes thin:
O that I might some other hearts convert,
            And so take up at use good store: 40
That to thy chests there might be coming in
            Both all my praise, and more!

Josephs coat

Wounded I sing, tormented I indite,
Thrown down I fall into a bed, and rest:
Sorrow hath chang'd its note: such is his will,
Who changeth all things, as him pleaseth best.
    For well he knows, if but one grief and smart   5
Among my many had his full career,
Sure it would carrie with it ev'n my heart,
And both would runne untill they found a biere
    To fetch the bodie; both being due to grief.
But he hath spoil'd the race; and giv'n to anguish   10
One of Joyes coats, ticing it with relief
To linger in me, and together languish.
    I live to shew his power, who once did bring
    My *joyes* to *weep*, and now my *griefs* to *sing*.

The Pulley

When God at first made man,
Having a glasse of blessings standing by;
Let us (said he) poure on him all we can:
Let the worlds riches, which dispersed lie,
            Contract into a span.   5

33. *streamers:* flags hung after a victory.
40. *use:* interest.

Josephs coat. Symbolic of a father's love, the 'coat of many colours'
    which Jacob gave to Joseph (Genesis 37.3) came to be regarded as a
    type of the humanity assumed by Christ upon his Incarnation
    [§ 219].
  8. *both:* 'grief and smart' and 'my heart'.
  9. *both:* i.e. heart and body, alike subject to sin and therefore to *grief.*

The Pulley. The poem inverts the legend of Pandora's box which re-

> So strength first made a way;
> Then beautie flow'd, then wisdome, honour, pleasure:
> When almost all was out, God made a stay,
> Perceiving that alone of all his treasure
>> Rest in the bottome lay.　　　　　　10
>
> For if I should (said he)
> Bestow this jewell also on my creature,
> He would adore my gifts in stead of me,
> And rest in Nature, not the God of Nature:
>> So both should losers be.　　　　　　15
>
> Yet let him keep the rest,
> But keep them with repining restlessnesse:
> Let him be rich and wearie, that at least,
> If goodnesse leade him not, yet wearinesse
>> May tosse him to my breast.　　　　　　20

The Priesthood

> Blest Order, which in power dost so excell,
> That with th' one hand thou liftest to the sky,
> And with the other throwest down to hell
> In thy just censures; fain would I draw nigh,
> Fain put thee on, exchanging my lay-sword　　　5
>> For that of th' holy word.
>
> But thou art fire, sacred and hallow'd fire;
> And I but earth and clay: should I presume
> To wear thy habit, the severe attire
> My slender compositions might consume.　　　10
> I am both foul and brittle; much unfit
>> To deal in holy Writ.
>
> Yet have I often seen, by cunning hand
> And force of fire, what curious things are made
> Of wretched earth. Where once I scorn'd to stand,　　　15
> That earth is fitted by the fire and trade
> Of skilfull artists, for the boards of those
>> Who make the bravest shows.

leased Sickness, Old Age, Vice, etc., save that Hope remained to comfort man so afflicted. For a contemporary reiteration of Herbert's argument, see above, p. 12.

10. *Rest:* see above, p. 12.

The Priesthood

8. *earth and clay:* i.e. shaped by *fire* (7). The implied image is Biblical, e.g. Jeremiah 18.6: 'as the clay is in the potter's hand, so are ye in mine hand' (so also Isaiah 64.8 and Romans 9.21–3).

But since those great ones, be they ne're so great,
Come from the earth, from whence those vessels come;   20
So that at once both feeder, dish, and meat
Have one beginning and one finall summe:
I do not greatly wonder at the sight,
                    If earth in earth delight.

But th' holy men of God such vessels are,   25
As serve him up, who all the world commands:
When God vouchsafeth to become our fare,
Their hands convey him, who conveys their hands.
O what pure things, most pure must those things be,
                    Who bring my God to me!   30

Wherefore I dare not, I, put forth my hand
To hold the Ark, although it seem to shake
Through th' old sinnes and new doctrines of our land.
Onely, since God doth often vessels make
Of lowly matter for high uses meet,   35
                    I throw me at his feet.

There will I lie, untill my Maker seek
For some mean stuffe whereon to show his skill:
Then is my time. The distance of the meek
Doth flatter power. Lest good come short of ill   40
In praising might, the poore do by submission
                    What pride by opposition.

The Search

Whither, O, whither art thou fled,
                    My Lord, my Love?
My searches are my daily bread;
                    Yet never prove.

My knees pierce th' earth, mine eies the skie;   5
                    And yet the sphere
And centre both to me denie
                    That thou art there.

28. *Their hands convey him:* i.e. in the Eucharist.
32. *To hold the Ark:* Uzzah elicited God's anger when he tried to pre-
    vent the Ark from toppling. Here as before the Ark is a type of the
    Church (above, *Affliction V*, p. 111, note on 3).

The Search
 3. *bread:* the dramatic irony is obvious. Just as *bread* looks to the
    Eucharist, so other words—e.g. *pierce* (5), *keyes* (15), etc.—anticipate
    the ministry of Christ (see above, pp. 18 ff.).
6-7. *the sphere | And centre:* cf. above, p. 117, note on 9.

Yet can I mark how herbs below
        Grow green and gay,   10
As if to meet thee they did know,
        While I decay.

Yet can I mark how starres above
        Simper and shine,
As having keyes unto thy love,   15
        While poore I pine.

I sent a sigh to seek thee out,
        Deep drawn in pain,
Wing'd like an arrow: but my scout
        Returns in vain.   20

I tun'd another (having store)
        Into a grone;
Because the search was dumbe before:
        But all was one.

Lord, dost thou some new fabrick mold,   25
        Which favour winnes,
And keeps thee present, leaving th' old
        Unto their sinnes?

Where is my God? what hidden place
        Conceals thee still?   30
What covert dare eclipse thy face?
        Is it thy will?

O let not that of any thing;
        Let rather brasse,
Or steel, or mountains be thy ring,   35
        And I will passe.

Thy will such an intrenching is,
        As passeth thought:
To it all strength, all subtilties
        Are things of nought.   40

Thy will such a strange distance is,
        As that to it
East and West touch, the poles do kisse,
        And parallels meet.

Since then my grief must be as large,   45
        As is thy space,
Thy distance from me; see my charge,
        Lord, see my case.

14. *Simper:* twinkle.
47. *charge:* burden.

O take these barres, these lengths away;
         Turn, and restore me: 50
Be not Almightie, let me say,
         Against, but for me.

When thou dost turn, and wilt be neare;
         What edge so keen,
What point so piercing can appeare   55
         To come between?

For as thy absence doth excell
         All distance known:
So doth thy nearnesse bear the bell,
         Making two one.

Grief

O who will give me tears? Come all ye springs,
Dwell in my head & eyes: come clouds, & rain:
My grief hath need of all the watry things,
That nature hath produc'd. Let ev'ry vein
Suck up a river to supply mine eyes,   5
My weary weeping eyes too drie for me,
Unlesse they get new conduits, new supplies
To bear them out, and with my state agree.
What are two shallow foords, two little spouts
Of a lesse world? the greater is but small,   10
A narrow cupboard for my griefs and doubts,
Which want provision in the midst of all.
Verses, ye are too fine a thing, too wise
For my rough sorrows: cease, be dumbe and mute,
Give up your feet and running to mine eyes,   15
And keep your measures for some lovers lute,
Whose grief allows him musick and a ryme:
For mine excludes both measure, tune, and time.
                  Alas, my God!

The Crosse

        What is this strange and uncouth thing?
To make me sigh, and seek, and faint, and die,
Untill I had some place, where I might sing,
        And serve thee; and not onely I,

Grief
1-2. Cf. Jeremiah 9.1: 'Oh that my head were waters, and mine eyes a
     fountain of tears . . .'
10. *a lesse world:* the microcosm of man (see above, p. 106, note on
     13–18).
15. *feet:* a pun on metrical feet.

But all my wealth, and familie might combine   5
To set thy honour up, as our designe.

    And then when after much delay,
Much wrastling, many a combate, this deare end,
So much desir'd, is giv'n, to take away
    My power to serve thee; to unbend   10
All my abilities, my designes confound,
And lay my threatnings bleeding on the ground.

    One ague dwelleth in my bones,
Another in my soul (the memorie
What I would do for thee, if once my grones   15
    Could be allow'd for harmonie)
I am in all a weak disabled thing,
Save in the sight thereof, where strength doth sting.

    Besides, things sort not to my will,
Ev'n when my will doth studie thy renown: 20
Thou turnest th' edge of all things on me still,
    Taking me up to throw me down:
So that, ev'n when my hopes seem to be sped,
I am to grief alive, to them as dead.

    To have my aim, and yet to be   25
Farther from it then when I bent my bow;
To make my hopes my torture, and the fee
    Of all my woes another wo,
Is in the midst of delicates to need,
And ev'n in Paradise to be a weed.   30

    Ah my deare Father, ease my smart!
These contrarieties crush me: these crosse actions
Doe winde a rope about, and cut my heart:
    And yet since these thy contradictions
Are properly a crosse felt by thy sonne,   35
With but foure words, my words, *Thy will be done.*

The Flower

    How fresh, O Lord, how sweet and clean
Are thy returns! ev'n as the flowers in spring;
    To which, besides their own demean,
The late-past frosts tributes of pleasure bring.

The Crosse.   23. *sped:* brought to a successful issue.
32. *crosse actions:* see above, p. 33, note on 24.

The Flower. Singled out by Coleridge for particular praise: '*A delicious poem*' [§ 147].
  3. *demean:* demeanour; also, demesne [*FEH*].

Grief melts away   5
Like snow in May,
As if there were no such cold thing.

Who would have thought my shrivel'd heart
Could have recover'd greennesse? It was gone
Quite under ground; as flowers depart   10
To see their mother-root, when they have blown;
Where they together
All the hard weather,
Dead to the world, keep house unknown.

These are thy wonders, Lord of power,   15
Killing and quickning, bringing down to hell
And up to heaven in an houre;
Making a chiming of a passing-bell.
We say amisse,
This or that is:
Thy word is all, if we could spell.   20

O that I once past changing were,
Fast in thy Paradise, where no flower can wither!
Many a spring I shoot up fair,
Offring at heav'n, growing and groning thither: 25
Nor doth my flower
Want a spring-showre,
My sinnes and I joining together:

But while I grow in a straight line,
Still upwards bent, as if heav'n were mine own,   30
Thy anger comes, and I decline:
What frost to that? what pole is not the zone,
Where all things burn,
When thou dost turn,
And the least frown of thine is shown?   35

And now in age I bud again,
After so many deaths I live and write;
I once more smell the dew and rain,
And relish versing: O my onely light,
It cannot be   40
That I am he
On whom thy tempests fell all night.

25. *Offring:* aiming.
29-30. In restating this commonplace, Donne asserted that man's body
'is not as others, groveling, but of an erect, of an upright form,
naturally built, and disposed to the contemplation of *Heaven*'
(*Devotions*, ed. John Sparrow [Cambridge, 1923], p. 10).

These are thy wonders, Lord of love,
To make us see we are but flowers that glide:
    Which when we once can finde and prove,   45
Thou hast a garden for us, where to bide.
        Who would be more,
        Swelling through store,
Forfeit their Paradise by their pride.

Dotage

False glozing pleasures, casks of happinesse,
Foolish night-fires, womens and childrens wishes,
Chases in Arras, guilded emptinesse,
Shadows well mounted, dreams in a career,
Embroider'd lyes, nothing between two dishes;   5
    These are the pleasures here.
True earnest sorrows, rooted miseries,
Anguish in grain, vexations ripe and blown,
Sure-footed griefs, solid calamities,
Plain demonstrations, evident and cleare,   10
Fetching their proofs ev'n from the very bone;
    These are the sorrows here.
But oh the folly of distracted men,
Who griefs in earnest, joyes in jest pursue;
Preferring, like brute beasts, a lothsome den   15
Before a court, ev'n that above so cleare,
Where are no sorrows, but delights more true,
    Then miseries are here!

The Sonne

Let forrain nations of their language boast,
What fine varietie each tongue affords:
I like our language, as our men and coast:
Who cannot dresse it well, want wit, not words.
How neatly doe we give one onely name   5
To parents issue and the sunnes bright starre!

Dotage
  2. *Foolish night-fires:* will o' the wisps.
  3. *Chases in Arras:* hunting scenes depicted on tapestries [GR].
  4. *in a career:* i.e. unfolding swiftly.
  8. *in grain:* indelible.

The Sonne
  1-3. Herbert's relative Sir Philip Sidney in *An Apologie for Poetrie*
  (1595) likewise placed the English language 'before any other vulgar
  language I know'.
  3. *coast:* region.
  5-6. See above, p. 12; also p. 36, note on 98.

A sonne is light and fruit; a fruitfull flame
Chasing the fathers dimnesse, carri'd farre
From the first man in th' East, to fresh and new
Western discov'ries of posteritie.   10
So in one word our Lords humilitie
We turn upon him in a sense most true:
　　　For what Christ once in humblenesse began,
　　　We him in glorie call, *The Sonne of Man.*

A true Hymne

　　　　　My joy, my life, my crown!
　　　My heart was meaning all the day,
　　　　　Somewhat it fain would say:
And still it runneth mutt'ring up and down
With onely this, *My joy, my life, my crown.*   5

　　　　　Yet slight not these few words:
　　　If truly said, they may take part
　　　　　Among the best in art.
The finenesse which a hymne or psalme affords,
Is, when the soul unto the lines accords.   10

　　　　　He who craves all the minde,
　　　And all the soul, and strength, and time,
　　　　　If the words onely ryme,
Justly complains, that somewhat is behinde
To make his verse, or write a hymne in kinde.   15

　　　　　Whereas if th' heart be moved,
　　　Although the verse be somewhat scant,
　　　　　God doth supplie the want.
As when th' heart sayes (sighing to be approved)
O, could I love! and stops: God writeth, *Loved.*   20

The Answer

My comforts drop and melt away like snow:
I shake my head, and all the thoughts and ends,
Which my fierce youth did bandie, fall and flow
Like leaves about me: or like summer friends,

8. *Chasing:* chasing away, dispelling.

A true Hymne
9. *finenesse:* 'subtlety or brave splendour, perhaps both' [§ 219].
14. *behinde:* lacking.

The Answer
4. *summer friends:* i.e. 'friends' mindful of us only in the summer of
　　our prosperity.

Flyes of estates and sunne-shine. But to all,   5
Who think me eager, hot, and undertaking,
But in my prosecutions slack and small;
As a young exhalation, newly waking,
Scorns his first bed of dirt, and means the sky;
But cooling by the way, grows pursie and slow,   10
And setling to a cloud, doth live and die
In that dark state of tears: to all, that so
    Show me, and set me, I have one reply,
    Which they that know the rest, know more than I.

A Dialogue-Antheme

Christian. Death

Chr. Alas, poore Death, where is thy glorie?
      Where is thy famous force, thy ancient sting?
Dea. *Alas poore mortall, void of storie,*
      Go spell and reade how I have kill'd thy King.
Chr. Poore death! and who was hurt thereby?   5
      Thy curse being laid on him, makes thee accurst.
Dea. *Let losers talk: yet thou shalt die;*
      These arms shall crush thee.
Chr.   Spare not, do thy worst.
      I shall be one day better then before:
      Thou so much worse, that thou shalt be no more.   10

The Water-course

Thou who dost dwell and linger here below,
Since the condition of this world is frail,
Where of all plants afflictions soonest grow;
If troubles overtake thee, do not wail:

For who can look for lesse, that loveth $\left\{ \begin{array}{l} \text{Life.} \\ \text{Strife.} \end{array} \right.$ 5

8. *exhalation:* vapour rising from the damp ground. In *Paradise Lost*
    the word, associated with meteors, is ominously foreboding—as in
    Pandemonium rising 'like an exhalation' (I, 711).
10. *pursie:* swollen.
13. *one reply:* the 'answer', intentionally elusive, depends on the inter-
    pretation of *the rest* (14). One suggestion is ventured later: see
    below, *The Rose,* p. 182, ll. 15–16 and 32.

A Dialogue-Antheme
1-2. Cf. 1 Corinthians 15.55: 'O death, where is thy sting? O grave,
    where is thy victory?'
  6. *Thy curse being laid on him:* as above, p. 117, note on 15.

But rather turn the pipe, and waters course
To serve thy sinnes, and furnish thee with store
Of sov'raigne tears, springing from true remorse:
That so in purenesse thou mayest him adore,
   Who gives to man, as he sees fit $\begin{cases} \text{Salvation.} \\ \text{Damnation.} \end{cases}$ 10

Self-condemnation

    Thou who condemnest Jewish hate,
For choosing Barabbas a murderer
      Before the Lord of Glorie;
    Look back upon thine own estate,
Call home thine eye (that busie wanderer)   5
      That choice may be thy storie.

    He that doth love, and love amisse
This worlds delights before true Christian joy,
      Hath made a Jewish choice:
    The world an ancient murderer is;   10
Thousands of souls it hath and doth destroy
      With her enchanting voice.

    He that hath made a sorrie wedding
Between his soul and gold, and hath preferr'd
      False gain before the true,   15
    Hath done what he condemnes in reading:
For he hath sold for money his deare Lord,
      And is a Judas-Jew.

    Thus we prevent the last great day,
And judge our selves. That light, which sin & passion   20
      Did before dimme and choke,
    When once those snuffes are ta'ne away,
Shines bright and cleare, ev'n unto condemnation,
      Without excuse or cloke.

Bitter-sweet

Ah my deare angrie Lord,
Since thou dost love, yet strike;
Cast down, yet help afford;
Sure I will do the like.

Self-condemnation
10-12. A reference to the Sirens who, according to the Christian tra-
    dition, 'embody both the general notion of worldliness and the
    more specific vice of sensuality' [§ 204].
19. *prevent the last great day:* anticipate the Last Judgement.

I will complain, yet praise;
I will bewail, approve:
And all my sowre-sweet dayes
I will lament, and love.

5

The Glance

When first thy sweet and gracious eye
Vouchsaf'd ev'n in the midst of youth and night
To look upon me, who before did lie
      Weltring in sinne;
I felt a sugred strange delight,
Passing all cordials made by any art,
Bedew, embalme, and overrunne my heart,
      And take it in.

5

Since that time many a bitter storm
My soul hath felt, ev'n able to destroy,
Had the malicious and ill-meaning harm
      His swing and sway:
But still thy sweet originall joy
Sprung from thine eye, did work within my soul,
And surging griefs, when they grew bold, controll,
      And got the day.

10

15

If thy first glance so powerfull be,
A mirth but open'd and seal'd up again;
What wonders shall we feel, when we shall see
      Thy full-ey'd love!
When thou shalt look us out of pain,
And one aspect of thine spend in delight
More then a thousand sunnes disburse in light,
      In heav'n above.

20

The 23rd Psalme

The God of love my shepherd is,
    And he that doth me feed:
While he is mine, and I am his,
    What can I want or need?

The Glance
16. *got:* won.

He leads me to the tender grasse,   5
    Where I both feed and rest;
Then to the streams that gently passe:
    In both I have the best.

Or if I stray, he doth convert
    And bring my minde in frame: 10
And all this not for my desert,
    But for his holy name.

Yea, in deaths shadie black abode
    Well may I walk, not fear:
For thou art with me; and thy rod   15
    To guide, thy staffe to bear.

Nay, thou dost make me sit and dine,
    Ev'n in my enemies sight:
My head with oyl, my cup with wine
    Runnes over day and night.   20

Surely thy sweet and wondrous love
    Shall measure all my dayes;
And as it never shall remove,
    So neither shall my praise.

Marie Magdalene

When blessed Marie wip'd her Saviours feet,
(Whose precepts she had trampled on before)
And wore them for a jewell on her head,
    Shewing his steps should be the street,
    Wherein she thenceforth evermore   5
With pensive humblenesse would live and tread:

The 23rd Psalme. The King James ('Authorized') Version of 1611
    reads:

    The Lord is my shepherd; I shall not want.
    He maketh me to lie down in green pastures:
    He leadeth me beside the still waters.
    He restoreth my soul:
    He leadeth me in the paths of righteousness for his name's sake.
    Yea, though I walk through the valley of the shadow of death,
    I will fear no evil: for thou art with me;
    Thy rod and thy staff they comfort me.
    Thou preparest a table before me in the presence of thine enemies:
    Thou anointest my head with oil; my cup runneth over.
    Surely goodness and mercy shall follow me all the days of my life:
    And I will dwell in the house of the Lord for ever.

10.   *in frame:* into appropriate order.
24.   *my praise:* 'thy praise' (*B*).

She being stain'd her self, why did she strive
To make him clean, who could not be defil'd?
Why kept she not her tears for her own faults,
  And not his feet? Though we could dive   10
  In tears like seas, our sinnes are pil'd
Deeper then they, in words, and works, and thoughts.

Deare soul, she knew who did vouchsafe and deigne
To bear her filth; and that her sinnes did dash
Ev'n God himself: wherefore she was not loth, 15
  As she had brought wherewith to stain,
  So to bring in wherewith to wash:
And yet in washing one, she washed both.

Aaron

   Holinesse on the head,
  Light and perfections on the breast,
Harmonious bells below, raising the dead
  To leade them unto life and rest.
   Thus are true Aarons drest.   5

   Profanenesse in my head,
  Defects and darknesse in my breast,
A noise of passions ringing me for dead
  Unto a place where is no rest.
   Poore priest thus am I drest.   10

   Onely another head
  I have, another heart and breast,
Another musick, making live not dead,
  Without whom I could have no rest:
   In him I am well drest.   15

   Christ is my onely head,
  My alone onely heart and breast,
My onely musick, striking me ev'n dead;
  That to the old man I may rest,
   And be in him new drest.   20

Aaron—i.e. a type of Christ's priestly role.
1-4. Aaron's priestly garments are detailed in Exodus 28.4 ff.: *on the head*, a mitre with a gold plate engraved 'Holiness to the Lord'; *on the breast*, a pouch bearing the Urim and the Thummim who signify *Light* and *perfections*; and *below* (i.e. on the robe's hem), 'pomegranates of blue, and of purple, and of scarlet . . .; and *bells* of gold between them round about'.
19. *old man:* cf. above, *The Reprisall*, p. 58, note on 15–16.

                        So holy in my head,
                  Perfect and light in my deare breast,
      My doctrine tun'd by Christ, (who is not dead,
                  But lives in me while I do rest)
                        Come people; Aaron's drest.   25

The Odour, 2.Cor.2

How sweetly doth *My Master* sound! *My Master!*
            As Amber-greese leaves a rich sent
                  Unto the taster:
            So do these words a sweet content,
An orientall fragrancie, *My Master*.   5

With these all day I do perfume my minde,
            My minde ev'n thrust into them both:
                  That I might finde
            What cordials make this curious broth,
This broth of smells, that feeds and fats my minde.   10

My Master, shall I speak? O that to thee
            My servant were a little so,
                  As flesh may be;
            That these two words might creep & grow
To some degree of spicinesse to thee!   15

Then should the Pomander, which was before
            A speaking sweet, mend by reflection,
                  And tell me more:
            For pardon of my imperfection
Would warm and work it sweeter then before.   20

For when *My Master*, which alone is sweet,
            And ev'n in my unworthinesse pleasing,
                  Shall call and meet,
            My servant, as thee not displeasing,
That call is but the breathing of the sweet.   25

This breathing would with gains by sweetning me
            (As sweet things traffick when they meet)
                  Return to thee.
            And so this new commerce and sweet
Should all my life employ, and busie me.   30

The Odour. 2 Corinthians 2.15–16 reads: 'we are unto God a sweet
    savour of Christ, in them that are saved, and in them that perish:
    to the one we are the savour of death unto death; and to the other
    the savour of life unto life'.
2. *Amber-greese:* 'gray amber, a secretion of the spermaceti whale,
    much prized in perfumery' [*GHP*].
16. *Pomander:* a scent ball, yielding its odour when warmed or squeezed.

The Foil

If we could see below
The sphere of vertue, and each shining grace
As plainly as that above doth show;
This were the better skie, the brighter place.

God hath made starres the foil   5
To set off vertues; griefs to set off sinning:
Yet in this wretched world we toil,
As if grief were not foul, nor vertue winning.

The Forerunners

The harbingers are come. See, see their mark;
White is their colour, and behold my head.
But must they have my brain? must they dispark
Those sparkling notions, which therein were bred?
Must dulnesse turn me to a clod?   5
Yet have they left me, *Thou art still my God.*

Good men ye be, to leave me my best room,
Ev'n all my heart, and what is lodged there:
I passe not, I, what of the rest become,
So *Thou art still my God*, be out of fear.   10
He will be pleased with that dittie;
And if I please him, I write fine and wittie.

Farewell sweet phrases, lovely metaphors.
But will ye leave me thus? when ye before
Of stews and brothels onely knew the doores,   15
Then did I wash you with my tears, and more,
Brought you to Church well drest and clad:
My God must have my best, ev'n all I had.

The Foil—i.e. the thin leaf of metal placed under a jewel to enhance its brilliance; but also the standard weapon [§ 204].
7. *toil*: labour; also, fight.

The Forerunners. Messengers sent in advance of a royal progress would secure lodgings by chalking the doors (cf. l. 35); now the harbingers of old age and death mark the narrator's hair white.
3. *dispark:* i.e. disempark, or turn out of a park; also, to take the sparkle away, to dull [§ 204].
6. Cf. Psalm 31.14: 'I trusted in thee, O Lord: I said, Thou art my God'.
9. *passe not* (also in 31): care not.

Lovely enchanting language, sugar-cane,
Hony of roses, whither wilt thou flie?   20
Hath some fond lover tic'd thee to thy bane?
And wilt thou leave the Church, and love a stie?
      Fie, thou wilt soil thy broider'd coat,
And hurt thy self, and him that sings the note.

Let foolish lovers, if they will love dung,   25
With canvas, not with arras clothe their shame:
Let follie speak in her own native tongue.
True beautie dwells on high: ours is a flame
      But borrow'd thence to light us thither.
Beautie and beauteous words should go together.   30

Yet if you go, I passe not; take your way:
For, *Thou art still my God*, is all that ye
Perhaps with more embellishment can say,
Go birds of spring: let winter have his fee,
      Let a bleak palenesse chalk the doore,   35
So all within be livelier then before.

The Rose

Presse me not to take more pleasure
      In this world of sugred lies,
And to use a larger measure
      Then my strict, yet welcome size.

First, there is no pleasure here: 5
      Colour'd griefs indeed there are,
Blushing woes, that look as cleare
      As if they could beautie spare.

Or if such deceits there be,
      Such delights I meant to say;   10
There are no such things to me,
      Who have pass'd my right away.

But I will not much oppose
      Unto what you now advise:
Onely take this gentle rose,   15
      And therein my answer lies.

The Rose. Cf. 'the rose of Sharon', the Church (above, p. 150, note on
    1).
  4. *size:* status (as above, p. 147).
  6. *Colour'd:* disguised.
  16. *my answer* (also in 32): see above, p. 175, note on 13.

What is fairer then a rose?
    What is sweeter? yet it purgeth.
Purgings enmitie disclose,
    Enmitie forbearance urgeth.   20

If then all that worldlings prize
    Be contracted to a rose;
Sweetly there indeed it lies,
    But it biteth in the close.

So this flower doth judge and sentence   25
    Worldly joyes to be a scourge:
For they all produce repentance.
    And repentance is a purge.

But I health, not physick choose:
    Onely though I you oppose,   30
Say that fairly I refuse,
    For my answer is a rose.

Discipline

Throw away thy rod,
Throw away thy wrath:
      O my God,
Take the gentle path.

For my hearts desire   5
Unto thine is bent:
      I aspire
To a full consent.

Not a word or look
I affect to own,   10
      But by book,
And thy book alone.

Though I fail, I weep:
Though I halt in pace,
      Yet I creep   15
To the throne of grace.

Then let wrath remove;
Love will do the deed:
      For with love
Stonie hearts will bleed.   20

18. *it purgeth:* see above, p. 131, note on 78.
20. *forbearance:* abstinence.

Love is swift of foot;
Love's a man of warre,
   And can shoot,
And can hit from farre.

Who can scape his bow?   25
That which wrought on thee,
   Brought thee low,
Needs must work on me.

Throw away thy rod;
Though man frailties hath,   30
   Thou art God:
Throw away thy wrath.

The Invitation

Come ye hither all, whose taste
   Is your waste;
Save your cost, and mend your fare.
God is here prepar'd and drest,
   And the feast,   5
God, in whom all dainties are.

Come ye hither all, whom wine
   Doth define,
Naming you not to your good:
Weep what ye have drunk amisse,   10
   And drink this,
Which before ye drink is bloud.

Come ye hither all, whom pain
   Doth arraigne,
Bringing all your sinnes to sight: 15
Taste and fear not: God is here
   In this cheer,
And on sinne doth cast the fright.

Discipline
22. Cf. Exodus 15.3: 'The Lord is a man of war'. The allusion may also
be to Cupid with his bow, especially as the Biblical 'bow' is an
instrument of divine punishment (as above, p. 112, note on 24).

The Invitation
1-3. Cf. Isaiah 55.1–2: 'every one that thirsteth, come ye to the waters,
and he that hath no money. . . . Wherefore do ye spend money for
that which is not bread?' As usual, however, Herbert's emphasis is
on the eucharistic *feast* (5) which here links with the poem imme-
diately following.

Come ye hither all, whom joy
   Doth destroy,   20
While ye graze without your bounds:
Here is joy that drowneth quite
   Your delight,
As a floud the lower grounds.

Come ye hither all, whose love   25
   Is your dove,
And exalts you to the skie:
Here is love, which having breath
   Ev'n in death,
After death can never die.   30

Lord I have invited all,
   And I shall
Still invite, still call to thee:
For it seems but just and right
   In my sight,   35
Where is all, there all should be.

The Banquet

Welcome sweet and sacred cheer,
   Welcome deare;
With me, in me, live and dwell:
For thy neatnesse passeth sight,
   Thy delight   5
Passeth tongue to taste or tell.

O what sweetnesse from the bowl
   Fills my soul,
Such as is, and makes divine!
Is some starre (fled from the sphere)   10
   Melted there,
As we sugar melt in wine?

Or hath sweetnesse in the bread
   Made a head
To subdue the smell of sinne;   15
Flowers, and gummes, and powders giving
   All their living,
Lest the enemie should winne?

The Banquet
14. *Made a head:* pressed forward in opposition [*FEH*].

Doubtlesse, neither starre nor flower
                    Hath the power   20
Such a sweetnesse to impart:
Onely God, who gives perfumes,
                    Flesh assumes,
And with it perfumes my heart.

But as Pomanders and wood   25
                    Still are good,
Yet being bruis'd are better sented:
God, to show how farre his love
                    Could improve,
Here, as broken, is presented.   30

When I had forgot my birth,
                    And on earth
In delights of earth was drown'd;
God took bloud, and needs would be
                    Spilt with me,   35
And so found me on the ground.

Having rais'd me to look up,
                    In a cup
Sweetly he doth meet my taste.
But I still being low and short,   40
                    Farre from court,
Wine becomes a wing at last.

For with it alone I flie
                    To the skie:
Where I wipe mine eyes, and see   45
What I seek, for what I sue;
                    Him I view,
Who hath done so much for me.

Let the wonder of this pitie
                    Be my dittie,   50
And take up my lines and life:
Hearken under pain of death,
                    Hands and breath;
Strive in this, and love the strife.

The Posie

                    Let wits contest,
And with their words and posies windows fill:
                    Lesse then the least
Of all thy mercies, is my posie still.

The Posie—i.e. a short motto; also, poetry ('poesie').
3-4. Herbert's own motto (quoted above, p. 31).

This on my ring,   5
This by my picture, in my book I write:
        Whether I sing,
Or say, or dictate, this is my delight.

        Invention rest,
Comparisons go play, wit use thy will: 10
        Lesse then the least
Of all Gods mercies, is my posie still.

A Parodie

Souls joy, when thou art gone,
        And I alone,
        Which cannot be,
Because thou dost abide with me,
        And I depend on thee;   5

Yet when thou dost suppresse
        The cheerfulnesse
        Of thy abode,
And in my powers not stirre abroad,
        But leave me to my load: 10

O what a damp and shade
        Doth me invade!
        No stormie night
Can so afflict or so affright,
        As thy eclipsed light.   15

Ah Lord! do not withdraw,
        Lest want of aw
        Make Sinne appeare;
And when thou dost but shine lesse cleare,
        Say, that thou art not here.   20

And then what life I have,
        While Sinne doth rave,
        And falsly boast,
That I may seek, but thou art lost;
        Thou and alone thou know'st.   25

O what a deadly cold
        Doth me infold!
        I half beleeve,
That Sinne sayes true: but while I grieve,
        Thou com'st and dost relieve.   30

A Parodie. On 'sacred parody', see Appendix III, pp. 209 ff; and on
    the poem here parodied, p. 211.

The Elixer

    Teach me, my God and King,
      In all things thee to see,
And what I do in any thing,
      To do it as for thee:

    Not rudely, as a beast,   5
      To runne into an action;
But still to make thee prepossest,
      And give it his perfection.

    A man that looks on glasse,
      On it may stay his eye;   10
Or if he pleaseth, through it passe,
      And then the heav'n espie.

    All may of thee partake:
      Nothing can be so mean,
Which with his tincture (for thy sake)   15
      Will not grow bright and clean.

    A servant with this clause
      Makes drudgerie divine:
Who sweeps a room, as for thy laws,
      Makes that and th' action fine.   20

    This is the famous stone
      That turneth all to gold:
For that which God doth touch and own
      Cannot for lesse be told.

A Wreath

A wreathed garland of deserved praise,
Of praise deserved, unto thee I give,
I give to thee, who knowest all my wayes,
My crooked winding wayes, wherein I live,
Wherein I die, not live: for life is straight,   5
Straight as a line, and ever tends to thee,

The Elixer. On the earlier versions of this extensively revised poem, see
    Appendix II, pp. 207–8. The title is explained in ll. 21–2.
14-16. Cf. *A Priest to the Temple:* 'Nothing is little in Gods service'
    (Ch. 14).
15. *for thy sake:* the proper *tincture,* i.e. the alchemical term for 'a
    supposed spiritual principle or immaterial substance whose character
    or quality may be infused into material things' [*OED*].
23. *touch:* test with a touchstone.

To thee, who art more farre above deceit,
Then deceit seems above simplicitie.
Give me simplicitie, that I may live,
So live and like, that I may know thy wayes,   10
Know them and practise them: then shall I give
For this poore wreath, give thee a crown of praise.

Death

Death, thou wast once an uncouth hideous thing,
                Nothing but bones,
        The sad effect of sadder grones:
Thy mouth was open, but thou couldst not sing.

For we consider'd thee as at some six   5
                Or ten yeares hence,
        After the losse of life and sense,
Flesh being turn'd to dust, and bones to sticks.

We lookt on this side of thee, shooting short;
                Where we did finde   10
        The shells of fledge souls left behinde,
Dry dust, which sheds no tears, but may extort.

But since our Saviours death did put some bloud
                Into thy face;
        Thou art grown fair and full of grace,   15
Much in request, much sought for, as a good.

For we do now behold thee gay and glad,
                As at dooms-day;
        When souls shall wear their new aray,
And all thy bones with beautie shall be clad.   20

Therefore we can go die as sleep, and trust
                Half that we have
        Unto an honest faithfull grave;
Making our pillows either down, or dust.

Dooms-day

                Come away,
        Make no delay.
Summon all the dust to rise,
Till it stirre, and rubbe the eyes;

Death. The poem initiates a sequence of five eschatological poems,
    traditional in theory but distinctly individual in practice (see above,
    pp. 20–21).
Dooms-day. On the 'sacred parody' attempted by this poem, see below,
    Appendix III, especially, p. 212.

While this member jogs the other,   5
Each one whispring, *Live your brother?*

   Come away,
  Make this the day.
Dust, alas, no musick feels,
But thy trumpet: then it kneels,   10
As peculiar notes and strains
Cure Tarantulaes raging pains.

   Come away,
  O make no stay!
Let the graves make their confession,   15
Lest at length they plead possession:
Fleshes stubbornnesse may have
Read that lesson to the grave.

   Come away,
  Thy flock doth stray.   20
Some to windes their bodie lend,
And in them may drown a friend:
Some in noisome vapours grow
To a plague and publick wo.

   Come away,   25
  Help our decay.
Man is out of order hurl'd,
Parcel'd out to all the world.
Lord, thy broken consort raise,
And the musick shall be praise.   30

Judgement

Almightie Judge, how shall poore wretches brook
   Thy dreadfull look,
Able a heart of iron to appall,
    When thou shalt call
  For ev'ry mans peculiar book?   5

12. 'Tarantism, an hysterical malady, was supposed to be caused by
the bite of the tarantula and to be cured by music and wild dancing'
[*FEH*].

15. *their confession:* i.e. that they do not legally possess bodies.

27. *Man is out of order hurl'd:* i.e. in contrast to the rest of creation
where, as Vaughan wrote, 'All is hurl'd / In sacred *Hymnes,* and
Order' ('The Morning-watch', 16–17; § 332).

29. *consort:* cf. above, p. 62, note on 13.

What others mean to do, I know not well;
          Yet I heare tell,
That some will turn thee to some leaves therein
          So void of sinne,
   That they in merit shall excell.   10

But I resolve, when thou shalt call for mine,
          That to decline,
And thrust a Testament into thy hand:
          Let that be scann'd.
   There thou shalt finde my faults are thine.   15

Heaven

O who will show me those delights on high?
      Echo.   *I.*
Thou Echo, thou art mortall, all men know.
      Echo.   *No.*
Wert thou not born among the trees and leaves?   5
      Echo.   *Leaves.*
And are there any leaves, that still abide?
      Echo.   *Bide.*
What leaves are they? impart the matter wholly.
      Echo.   *Holy.*   10
Are holy leaves the Echo then of blisse?
      Echo.   *Yes.*
Then tell me, what is that supreme delight?
      Echo.   *Light.*
Light to the minde: what shall the will enjoy?   15
      Echo.   *Joy.*
But are there cares and businesse with the pleasure?
      Echo.   *Leisure.*
Light, joy, and leisure; but shall they persever?
      Echo.   *Ever.*   20

Heaven. On the 'sacred parody' attempted by this echo-poem, see
   below, Appendix III, especially p. 210. On the apparently naïve
   rhyme scheme, see above, pp. 12–13.

Love (III)

Love bade me welcome: yet my soul drew back,
      Guiltie of dust and sinne.
But quick-ey'd Love, observing me grow slack
      From my first entrance in,
Drew nearer to me, sweetly questioning,   5
      If I lack'd any thing.

A guest, I answer'd, worthy to be here:
      Love said, You shall be he.
I the unkinde, ungratefull? Ah my deare,
      I cannot look on thee.   10
Love took my hand, and smiling did reply,
      Who made the eyes but I?

Truth Lord, but I have marr'd them: let my shame
      Go where it doth deserve.
And know you not, sayes Love, who bore the blame?   15
      My deare, then I will serve.
You must sit down, sayes Love, and taste my meat:
      So I did sit and eat.

FINIS.

Glorie be to God on high, and on earth
peace, good will towards men.

Love III. The poem celebrates not the sacrament in the visible Church
but the final communion in Heaven when God 'shall gird himself,
and make them to sit down to meat, and will come forth and serve
them' (Luke 12.37; § 216).

The Church Militant

Almightie Lord, who from thy glorious throne
Seest and rulest all things ev'n as one:
The smallest ant or atome knows thy power,
Known also to each minute of an houre:
Much more do Common-weals acknowledge thee,   5
And wrap their policies in thy decree,
Complying with thy counsels, doing nought
Which doth not meet with an eternall thought.
But above all, thy Church and Spouse doth prove
Not the decrees of power, but bands of love.   10
Early didst thou arise to plant this vine,
Which might the more indeare it to be thine.
Spices come from the East; so did thy Spouse,
Trimme as the light, sweet as the laden boughs
Of *Noahs* shadie vine, chaste as the dove;   15
Prepar'd and fitted to receive thy love.
The course was westward, that the sunne might light
As well our understanding as our sight.
Where th' Ark did rest, there *Abraham* began
To bring the other Ark from *Canaan*.   20
Moses pursu'd this; but King *Solomon*
Finish'd and fixt the old religion.
When it grew loose, the Jews did hope in vain
By nailing Christ to fasten it again.
But to the Gentiles he bore crosse and all,   25
Rending with earthquakes the partition-wall:
Onely whereas the Ark in glorie shone,
Now with the crosse, as with a staffe, alone,
Religion, like a pilgrime, westward bent,
Knocking at all doores, ever as she went.   30
Yet as the sunne, though forward be his flight,
Listens behinde him, and allows some light,

15. *Noahs shadie vine:* see above, p. 139, headnote.
16. *W* reads: 'All, Emblems, which thy Darling doth improve'.
19-22. The place where Noah's ark landed after the Flood is here said
  to be the starting point of Abraham's sojourn toward Egypt with the
  Ark of the Covenant. The latter, which Moses endeavoured to
  bring to the Promised Land of Canaan, was eventually lodged in
  Solomon's Temple.
26. *partition-wall:* '[Christ] hath broken down the middle wall of
  partition between us' (Ephesians 2.14).
28. *as with a staffe:* see above, p. 58, note on 3.

Till all depart: so went the Church her way,
Letting, while one foot stept, the other stay
Among the eastern nations for a time,   35
Till both removed to the western clime,
To *Egypt* first she came, where they did prove
Wonders of anger once, but now of love.
The ten Commandments there did flourish more
Then the ten bitter plagues had done before.   40
Holy *Macarius* and great *Anthonie*
Made *Pharaoh Moses*, changing th' historie.
Goshen was darknesse, *Egypt* full of lights,
Nilus for monsters brought forth Israelites.
Such power hath mightie Baptisme to produce   45
For things misshappen, things of highest use.
How deare to me, O God, thy counsels are!
          Who may with thee compare?
Religion thence fled into *Greece,* where arts
Gave her the highest place in all mens hearts.   50
Learning was pos'd, Philosophie was set,
Sophisters taken in a fishers net.
Plato and *Aristotle* were at a losse,
And wheel'd about again to spell *Christ-Crosse.*
Prayers chas'd syllogismes into their den,   55
And *Ergo* was transform'd into *Amen.*
Though *Greece* took horse as soon as *Egypt* did,
And *Rome* as both; yet *Egypt* faster rid,
And spent her period and prefixed time
Before the other. *Greece* being past her prime,   60
Religion went to *Rome,* subduing those,
Who, that they might subdue, made all their foes.
The Warrier his deere skarres no more resounds,
But seems to yeeld Christ hath the greater wounds,
Wounds willingly endur'd to work his blisse,   65
Who by an ambush lost his Paradise.
The great heart stoops, and taketh from the dust
A sad repentance, not the spoils of lust:
Quitting his spear, lest it should pierce again
Him in his members, who for him was slain.   70
The Shepherds hook grew to a scepter here,

41-2. The fourth-century hermits Macarius and Anthony considered
    God's instrument to have been Egypt, not Israel.
44. *for:* instead of.
47-8. The reiterated lines (also in 99 f., 155 f., 209 f., 278 f.) are from
    Psalms 139.17 and 89.6 in the Book of Common Prayer.
51. *pos'd:* nonplussed.
    set: defeated.
54. *Christ-Crosse:* alphabet.
58. *rid:* rode.

Giving new names and numbers to the yeare.
But th' Empire dwelt in *Greece*, to comfort them
Who were cut short in *Alexanders* stemme.
In both of these Prowesse and Arts did tame   75
And tune mens hearts against the Gospel came:
Which using, and not fearing skill in th' one,
Or strength in th' other, did erect her throne.
Many a rent and struggling th' Empire knew,
(As dying things are wont) untill it flew   80
At length to *Germanie*, still westward bending,
And there the Churches festivall attending:
That as before Empire and Arts made way,
(For no lesse Harbingers would serve then they)
So they might still, and point us out the place   85
Where first the Church should raise her down-cast face.
Strength levels grounds, Art makes a garden there;
Then showres Religion, and makes all to bear.
Spain in the Empire shar'd with *Germanie*,
But *England* in the higher victorie: 90
Giving the Church a crown to keep her state,
And not go lesse then she had done of late.
Constantines British line meant this of old,
And did this mysterie wrap up and fold
Within a sheet of paper, which was rent   95
From times great Chronicle, and hither sent.
Thus both the Church and Sunne together ran
Unto the farthest old meridian.
How deare to me, O God, thy counsels are!
                    Who may with thee compare?   100
Much about one and the same time and place,
Both where and when the Church began her race,
Sinne did set out of Eastern *Babylon*,
And travell'd westward also: journeying on
He chid the Church away, where e're he came,   105
Breaking her peace, and tainting her good name.
At first he got to *Egypt*, and did sow
Gardens of gods, which ev'ry yeare did grow,

72. The reference is to the introduction of the Christian calendar
    which displaced pagan festivals.
73. *in Greece:* i.e. through the creation of the Byzantine Empire by
    Constantine the Great.
76. *against:* before.
93. *Constantines British line:* Constantine was proclaimed emperor in
    York in 306; his mother Helen was said to have been born in
    England. Hence also Milton's proud claim in 1643 that the Roman
    Empire was baptized by 'our English *Constantine*' (*Selected Prose*,
    ed. C. A. Patrides, Penguin Books, 1974, p. 120).
95. *a sheet of paper:* the 'Donation of Constantine' (actually a forgery)
    which had granted extensive privileges to the Pope.
98. *meridian:* highest point.

Fresh and fine deities. They were at great cost,
Who for a god clearely a sallet lost.   110
Ah, what a thing is man devoid of grace,
Adoring garlick with an humble face,
Begging his food of that which he may eat,
Starving the while he worshippeth his meat!
Who makes a root his god, how low is he,   115
If God and man be sever'd infinitely!
What wretchednesse can give him any room,
Whose house is foul, while he adores his broom?
None will beleeve this now, though money be
In us the same transplanted foolerie.   120
Thus Sinne in *Egypt* sneaked for a while;
His highest was an ox or crocodile,
And such poore game. Thence he to *Greece* doth passe,
And being craftier much then Goodnesse was,
He left behinde him garrisons of sinnes   125
To make good that which ev'ry day he winnes.
Here Sinne took heart, and for a garden-bed
Rich shrines and oracles he purchased:
He grew a gallant, and would needs foretell
As well what should befall, as what befell.   130
Nay, he became a poet, and would serve
His pills of sublimate in that conserve.
The world came both with hands and purses full
To this great lotterie, and all would pull.
But all was glorious cheating, brave deceit,   135
Where some poore truths were shuffled for a bait
To credit him, and to discredit those
Who after him should braver truths disclose.
From *Greece* he went to *Rome:* and as before
He was a God, now he's an Emperour.   140
Nero and others lodg'd him bravely there,
Put him in trust to rule the Romane sphere.
Glorie was his chief instrument of old:
Pleasure succeeded straight, when that grew cold.
Which soon was blown to such a mightie flame,   145
That though our Saviour did destroy the game,
Disparking oracles, and all their treasure,
Setting affliction to encounter pleasure;

110. *sallet:* salad.
112. *Adoring garlick:* so the Israelites on leaving Egypt missed 'the
      leeks, and the onions, and the garlick' (Numbers 11.15).
127. *for:* instead of.
131. *he became a poet:* i.e. through the versified utterances of the Greek
      oracles.
132. The poison *sublimate* was sugar-coated.
147. *Disparking:* as above, p. 181, note on 3.

Yet did a rogue with hope of carnall joy
Cheat the most subtill nations. Who so coy,   150
So trimme, as *Greece* and *Egypt*? yet their hearts
Are given over, for their curious arts,
To such Mahometan stupidities,
As the old heathen would deem prodigies.
How deare to me, O God, thy counsels are!   155
         Who may with thee compare?
Onely the West and *Rome* do keep them free
From this contagious infidelitie.
And this is all the Rock, whereof they boast,
As *Rome* will one day finde unto her cost.   160
Sinne being not able to extirpate quite
The Churches here, bravely resolv'd one night
To be a Church-man too, and wear a Mitre:
The old debauched ruffian would turn writer.
I saw him in his studie, where he sate   165
Busie in controversies sprung of late.
A gown and pen became him wondrous well:
His grave aspect had more of heav'n then hell:
Onely there was a handsome picture by,
To which he lent a corner of his eye.   170
As Sinne in *Greece* a Prophet was before,
And in old *Rome* a mightie Emperour;
So now being Priest he plainly did professe
To make a jest of Christs three offices:
The rather since his scatter'd jugglings were   175
United now in one both time and sphere.
From *Egypt* he took pettie deities,
From *Greece* oracular infallibilities,
And from old *Rome* the libertie of pleasure,
By free dispensings of the Churches treasure.   180
Then in memoriall of his ancient throne
He did surname his palace, *Babylon*.
Yet that he might the better gain all nations,
And make that name good by their transmigrations;
From all these places, but at divers times,   185
He took fine vizards to conceal his crimes:
From *Egypt* Anchorisme and retirednesse,
Learning from *Greece*, from old *Rome* statelinesse:
And blending these he carri'd all mens eyes,
While Truth sat by, counting his victories: 190
Whereby he grew apace and scorn'd to use

149. *a rogue:* Mohammed.
174. *Christ's three offices:* i.e. as prophet, priest, and king, here per-
      verted by Sin (171–3, 177–80, 187–8).
182. *Babylon:* the *Western* one (211), in extension of the Eastern
      prototype.

Such force as once did captivate the Jews;
But did bewitch, and finely work each nation
Into a voluntarie transmigration.
All poste to *Rome*: Princes submit their necks   195
Either t' publick foot or private tricks.
It did not fit his gravitie to stirre,
Nor his long journey, nor his gout and furre.
Therefore he sent out able ministers,
Statesmen within, without doores cloisterers: 200
Who without spear, or sword, or other drumme
Then what was in their tongue, did overcome;
And having conquer'd, did so strangely rule,
That the whole world did seem but the Popes mule.
As new and old *Rome* did one Empire twist;   205
So both together are one Antichrist,
Yet with two faces, as their *Janus* was;
Being in this their old crackt looking-glasse.
How deare to me, O God, thy counsels are!
       Who may with thee compare?   210
Thus Sinne triumphs in Western *Babylon*;
Yet not as Sinne, but as Religion.
Of his two thrones he made the latter best,
And to defray his journey from the east.
Old and new *Babylon* are to hell and night,   215
As is the moon and sunne to heav'n and light.
When th' one did set, the other did take place,
Confronting equally the law and grace,
They are hells land-marks, Satans double crest:
They are Sinnes nipples, feeding th' east and west.   220
But as in vice the copie still exceeds
The pattern, but not so in vertuous deeds;
So though Sinne made his latter seat the better,
The latter Church is to the first a debter,
The second Temple could not reach the first: 225
And the late reformation never durst
Compare with ancient times and purer yeares;
But in the Jews and us deserveth tears.
Nay, it shall ev'ry yeare decrease and fade;
Till such a darknesse do the world invade   230
At Christs last coming, as his first did finde:
Yet must there such proportions be assign'd
To these diminishings, as is between
The spacious world and *Jurie* to be seen.

192. *captivate:* make captive.
204. *the Popes mule:* the ceremonial kiss bestowed on the Pope's *publick
     foot* (196).
206. *Antichrist:* Herbert echoes the usual prejudice of his Protestant
     contemporaries [§ 92].

Religion stands on tip-toe in our land,   235
Readie to passe to the *American* strand.
When height of malice, and prodigious lusts,
Impudent sinning, witchcrafts, and distrusts
(The marks of future bane) shall fill our cup
Unto the brimme, and make our measure up;   240
When *Sein* shall swallow *Tiber*, and the *Thames*
By letting in them both, pollutes her streams:
When *Italie* of us shall have her will,
And all her calender of sinnes fulfill;
Whereby one may fortell, what sinnes next yeare   245
Shall both in *France* and *England* domineer:
Then shall Religion to *America* flee:
They have their times of Gospel, ev'n as we.
My God, thou dost prepare for them a way
By carrying first their gold from them away: 250
For gold and grace did never yet agree:
Religion alwaies sides with povertie.
We think we rob them, but we think amisse:
We are more poore, and they more rich by this.
Thou wilt revenge their quarrell, making grace   255
To pay our debts, and leave our ancient place
To go to them, while that which now their nation
But lends to us, shall be our desolation.
Yet as the Church shall thither westward flie,
So Sinne shall trace and dog her instantly: 260
They have their period also and set times
Both for their vertuous actions and their crimes.
And where of old the Empire and the Arts
Usher'd the Gospel ever in mens hearts,
Spain hath done one; when Arts perform the other,   265
The Church shall come, & Sinne the Church shall smother:
That when they have accomplished the round,
And met in th' east their first and ancient sound,
Judgement may meet them both & search them round.
Thus do both lights, as well in Church as Sunne,   270
Light one another, and together runne.
Thus also Sinne and Darknesse follow still
The Church and Sunne with all their power and skill.
But as the Sunne still goes both west and east;
So also did the Church by going west   275
Still eastward go; because it drew more neare

235-6. In licensing *The Temple* for publication, the Vice-Chancellor
      at Cambridge objected to these lines; but Nicholas Ferrar 'would
      by no means allow the Book to be printed, and want them' [*IW*,
      p. 315; cf. § 270].
265. *Spain hath done one:* i.e. used her empire to christianize South
      America.
268. *sound:* inlet, haven.

To time and place, where judgement shall appeare.
How deare to me, O God, thy counsels are!
        Who may with thee compare?

L'Envoy

King of Glorie, King of Peace,
With the one make warre to cease;
With the other blesse thy sheep,
Thee to love, in thee to sleep.
Let not Sinne devoure thy fold,   5
Bragging that thy bloud is cold,
That thy death is also dead,
While his conquests dayly spread;
That thy flesh hath lost his food,
And thy Crosse is common wood.   10
Choke him, let him say no more,
But reserve his breath in store,
Till thy conquests and his fall
Make his sighs to use it all,
And then bargain with the winde   15
To discharge what is behinde.

        Blessed be God alone,
        Thrice blessed Three in One.

            FINIS.

L'Envoy
    1. The line is repeated from *Praise II* (above, p. 155).
    2. Cf. Psalm 46.9: 'He maketh wars to cease unto the end of the earth'.

appendix I
Poems not included in *The Temple**

The H. Communion

O gratious Lord how shall I know
Whether in these gifts thou bee so
    As thou art evry-where;
Or rather so, as thou alone
Tak'st all the Lodging, leaving none   5
    ffor thy poore creature there

ffirst I am sure, whether bread stay
Or whether Bread doe fly away
    Concerneth bread not mee.
But that both thou, and all thy traine   10
Bee thee, to thy truth, & my gaine
    Concerneth mee & Thee.

And if in comming to thy foes
Thou dost come first to them, that showes
    The hast of thy good will.
Or if that thou two stations makest   15
In Bread & mee, the way thou takest
    Is more, but for mee still.

Then of this also I am sure
That thou didst all those pains endure
    To' abolish Sinn, not Wheat.   20
Creatures are good, & have their place
Sinn onely, which did all deface
    Thou drivest from his seat.

I could beleeve an Impanation   25
At the rate of an Incarnation
    If thou hadst dyde for Bread.
But that which made my soule to dye
My flesh, & fleshly villany,
    That allso made thee dead.   30

---

* The first six poems are from the Williams MS (*W*); the last three (pp.
205–6) from Walton's *Life* (*IW*).

The H. Communion
25. *Impanation:* a theory of the Eucharist which asserts Christ's local
presence or inclusion after the consecration of the bread.

That flesh is there, mine eyes deny:
And what shold flesh but flesh discry,
   The noblest sence of five.
If glorious bodies pass the sight
Shall they be food & strength, & might   **35**
   Even there, where they deceive?

Into my soule this cannot pass
fflesh (though exalted) keeps his grass
   And cannot turn to soule.
Bodyes & Minds are different Spheres   **40**
Nor can they change their bounds & meres,
   But keep a constant Pole.

This gift of all gifts is the best,
Thy flesh the least that I request.
   Thou took'st that pledg from mee: **45**
Give me not that I had before,
Or give mee that, so I have more
   My God, give mee all Thee.

Love

   Thou art too hard for me in Love:
There is no dealing with thee in that Art:
   That is thy Master-peece I see
   When I contrive & plott to prove
Something that may be conquest on my part   **5**
   Thou still, O Lord, outstrippest mee.

   Sometimes, when as I wash, I say
And shrodely, as I think Lord wash my soule
   More spotted then my flesh can bee.
   But then there comes into my way   **10**
Thy ancient baptism which when I was foule
   And knew it not, yet cleansed mee.

   I took a time when thou didst sleep
Great waves of trouble combating my brest:
   I thought it brave to praise thee then,
   Yet then I found, that thou didst creep   **15**
Into my hart with joye, giving more rest
   Then flesh did lend thee, back agen,

Love. 8. *shrodely:* shrewdly.

```
      Let mee but once the conquest have
Upon the matter 'twill thy conquest prove:                        20
   If thou subdue mortalitie
   Thou do'st no more, then doth the grave:
Whereas if I orecome thee & thy Love
   Hell, Death & Divel come short of mee.
```

Trinity Sunday

```
      He that is one,
         Is none.
      Two reacheth thee
      In some degree.
      Nature & Grace                                             5
With Glory may attaine thy Face.
      Steele & a flint strike fire,
         Witt & desire
      Never to thee aspire,
Except life catch & hold those fast.                             10
      That which beleefe
Did not confess in the first Theefe
      His fall can tell,
   ffrom Heaven, through Earth, to Hell.
      Lett two of those alone                                    15
         To them that fall,
Who God & Saints and Angels loose at last.
      Hee that has one,
         Has all.
```

Even-song

```
The Day is spent, & hath his will on mee:
   I and the Sunn have runn our races,
   I went the slower, yet more paces,
      ffor I decay not hee.

Lord make my Losses up, & sett mee free:                          5
   That I who cannot now by day
   Look on his daring brightnes, may
      Shine then more bright then hee.

If thou deferr this light, then shadow mee:
   Least that the Night, earths gloomy shade                     10
   ffouling her nest, my earth invade,
      As if shades knew not Thee.
```

Trinity Sunday
12. *the first Theefe:* Satan.

But thou art Light & darknes both togeather:
  If that bee dark we can not see:
    The sunn is darker then a Tree,   15
      And thou more dark then either.

Yet Thou art not so dark, since I know this,
  But that my darknes may touch thine:
  And hope, that may teach it to shine,
    Since Light thy Darknes is.   20

O lett my Soule, whose keyes I must deliver
  Into the hands of senceles Dreames
  Which know not thee; suck in thy beames
    And wake with thee for ever.

The Knell

  The Bell doth tolle
Lord help thy servant whose perplexed Soule
    Doth wishly look
    On either hand
And sometimes offers, sometimes makes a stand   5
    Strugling on th' hook.

  Now is the season
Now the great combat of our flesh & reason
    O help my God!
    See, they breake in   10
Disbanded humours, sorrows troops of Sinn
    Each with his rodd.

  Lord make thy Blood
Convert & colour all the other flood
    And streams of grief   15
    That they may bee
Julips & Cordials when wee call on thee
    ffor some relief.

Perseverance

My God, the poore expressions of my Love
Which warme these lines, & serve them up to thee
Are so, as for the present, I did move
  Or rather as thou movedst mee.

But what shall issue, whither these my words   5
Shal help another, but my judgment bee;
As a burst fouling-peece doth save the birds
  But kill the man, is seald with thee.

The Knell
  3. *wishly:* wistfully.

ffor who can tell, though thou hast dyde to winn
And wedd my soule in glorious paradise;   10
Whither my many crymes and use of sinn
    May yet forbid the bancs and bliss.

Onely my soule hangs on thy promisses
With face and hands clinging unto thy brest,
Clinging and crying, crying without cease   15
    Thou art my rock, thou art my rest.

[Sonnet (I)]

My God, where is that ancient heat towards thee,
    Wherewith whole showls of *Martyrs* once did burn,
    Besides their other flames? Doth Poetry
Wear *Venus* Livery? only serve her turn?
Why are not *Sonnets* made of thee? and layes   5
    Upon thine Altar burnt? Cannot thy love
    Heighten a spirit to sound out thy praise
As well as any she? Cannot thy *Dove*
Out-strip their *Cupid* easily in flight?
    Or, since thy wayes are deep, and still the same,   10
    Will not a verse run smooth that bears thy name!
Why doth that fire, which by thy power and might
    Each breast does feel, no braver fuel choose
    Than that, which one day, Worms, may chance refuse?

[Sonnet (II)]

Sure Lord, there is enough in thee to dry
    Oceans of *Ink*; for, as the Deluge did
    Cover the Earth, so doth thy Majesty:
Each Cloud distills thy praise, and doth forbid
Poets to turn it to another use.   5
    Roses and *Lillies* speak thee; and to make
    A pair of Cheeks of them, is thy abuse.
Why should I *Womens eyes* for Chrystal take?
Such poor invention burns in their low mind,

Perseverance
12. *banes:* i.e. banns.

Sonnets I & II, first printed by Walton [*IW*, pp. 268–9], were sent by
    Herbert to his mother in 1610 'as a New-years gift'; they declare,
    he told her, 'my resolution to be, that my poor Abilities in Poetry
    shall be all, and ever consecrated to Gods glory'.

Whose fire is wild, and doth not upward go   10
To praise, and on thee Lord, some *Ink* bestow.
Open the bones, and you shall nothing find
In the best *face* but *filth*, when Lord, in thee
The *beauty* lies, in the *discovery*.

To my Successor

If thou chance for to find
A new House to thy mind,
And built without thy Cost:
Be good to the Poor,
As God gives thee store,   5
And then, my Labour's not lost.

To my Successor, first printed by Walton [*IW*, p. 293] and composed
    after Herbert had rebuilt the Bemerton rectory, was 'writ upon, or
    ingraven in the Mantle of the Chimney in his Hall'. Another version
    is provided anonymously in Thomas Fuller's *The Holy State* (1642):

If thou dost find an house built to thy mind
        Without thy cost,
Serve thou the more God and the poore;
    My labour is not lost.

appendix II
Three Versions of a Poem by Herbert

Many poems in W^1 were considerably altered before they reappeared in B, but few underwent more drastic revisions than 'The Elixer'. Its earliest extant version is in W, transcribed by an amanuensis (see below, #1); its second version is again from W but with corrections in Herbert's hand (#2); and its third is from B (#3), which is also the version in the 1633 edition reproduced above, p. 188.

#1

Perfection

    Lord teach me to referr
    All things I doe to thee
That I not only may not erre
    But allso pleasing bee.

    A man that looks on glass   5
    On it may stay his eye:
Or if he pleaseth, through it pass
    And then the Heav'en espy.

    He that does ought for thee,
    Marketh that deed for thine: 10
And when the Divel shakes the tree,
    Thou saist, this fruit is mine.

    All may of thee pertake:
    Nothing can be so low
Which with his tincture (for thy sake)   15
    Will not to Heaven grow.

    A servant with this clause,
    Makes drudgery divine.
Who sweeps a chamber for thy Lawes,
    Makes that, and th' action fine.   20

[1] The abbreviations are explained above, p. 1. In transcribing the versions I have expanded all contractions. The two W versions are reproduced in facsimile in *English Poetical Autographs*, ed. Desmond Flower and A. N. L. Munby (1938), No. 10.

But these are high perfections:
Happy are they that dare
Lett in the light to all their actions
And show them as they are.

#2

Perfection   The Elixir[2]

[Herbert retained the first two stanzas of the previous version without any changes (ll. 1–8); eliminated the third stanza (ll. 9–12); amended the next two stanzas (see below); and added the final one shown:]

All may of thee pertake:
Nothing can be so meane
Which with his tincture (for thy sake)
Will not grow bright & cleane.

A servant with this clause,
Makes drudgery divine.
Who sweeps a roome as for thy Lawes,
Makes that, and th' action fine.

This is the famous stone
That turneth all to gold;
For that which God doth touch & owne
Can not for less be told.

#3

The Elixer

[The amended version in *B* is the same as the printed one, above, p. 188, except for some variants in punctuation].

[2] Herbert added the new title without crossing out the former one.

appendix III
Some Secular Poems
parodied by Herbert

Herbert's aspiration to curtail poetry's excessive attachment to the
secular muse, involved in particular an attempt to re-dedicate the poems
of his predecessors to a sacred use. The result was often, nominally at
least, 'sacred parody'—especially 'parody' in the musical sense of
providing new words for a familiar tune [§ 295].

Instances abound [cf. §§ 165, 193]. Herbert's general aim—clearly
enunciated in the poem 'My God, where is that ancient heat towards
thee', itself pointedly cast in the form of a sonnet (above, p. 205)—is
enacted in the external form of his 'pattern poems' (see below, #1),
in his deployment of the equally traditional 'echo device' (#2), and
especially in his conscious inversion of the language common to secular
poets (#3 through #5).

#1

An Altare and Sacrifice to Disdaine,
for freeing him from loue
(Anonymous)[1]

My Muse by thee restor'd to life,
To thee Disdaine, this Altare reares,
Whereon she offers causlesse strife,
Self-spending sighs, and bootlesse teares
       Long Sutes in vaine,   5
       Hats for Good will:
       Still-dying paine,
       Yet living still.
       Self-loving pride,
       Lookes coyly strange,   10
       Will Reasons guide,
       Desire of change.
       And last of all,
       Blinde Beauties thrall,
       That bindes desire.   15
All these I offer to Disdaine,
By whom I live from fancie free.
With vow, that if I love againe,
My life the sacrifice shall bee.

Cf. 'The Altar' (above, p. 48).

#2

Echo to a Rock
by Lord Herbert of Cherbury[2]

Thou heaven-threat'ning Rock, gentler then she!
      Since of my pain
   Thou still more sensible wilt be,
Only when thou giv'st leave but to complain.
          Echo Complain.   5
But thou dost answer too, although in vain
   Thou answer'st when thou canst no pity show.
          Echo Oh.
   What canst thou speak and pity too?
   Then yet a further favour do,   10
And tell if of my griefs I any end shall know.
          Echo No.

Sure she will pity him that loves her so truly.
          Echo You ly.
   Vile Rock, thou now grow'st so unruly,   15
   That had'st thou life as thou hast voice,
     Thou should'st dye at my foot.
          Echo Dye at my foot.
   Thou canst not make me do't,
   Unless thou leave it to my choice,   20
   Who thy hard sentence shall fulfill,
When thou shalt say, I dye to please her only will.
          Echo I will.
   When she comes hither, then, I pray thee, tell,
Thou art my Monument, and this my last farewell.   25
          Echo Well.

Cf. 'Heaven' (above, p. 191).

#3

from *Astrophil and Stella* (I)
by Sir Philip Sidney[3]

Loving in truth, and faine in verse my love to show,
That the deare She might take some pleasure of my paine:
Pleasure might cause her reade, reading might make her know,
Knowledge might pitie winne, and pitie grace obtaine,
   I sought fit words to paint the blackest face of woe,   5
Studying inventions fine, her wits to entertaine:
Oft turning others' leaves, to see if thence would flow

Some fresh and fruitfull showers upon my sunne-burn'd braine.
   But words came halting forth, wanting Invention's stay,
Invention, Nature's child, fled step-dame Studie's blowes,   10
And others' feete still seem'd but strangers in my way.
Thus great with child to speake, and helplesse in my throwes,
   Biting my trewand pen, beating my self for spite,
    'Foole', said my Muse to me, 'looke in thy heart and write'.

Cf. 'Jordan II' (above, p. 116).

#4

Song

(attributed to William Herbert, 3rd earl of Pembroke)[4]

Soules joy, now I am gone,
   And you alone,
    (Which cannot be,
Since I must leave my selfe with thee,
   And carry thee with me)   5
   Yet when unto our eyes
    Absence denyes
    Each others sight,
And makes to us a constant night,
   When others change to light;   10
     O give no way to griefe,
     But let beliefe
      Of mutuall love,
     This wonder to the vulgar prove
     Our Bodyes, not wee move.   15

Let not thy wit beweepe
   Wounds but sense-deepe,
   For when we misse
By distance our lipp-joying blisse,
   Even then our soules shall kisse,   20
   Fooles have no meanes to meet,
   But by their feet.
   Why should our clay,
Over our spirits so much sway,
   To tie us to that way?   25
    O give no way to griefe, &c.

Cf. 'A Parodie' (above, p. 187).

#5

To his Love
(Anonymous)[5]

Come away, come sweet Love,
The golden morning breakes:
All the earth, all the ayre,
Of love and pleasure speakes.
Teach thine armes then to embrace,   5
And sweet Rosie lips to kisse:
And mixe our soules in mutuall blisse.
Eyes were made for beauties grace,
Viewing, ruing Loves long paine:
Procur'd by beauties rude disdaine.   10

Come away, come my sweet Love,
The golden morning wasts:
While the Sunne from his Sphere
His fierie arrowes casts,
Making all the shadowes flie,   15
Playing, staying in the Groave:
To entertaine the stealth of love.
Thither sweet Love let us hie
Flying, dying in desire:
Wing'd with sweet hopes and heavenly fire.   20

Come away, come sweet Love,
Doo not in vaine adorne
Beauties grace that should rise
Like to the naked morne.
Lillies on the Rivers side,   25
And faire *Cyprian* flowers new blowne,
Desire no beauties but their owne.
Ornament is Nurse of pride,
Pleasure, measure, Loves delight:
Hast then sweet Love our wished flight.   30

Cf. 'Dooms-day' (above, p. 189).

[1] Reprinted from *A Poetical Rhapsody* (1602), ed. H. H. Rollins (Cambridge, Mass., 1931), I, 180. First cited by Hutchinson as a poem 'shaped like a pagan altar' [*FEH*, pp. 484–5], it has since been said to form the background to Herbert's 'deliberate parody' [§ 190]. The tradition of 'pattern poetry' is certainly formidable: firmly established in the Greek anthology, it was so greatly extended during the Renaissance that Gabriel Harvey was driven to protest against poems which 'represente the form and figure of an egg, an ape, a winge, and sutche ridiculous and madd gugawes and crockchettes' [§ 23]. On this clearly-defined poetic practice see also the discussion of 'oracular representation' in George Puttenham's (?) *The Arte of English Poesie* (1589), Bk. II, Ch. XI, 'Of Proportion in figure'.

[2] Reprinted from *The Poems English and Latin of Edward, Lord Herbert of Cherbury*, ed. G. C. Moore Smith (Oxford, 1923), pp. 46–7. Numerous other examples of the device, from Greek and Latin poetry to the poetry of the Renaissance generally (including Spenser's), are given in the survey by Elbridge Colby, *The Echo Device in Literature* (1920; reprinted from *BNYPL*, XXIII [1919], 683–713, 783–804). It should be noted that Lord Herbert also composed 'Echo in a Church', said to be 'the first example in English of the use of the echo form for devotional purposes' [§ 205].

[3] Reprinted from *The Poems of Sir Philip Sidney*, ed. William A. Ringler, Jr. (Oxford, 1962), p. 166; discussed in relation to Herbert by Martz [§ 190].

[4] Reprinted from *The Poetical Works of John Donne*, ed. Herbert J. C. Grierson (Oxford, 1912), I, 429–30; discussed in relation to Herbert by Tuve [§ 295].

[5] Reprinted from *Englands Helicon* (1600), ed. H. H. Rollins (Cambridge, Mass., 1935), I, 158–9; first published in John Dowland's *First Booke of Songes or Ayres* (1597), as noted by Martz [§ 191].

Bibliography

Contents

Abbreviations

B	The Bodleian MS of *The Temple* (above, p. 1)
BNYPL	*Bulletin of the New York Public Library*
BO	Barnabas Oley, 'A Prefatory View of the Life and Vertues of the Authour', prefixed to *Herbert's Remains* (1652)
CE	*College English*
CLAJ	*College Language Association Journal*
Donne, Sermons	*The Sermons of John Donne*, ed. E. M. Simpson and G. R. Potter (Berkeley, 1953–62), 10 vols.
EC	*Essays in Criticism*
ELH	*Journal of English Literary History*
ELN	*English Language Notes*
E & S	*Essays and Studies* by Members of the English Association
Exp	*Explicator*
FEH	F. E. Hutchinson, ed., *The Works of George Herbert* (Oxford, 1941)
FP	*The Ferrar Papers*, ed. B. Blackstone (Cambridge, 1938)
GHP	George Herbert Palmer, ed., *The English Works of George Herbert* (Cambridge, Mass., 1905), 3 vols.
GR	Gareth Reeves, ed., *Selected Poems of George Herbert* (1971)
HLQ	*Huntingdon Library Quarterly*
IW	Izaac Walton, *The Life of Mr George Herbert* (1670), in *Lives* (World's Classics edn, n.d.), pp. 251–321
JEGP	*Journal of English and Germanic Philology*

JHS	Joseph H. Summers, ed., *George Herbert: Selected Poetry* (1967)
JWCI	*Journal of the Warburg and Courtauld Institutes*
LPH	*The Latin Poetry of George Herbert: A Bilingual Edition*, trans. Mark McCloskey and Paul R. Murphy (Athens, Ohio, 1965)
LS	Barbara K. Lewalski and Andrew J. Sabol, eds, *George Herbert*, in their *Major Poets of the Earlier Seventeenth Century* (1973), pp. 173–389
MLN	*Modern Language Notes*
MLQ	*Modern Language Quarterly*
MP	*Modern Philology*
N & Q	*Notes and Queries*
OED	*The Oxford English Dictionary*
PLL	*Papers on Language and Literature*
PMLA	*Publications of the Modern Language Association*
PQ	*Philological Quarterly*
RES	*Review of English Studies*
RN	*Renaissance News*
SCN	*Seventeenth Century News*
SEL	*Studies in English Literature*
SP	*Studies in Philology*
SR	*Studies in the Renaissance*
TLS	*Times Literary Supplement*
UTQ	*University of Toronto Quarterly*
W	The Williams MS of *The Temple* (above, p. 1)

See also 'A Note on Abbreviations', above, p. 1.

A Bibliographical Note

There are detailed bibliographies in C. S. Lewis [§ 66]; Douglas Bush [§ 17]; and *The New Cambridge Bibliography of English Literature*, ed. George Watson, Vol. I (1974). More modest bibliographies will be found in the various Folger Booklets on Tudor and Stuart Civilization, and in *A Guide to English Literature*, ed. Boris Ford, II: *The Age of Shakespeare*, and III: *From Donne to Marvell* (revised edn, 1961–2).

Annual bibliographies include: The English Association's *The Year's Work in English Studies* (1919 ff.); the Modern Humanities Research Association's *Annual Bibliography of English Language and Literature* (1920 ff.); *PMLA* (1922 ff.); and *SP* (1922 ff.).

Studies of Herbert and the poets once associated with him in 'the school of Donne', are included in Theodore Spencer, *Studies in Metaphysical Poetry* (1939), pp. 31–83, and Lloyd E. Berry, *A Bibliography of Studies in Metaphysical Poetry 1939–1960* (Madison, 1964). On Herbert himself see below, p. 223.

Background Studies

Studies of the theological background as it relates to Herbert, may be divided into studies of the Church, the Sacraments, and Parabolic Teaching. As regards the first: for a rather technical examination of 'ecclesia', see the *Theological Dictionary of the New Testament*, ed. Gerhard Kittel, trans. G. W. Bromiley (Grand Rapids, Mich., 1965), III, 501–36; and for a sustained exposition: George Johnston, *The Doctrine of the Church in the New Testament* (Cambridge, 1943). On the analogies commonly deployed by Biblical writers, consult Paul S. Minear, *Images of the Church in the New Testament* (1961), and Stephen J. Brown's more general survey, *Image and Truth: Studies in the Imagery of the Bible* (Rome, 1955).

The literature on the sacraments is extensive. For a general introduction, see: Oliver C. Quick, *The Christian Sacraments* (1927); and for the Calvinistic interpretation: Ronald S. Wallace, *Calvin's Doctrine of the Word and Sacrament* (Edinburgh, 1953). On baptism, consult: G. W. H. Lampe, *The Seal of the Spirit*, 2nd edn (1967), and its bibliography. On the Eucharist, there are studies of the Biblical and early Christian contexts by C. H. Dodd, 'The Sacrament of the Lord's Supper in the New Testament', in *Christian Worship*, ed. Nathaniel Micklem (Oxford, 1936), Ch. V; A. J. B. Higgins, *The Lord's Supper in the New Testament* (1952); Oscar Cullmann and F. J. Leenhardt, *Essays on the Lord's Supper*, trans. J. G. Davies (1958); as well as the more general study by D. Gerhard Delling, *Worship in the New Testament*, trans. P. Scott (1962), and the more technical one by Joachim Jeremias, *The Eucharistic Words of Jesus* (1966). The best survey of the doctrinal developments is by Darwell Stone, *A History of the Doctrine of the Holy Eucharist* (1909), 2 vols; carried forward to the 16th century in England by C. W. Dugmore, *Eucharistic Doctrine in England from Hooker to Waterland* (1942), and *The Mass and the English Reformers* (1958). On the relationship of the Eucharist to sacrifice, see F. C. N. Hicks, *The Fullness of Sacrifice* (1930), and Eugene Masure, *The Christian Sacrifice*, trans. Illtyd Trethowan (1944). Related studies include: J. W. C. Wand, *The Development of Sacramentalism* (1928); Dom Gregory Dix, *The Shape of the Liturgy* (1945); and Yngve Brilioth, *Eucharistic Faith and Practice, Evangelical and Catholic*, trans. A. G. Hebert (1930).

Studies of parabolic teaching include: A. T. Cadoux, *The Parables of Jesus* (1931); C. H. Dodd, *The Parables of the Kingdom* (1935); W. O. E. Oesterley, *The Gospel Parables in the Light of their Jewish Background* (1936); J. Alexander Findlay, *Jesus and his Parables* (1950); A. M. Hunter, *Interpreting the Parables*, 2nd edn (1964); Geraint V. Jones, *The Art and Truth of the Parables* (1964); Eta Linnemann, *Parables of Jesus: Introduction and Exposition*, trans. John Sturdy (1966); Joachim Jeremias, *The Parables of Jesus*, trans. S. H. Hooke, 3rd edn (1972); etc.

On the language of theology, see the extensive reading list in *Bright Essence: Studies in Milton's Theology*, by W. B. Hunter, C. A. Patrides and J. H. Adamson (Salt Lake City, 1971), pp. 179–81.

Studies of the general background include the following:

§ 1. ADDLESHAW, G. W. O.: *High Church Tradition: A Study in the Liturgical Thought of the Seventeenth Century* (1941).

§ 2. ADDLESHAW, G. W. O., and FREDERICK ETCHELLS: *The Architectural Setting of Anglican Worship* (1948).

§ 3. AKRIGG, G. P. V.: *Jacobean Pageant; or the Court of James I* (1962).

§ 4. ASHLEY, MAURICE: *Life in Stuart England* (1964).

§ 5. ASHLEY, MAURICE: *The Golden Century: Europe 1598–1715* (1969).

§ 6. ASHTON, TREVOR (ed.): *Crisis in Europe 1560–1660* (1965).

§ 7. ATKINS, J. W. H.: *English Literary Criticism: The Renascence* (2nd edn, 1951).

§ 8. AYLMER, G. E.: *The Struggle for the Constitution 1603–1689* (1963; American edn: *A Short History of 17th-Century England*).

§ 9. BAKER, HERSCHEL: *The Image of Man: A Study of the Idea of Human Dignity in Classical Antiquity, the Middle Ages, and the Renaissance* (1961; former title: *The Dignity of Man*, Cambridge, Mass., 1947), and *The Wars of Truth: Studies in the Decay of Christian Humanism in the Earlier 17th Century* (1952).

§ 10. BAROWAY, ISRAEL: Four essays on the Bible as poetry during the English Renaissance: *JEGP*, XXXII (1933), 447–80; *ELH*, II (1935), 66–91; *ELH*, VIII (1941), 119–42; and *ELH*, XVII (1950), 115–35.

§ 11. BEARDSLEE, JOHN W. (ed. and trans.): *Reformed Dogmatics* (1965). Primary sources. Cf. § 48.

§ 12. BENNETT, H. S.: *English Books and Readers 1558 to 1603* and *1603 to 1640* (Cambridge, 1965 and 1970).

§ 13. BETHEL, S. L.: 'The Nature of Metaphysical Wit', *Northern Miscellany of Literary Criticism*, I (1953), 19–40; repr. in *Discussions of John Donne*, ed. Frank Kermode (Boston, 1962), pp. 136–49.

§ 14. BETTENSON, HENRY (ed.): *Documents of the Christian Church* (2nd edn, 1963). Primary sources.

§ 15. BRADBURY, MALCOLM, and DAVID PALMER (eds): *Metaphysical Poetry* (Stratford-upon-Avon Studies XI, 1970).

§ 16. BURTON, ELIZABETH: *The Jacobeans at Home* (1962).

§ 17. BUSH, DOUGLAS: *English Literature in the Earlier 17th Century* (2nd revised edn, Oxford, 1962). The best single survey of the period.

§ 18. BUSH, DOUGLAS: *Prefaces to Renaissance Literature* (Cambridge, Mass., 1965).

§ 19. BUSH, DOUGLAS: *The Renaissance and English Humanism* (Toronto, 1939).

§ 20. CAMPBELL, LILY B.: *Divine Poetry and Drama in 16th Century England* (Cambridge, 1959).

§ 21. CHANDOS, JOHN (ed.): *In God's Name: Examples of Preaching in England . . . 1534–1662* (1971).

§ 22. CHARLTON, KENNETH: *Education in Renaissance England* (1965).

§ 23. CHURCH, MARGARET: 'The First English Pattern Poems', *PMLA*, LXI (1946), 636–50. Cf. § 37.

§ 24. CLARKE, W. K. LOWTHER (ed.): *Liturgy and Worship: A Companion to the Prayer Books of the Anglican Communion* (1932).

§ 25. COCHRANE, ERIC (ed.): *The Late Italian Renaissance 1525–1630* (1970).

§ 26. COFFIN, CHARLES M.: *John Donne and the New Philosophy* (1937).

§ 27. COHEN, J. M.: *The Baroque Lyric* (1963).

§ 28. COLIE, ROSALIE L.: *Paradoxia Epidemica: The Renaissance Tradition of Paradox* (Princeton, 1966), Cf. § 148.

§ 29. COLLINSON, PATRICK: *The Elizabethan Puritan Movement* (1967).

§ 30. CURTIS, MARK H.: *Oxford and Cambridge in Transition, 1558–1642* (Oxford, 1959).

§ 31. DAVIES, GODFREY: *The Early Stuarts 1603–1660* (2nd edn, Oxford, 1959).

§ 32. DELANY, PAUL: *British Autobiography in the 17th Century* (1969).

§ 33. DIECKMANN, LISELOTTE: *Hieroglyphics: The History of a Literary Symbol* (St Louis, 1970).

§ 34. ELLRODT, ROBERT: *L'Inspiration personelle et l'esprit du temps chez les poètes métaphysiques anglais* (Paris, 1960), 2 vols. Cf. § 156.

§ 35. ELLRODT, ROBERT: 'Scientific Curiosity and Metaphysical Poetry in the 17th Century', *MP*, LXI (1964), 180–97.

§ 36. FLINDALL, R. P.: 'Theological Reading in the 17th Century', *Church Quarterly Review*, CLXVI (1965), 171–8.

§ 37. FREEMAN, ROSEMARY: *English Emblem Books* (1948). Cf. § 164.

§ 38. GARIN, EUGENIO: *Italian Humanism*, trans. Peter Munz (1965).

§ 39. GEORGE, CHARLES H. and KATHERINE: *The Protestant Mind of the English Reformation* (Princeton, 1961).

§ 40. GRIERSON, SIR HERBERT: *Cross-Currents in English Literature of the 17th Century* (1929).

§ 41. HAGSTRUM, JEAN H.: *The Sister Arts: The Tradition of*

Literary Pictorialism and English Poetry from Dryden to Gray (Chicago, 1958). Touches on Herbert in 'The Baroque Century'.

§ 42. HALL, MARIE BOAS: *The Scientific Renaissance 1450–1630* (1962).

§ 43. HAMILTON, K. G.: *The Two Harmonies: Poetry and Prose in the 17th Century* (Oxford, 1963).

§ 44. HARRISON, A. W.: *Arminianism* (1937).

§ 45. HART, ROGER: *English Life in the 17th Century* (1970).

§ 46. HATHAWAY, BAXTER: *Marvels and Commonplaces: Renaissance Literary Criticism* (1968).

§ 47. HAVRAN, MARTIN J.: *The Catholics in Caroline England* (Stanford, 1962).

§ 48. HEPPE, HEINRICH (ed.): *Reformed Dogmatics*, trans. G. T. Thomson (1950). Primary sources. Cf. § 11.

§ 49. HILL, CHRISTOPHER: *Society and Puritanism in Pre-Revolutionary England* (1964).

§ 50. HOLLANDER, JOHN: *The Untuning of the Sky: Ideas of Music in English Poetry 1500–1700* (Princeton, 1961). Cf. § 261.

§ 51. HOWELL, WILBUR S.: *Logic and Rhetoric in England, 1500–1700* (Princeton, 1956).

§ 52. HUGHES, PHILIP: *Rome and the Counter-Reformation in England* (1942).

§ 53. HUNT, JOHN DIXON (ed.): *Encounters: Essays on Literature and the Visual Arts* (1971). Especially the essays by Douglas Chambers and Dean T. Mace.

§ 54. JOHNSON, FRANCIS R.: *Astronomical Thought in Renaissance England* (Baltimore, 1937).

§ 55. JOHNSON, PAULA: *Form and Transformation in Music and Poetry in the English Renaissance* (New Haven, 1972).

§ 56. JONAS, LEAH: *The Divine Science: The Aesthetic of some representative 17th-Century English Poets* (1940).

§ 57. JOSEPH, B. L.: *Shakespeare's Eden: The Commonwealth of England 1558–1629* (1971).

§ 58. KAMEN, HENRY: *The Iron Century: Social Change in Europe 1550–1660* (1971).

§ 59. KNAPPEN, M. M.: *Tudor Puritanism* (Chicago, 1939).

§ 60. KNIGHTS, L. C.: *Drama and Society in the Age of Jonson* (1937), and 'On the Social Background of Metaphysical Poetry', *Scrutiny*, XIII (1945), 37–52.

§ 61. KOENIGSBERGER, H. G.: *The Habsburgs and Europe, 1516–1660* (Ithaca, N.Y., 1971).

§ 62. KOCHER, PAUL H.: *Science and Religion in Elizabethan England* (San Marino, Calif., 1953).

§ 63. KRISTELLER, PAUL O., and PHILIP P. WIENER (eds): *Renaissance Essays* (1968).

§ 64. LEES-MILNE, JAMES: *The Age of Inigo Jones* (1953).

§ 65. LEWIS, C. S.: *The Discarded Image: An Introduction to*

Medieval and Renaissance Literature (Cambridge, 1964).

§ 66. LEWIS, C. S.: *English Literature in the 16th Century excluding drama* (Oxford, 1954).

§ 67. LOCKYER, ROGER: *Tudor and Stuart Britain 1471–1714* (1964).

§ 68. LONG, KENNETH R.: *The Music of the English Church* (1971). With eight chapters on developments in the 16th and early 17th centuries.

§ 69. LOVEJOY, ARTHUR O.: *The Great Chain of Being: A Study of the History of an Idea* (Cambridge, Mass., 1936).

§ 70. MCADOO, H. R.: *The Structure of Caroline Moral Theology* (1949).

§ 71. MCADOO, H. R.: *The Spirit of Anglicanism: A Survey of Anglican Theological Method in the 17th Century* (1965).

§ 72. MACLURE, MILLAR: *The Paul's Cross Sermons, 1534–1642* (Toronto, 1958).

§ 73. MALAND, DAVID: *Europe in the 17th Century* (1966).

§ 74. MARTZ, LOUIS L.: *The Poetry of Meditation: A Study in English Religious Literature of the 17th Century* (New Haven, 1954). Cf. §§ 190–1.

§ 75. MATHEW, DAVID: *The Jacobean Age* (1938), and *The Age of Charles I* (1951).

§ 76. MAZZARO, JEROME: *Transformations in the Renaissance English Lyric* (Ithaca, N.Y., 1970).

§ 77. MAZZEO, JOSEPH A.: *Renaissance and Revolution: Backgrounds to 17th-Century English Literature* (1965).

§ 78. MAZZEO, JOSEPH A.: 'A 17th-Century Theory of Metaphysical Poetry', in *Renaissance and 17th-Century Studies* (1964), Ch. II.

§ 79. MERCER, ERIC: *English Art 1553–1625* (Oxford, 1962).

§ 80. MILES, JOSEPHINE: *The Primary Language of Poetry in the 1640s*, University of California Publications in English, XIX (1948), 1–160. Cf. § 192.

§ 81. MINER, EARL: *The Metaphysical Mode from Donne to Cowley* (Princeton, 1969).

§ 82. MIRIAM JOSEPH, SISTER, C. S. C.: *Rhetoric in Shakespeare's Time: Literary Theory of Renaissance Europe* (1962), abridged from *Shakespeare's Use of the Arts of Language* (1947).

§ 83. MITCHELL, W. FRASER: *English Pulpit Oratory from Andrewes to Tillotson* (1932).

§ 84. MORE, PAUL E. and FRANK L. CROSS (eds): *Anglicanism: The Thought and Practice of the Church of England, illustrated from the Religious Literature of the 17th Century* (1935).

§ 85. MORISON, STANLEY: *English Prayer Books: An Introduction to the Literature of Christian Public Worship* (3rd edn, Cambridge, 1949).

§ 86. MORRIS, CHRISTOPHER: *Political Thought in England: Tyndale to Hooker* (1953).

§ 87. MULDER, JOHN R.: *The Temple of the Mind: Education and Literary Taste in 17th-Century England* (1969). Cf. § 197.

§ 88. NEW, J. F. H.: *Anglican and Puritan: The Basis of their Opposition, 1558–1640* (1964).

§ 89. NICOLSON, MARJORIE H.: *The Breaking of the Circle: Studies in the Effect of the New Science upon 17th-Century Poetry* (revised edn, 1960).

§ 90. OGG, DAVID: *Europe in the 17th Century* (1925; 8th edn, 1961).

§ 91. PATRIDES, C. A.: *The Grand Design of God: The Literary Form of the Christian View of History* (1972). Cf. § 286.

§ 92. PATRIDES, C. A.: *Milton and the Christian Tradition* (Oxford, 1966). A survey of theology in the 16th and 17th centuries.

§ 93. PETERSON, DOUGLAS L.: *The English Lyric from Wyatt to Donne: A History of the Plain and Eloquent Styles* (Princeton, 1967).

§ 94. POWELL, CHILTON L.: *English Domestic Relations 1487–1653* (1917).

§ 95. POWICKE, SIR MAURICE: *The Reformation in England* (1941).

§ 96. PRAZ, MARIO: *Studies in 17th-Century Imagery* (2nd revised edn, Rome, 1964). With an exhaustive bibliography of emblem books. Cf. § 37.

§ 97. REESE, GUSTAVE: *Music in the Renaissance* (revised edn, 1959).

§ 98. ROBB, NESCA: *Neoplatonism of the Italian Renaissance* (1935).

§ 99. ROBINSON, H. WHEELER (ed.): *The Bible in its Ancient and English Versions* (Oxford, 1940).

§ 100. ROSSI, MARIO M.: *La vita, le opere, i tempi di Edoardo Herbert di Cherbury* (Florence, 1947), 3 vols.

§ 101. RUSSELL, CONRAD: *The Crisis of Parliaments: English History 1500–1660* (Oxford, 1971).

§ 102. SHARP, ROBERT L.: *From Donne to Dryden: The Revolt against Metaphysical Poetry* (Chapel Hill, 1940).

§ 103. SHUMAKER, WAYNE: *The Occult Sciences in the Renaissance* (Berkeley, 1972).

§ 104. SIMON, JOAN: *Education and Society in Renaissance England* (Cambridge, 1966).

§ 105. SMART, ALASTAIR: *The Renaissance and Mannerism in Italy*, and *The Renaissance and Mannerism outside Italy* (1972).

§ 106. SMITH, HALLETT: 'English Metrical Psalms in the 16th Century and their Literary Significance', *HLQ*, IX (1946), 249–71.

§ 107. SPITZER, LEO: *Classical and Christian Ideas of World Harmony*, ed. A. G. Hatcher (Baltimore, 1963).

§ 108. STEIN, ARNOLD: 'On Elizabethan Wit', *SEL*, I (1961), 75–91. Cf. § 213.

§ 109. STEWART, STANLEY: *The Enclosed Garden: The Tradition and the Image in 17th-Century Poetry* (Madison, 1966). Cf. § 214.

§ 110. STONE, LAWRENCE: *The Causes of the English Revolution 1529–1642* (1972).

§ 111. STRONG, ROY: *The English Icon: Elizabethan and Jacobean Portraiture* (1969). Also the collection of *Tudor and Jacobean Portraits* (1969), 2 vols.

§ 112. TULLOCH, JOHN: *Rational Theology and Christian Philosophy in England in the 17th Century* (2nd edn, 1874), 2 vols. Still a reliable survey.

§ 113. TUVE, ROSEMOND: *Elizabethan and Metaphysical Imagery* (Chicago, 1947). Cf. § 219.

§ 114. USHER, ROLAND G.: *The Reconstruction of the English Church* (1910), 2 vols.

§ 115. WALKER, D. P.: 'Orpheus the Theologian', in his *The Ancient Theology* (1972), Ch. I. A reliable survey of Orphism.

§ 116. WALTON, GEOFFREY: *Metaphysical to Augustan* (1955).

§ 117. WARNKE, FRANK J. (ed.): *European Metaphysical Poems* (New Haven, 1961). Texts with translations.

§ 118. WEBBER, JOAN: *Contrary Music: The Prose Style of John Donne* (Madison, 1963).

§ 119. WEBER, SARAH A.: *Theology and Poetry in the Middle English Lyric* (Columbus, 1969).

§ 120. WHALE, J. S.: *The Protestant Tradition* (Cambridge, 1955).

§ 121. WHIFFEN, MARCUS: *An Introduction to Elizabethan and Jacobean Architecture* (1952).

§ 122. WIENER, PHILIP P. (ed.): *Dictionary of the History of Ideas* (1973), 3 vols. A wide-ranging collection of authoritative studies.

§ 123. WILLIAMSON, GEORGE: *The Senecan Amble: A Study in Prose Form from Bacon to Collier* (1951).

§ 124. WILLIAMSON, GEORGE: *The Proper Wit of Poetry* (1961).

§ 125. WILLIAMSON, GEORGE: *Seventeenth Century Contexts* (1960).

§ 126. WILSON, F. P.: *Elizabethan and Jacobean* (Oxford, 1945). An excellent introduction to the period of transition.

§ 127. WILSON, F. P.: *Seventeenth Century Prose* (Berkeley, 1960). On Burton, Browne, biographies, and sermons.

§ 128. WOODFILL, WALTER L.: *Musicians in English Society from Elizabeth to Charles I* (Princeton, 1953).

§ 129. WRIGHT, LOUIS B.: *Middle-Class Culture in Elizabethan England* (Chapel Hill, 1935).

§ 130. WRIGHT, LOUIS B., and VIRGINIA A. LAMAR (eds): *Life and Letters in Tudor and Stuart England* (Ithaca, N.Y., 1962).
The emblem can now be studied through the impressive collection edited by Arthur Henkel and Albrecht Schöne, *Emblemata* (Stuttgart, 1967); see also the important bibliographical supplement in *Renaissance Quarterly*, XXIII (1970), 66–80. There is also a modest *Selection of Emblems* (an Augustan Reprint Society facsimile, Los Angeles, 1972), drawn from Herman Hugo (1624), Francis Quarles (1635), and Edmund Arwaker (1686). Cf. §§ 37, 96.

Studies of Herbert

Bibliographies of Herbert include several compilations—e.g., those by Theodore Spencer and Lloyd E. Berry (above, p. 215), etc.— but all have now been superseded by the sophisticated labours of John R. Roberts, *George Herbert: An Annotated Bibliography of Modern Criticism 1905-1974* (Columbia, Mo., 1978). An equally indispensable work is the edition by Mario A. DiCesare and Rigo Magnani of *A Concordance to the Complete Writings of George Herbert* (Ithaca, N.Y., 1977).

Early accounts of Herbert include Nicholas Ferrar's preface to *The Temple* (above, pp. 30-1), the biographies by Oley and Walton [*BO, IW*], and the brief comments by Thomas Fuller in *The History of the Worthies of England* (1662, under 'Montgomeryshire'; in the 1840 edn: III, 549–50) and by John Aubrey in *Brief Lives* (ed. Oliver L. Dick, 3rd edn, 1958, pp. 136-7). See the survey by Robert E. Reiter, 'George Herbert and his Biographers', *Cithara*, IX (1970), ii, 18–31; and on Walton's performance: Donald A. Stauffer, *English Biography before 1700* (Cambridge, Mass., 1930), Ch. IV; John Butt, 'Izaac Walton's Methods of Biography', *E & S*, XIX (1933), 67–84; Marchette Chute, 'Walton's Biography of Herbert', in her *Two Gentle Men* (1959), pp. 277–82; and especially David Novarr, *The Making of Walton's 'Lives'* (Ithaca, N.Y., 1958), Ch. X.

Later accounts might have included William Hazlitt's 'George Herbert' in his *Johnson's Lives of the English Poets, Completed* (1854), I, 286–9; but, expectations notwithstanding, it is a trite sketch at best. More recent biographies are by Margaret Cropper, *Flame touches Flame* (1949), pp. 1–28; Marchette Chute (as above), pp. 9–152; Hutchinson [*FEH*, pp. xxi–xxxix]; Summers [§216, Ch. II]; and Amy M. Charles, *A Life of George Herbert* (Ithaca, N.Y., 1977).

The head of the Herbert family, Lord Herbert of Cherbury, should be approached by way of his *Autobiography* (ed. C. H. Herford, 1928), his *Poems* (ed. G. C. Moore Smith, Oxford, 1923), and his philosophical treatise *De Veritate* (trans. Meyrick H. Carré, Bristol, 1937). The first is placed within a larger context

by Delany [§ 32]; the last is summarily expounded by W. R.
Sorley, 'The Philosophy of Herbert of Cherbury', *Mind*, n.s., III
(1894), 491–508; while a panoramic view is provided by Rossi
[§ 100]. On the matriarchal head of the household, consult William
Blackburn, 'Lady Margaret Herbert and her Son George', *South
Atlantic Quarterly*, L (1951), 378–88; Aubrey Noakes, 'The
Mother of George Herbert', *Contemporary Review*, CLXXXIII
(1953), 39–45; and especially the studies cited above, p. 23, note 2.

Most studies of the Ferrar circle are adversely affected by undue
piety, whether they are mediocre (e.g. Henry Collett's *Little
Gidding and its Founder*, 1925), or more scholarly (e.g. Maycock's
studies, cited below). The most reliable source is *Nicholas Ferrar:
Two Lives by his Brother John and by Dr Jebb*, ed. J. E. B. Mayor,
being Part I of *Cambridge in the 17th Century* (Cambridge, 1855).
Other biographical accounts include T. O. Beachcroft, 'Nicholas
Ferrar and George Herbert', *Criterion*, XII (1932), 24–42; R.
Balfour Daniels, 'George Herbert's Literary Executor', in his *Some
17th Century Worthies* (Chapel Hill, 1940), pp. 80–90; Margaret
Cropper, *Flame touches Flame* (1949), pp. 29–72; C. Leslie Craig,
Nicholas Ferrar Junior (1950); and Alan L. Maycock, *Nicholas
Ferrar of Little Gidding* (1938), with its continuation in *Chronicles
of Little Gidding* (1954). Indispensable material is included in
The Story Books of Little Gidding, ed. E. Cruwys Sharland (1899);
*Conversations at Little Gidding ... Dialogues by Members of the
Ferrar Family*, ed. A. M. Williams (Cambridge, 1970); and
especially *FP*. [The celebrated account of Little Gidding in J. H.
Shorthouse's novel *John Inglesant* (1881), is blatant plagiarism;
see W. K. Fleming, 'Some Truths about *John Inglesant*', *Quarterly
Review*, CCXLV (1925), 130–48, and Maycock, *Nicholas Ferrar*
(as above), App. I].

F. E. Hutchinson describes 'The First Edition of Herbert's
Temple [1633]' in *Papers of the Oxford Bibliographical Society*, V
(1936–9), 187–97. There are two facsimiles of this edition, one with
an introduction by Alexander B. Grosart (1876), the other published
by the Scolar Press (1968). [On *Herbert's Remains*, see below,
p. 235]. *W* has been edited by Amy M. Charles in *The Williams
Manuscript of George Herbert's Poems: A Facsimile Reproduction*
(Delmar, N.Y.: Scholars' Facsimiles and Reprints, 1977); see also
Renaissance Papers 1971, pp. 59–77.

The first Everyman's edition of *The Temple*, with a laconic intro-
duction by Edward Thomas and an inadequate text (1908), is
obsolete; so is the Nonesuch Press edition by Francis Meynell
(1927). Palmer's magisterial three-volume edition [*GHP*] has a full
commentary even if the arrangement of the poems is distinctly per-
sonal and inevitably controversial. More recent editions are often
distinguished by their haphazard selections and elementary intro-
ductions, as in the *Selected Poems* gathered by Douglas Brown
(1960), *A Choice of George Herbert's Verse* attempted by R. S.
Thomas (1967), and the few poems casually put together by W. H.

Auden (Penguin Books, 1973). On the other hand, the *Selected Poems* ventured by Gareth Reeves (1971) has extensive annotation—but also an uninspiring introduction—while the *Selected Poetry* edited by J. H. Summers (1971) has discreet notes *and* a suggestive introduction. The 'definitive' edition of *The Temple* by Hutchinson [*FEH*]—and its offshoot, the World's Classics edition with an introduction by Helen Gardner (1961)—will be much affected once the forthcoming edition by J. Max Patrick and John R. Mulder appears. Hutchinson's extensive indebtedness to *B*, like the more exclusive one in the Lewalski-Sabol edition [*LS*], has been heavily criticized by Patrick for disregarding the only reliable authority: the first edition (*SCN*, XXXI [1973], 53–4).

Herbert's appeal is by no means confined to the studies of critics and scholars listed below. Of late, the account of his peregrinations by Walton was imaginatively adapted for television in 'The Pilgrimage of George Herbert', directed and produced at the University of York by Tom Gutteridge (1972).

1. *General Studies*

§ 131. ALVAREZ, A.: 'The Poetry of Religious Experience: George Herbert', in his *The School of Donne* (1961), Ch. III (1).

§ 132. ANON.: 'From Court to Sanctuary: George Herbert's Songs', *TLS*, 12 July 1941 (pp. 334, 337).

§ 133. ASALS, HEATHER: 'George Herbert and Hugh of St Victor's "Soliloquium de Arrha Animae"', *N&Q*, CCXIV (1969), 368–70. Cf. above, p. 24, note 12.

§ 134. ASALS, HEATHER: 'The Tetragrammaton in *The Temple*', *SCN*, XXXI (1973), 48–50.

§ 135. ASALS, HEATHER: 'The Voice of George Herbert's "The Church"', *ELH*, XXXVI (1969), 511–28.

§ 136. BENNETT, JOAN: 'George Herbert', in her *Five Metaphysical Poets*, 3rd edn (Cambridge, 1964), Ch. IV.

§ 137. BLANCHARD, MARGARET M.: 'The Leap into Darkness: Donne, Herbert, and God', *Renascence*, XVII (1964), 38–50.

§ 138. BLUM, IRVING D.: 'The Paradox of Money Imagery in English Renaissance Poetry', *SR*, VIII (1961), 144–54.

§ 139. BOTTRALL, MARGARET: *George Herbert* (1954). Ch. IV ('Herbert's Craftsmanship') repr. in *Seventeenth-Century English Poetry*, ed. William R. Keast (1962), pp. 238–51.

§ 140. BRADBROOK, M. C.: 'The Liturgical Tradition in English Verse: Herbert and Eliot', *Theology*, XLIV (1942), 13–23.

§ 141. BRINKLEY, ROBERTA F. (ed.): *Coleridge on the Seventeenth Century* (Durham, N.C., 1955), pp. 533–40. His comments on Herbert's poetry [§ 147].

§ 142. BURKE, KENNETH: 'On Covery, Re— & Dis—', *Accent*, XIII (1953), 218–26. Reflections on Herbert *pace* Tuve [§ 219].

§ 143. CARNES, VALERIE: 'The Unity of George Herbert's *The Temple*: A Reconsideration', *ELH*, XXXV (1968), 505–26.

§ 144. CHARLES, AMY M.: 'George Herbert: Priest, Poet, Musician', *Journal of the Viola da Gamba Society of America*, IV (1967), 27–36.

§ 145. CHOSSONNERY, PAUL : 'La composition et la signification de *The Temple* de George Herbert', *Etudes Anglaises*, XXIV (1971), 113–25.

§ 146. CLARK, IRA: '"Lord, in Thee the Beauty Lies in the Discovery": "Love Unknown" and Reading Herbert', *ELH*, XXXIX (1972), 560–84.

§ 147. COLERIDGE, SAMUEL TAYLOR: *Biographia Literaria* (1817), Ch. XIX (Everyman edn, 1956, pp. 225–8); also 'Notes on *The Temple* and [Christopher Harvey's] *Synagogue*', appended to the William Pickering edn (1857), pp. 345–50. Reprinted in Brinkley [§ 141].

§ 148. COLIE, ROSALIE L.: '*Logos* in *The Temple*' (as above, § 28), Ch. VI; repr. from *JWCI*, XXVI (1963), 327–42.

§ 149. DOUDS, J. B.: 'George Herbert's Use of the Transferred Verb: A Study in the Structure of Poetic Imagery', *MLQ*, V (1944), 163–74.

§ 150. DOWDEN, E.: 'Anglo-Catholic Poets: Herbert', in his *Puritan and Anglican: Studies in Literature* (1900), pp. 97–120.

§ 151. DUNDAS, JUDITH: 'Levity and Grace: The Poetry of Sacred Wit', *The Yearbook of English Studies*, II (1972), 93–102.

§ 152. EL-GABALAWY, SAAD: 'George Herbert and the *Ars Amatoria*', *Xavier University Studies*, X (1971), iii, 28–33. Glances also at the inclinations of the indexer of *The Temple* (1656 ff.), more fully argued in his 'A 17th-Century Reading of George Herbert', *PLL*, VII (1971), 159–67.

§ 153. EL-GABALAWY, SAAD: 'George Herbert's Affinities with the Homiletical Mode', *Humanities Association Bulletin* (Canada), XXI (1970), iii, 38–48.

§ 154. EL-GABALAWY, SAAD: 'George Herbert's Christian Sensibility: A Resumé', *Cithara*, XI (1972), ii, 16–22.

§ 155. ELIOT, T. S.: *George Herbert* ('Writers and their Work', No. 152; 1962). On *The Temple* as 'a structure' (cited above, p. 15), see p. 17. Elsewhere he calls it 'a book constructed according to a plan', 'a continued religious meditation within an intellectual framework' (*The Welsh Review*, III [1944], 261).

§ 156. ELLRODT, ROBERT: 'George Herbert and the Religious Lyric', in *English Poetry and Prose 1540–1674*, ed. Christopher Ricks (1970), Ch. VIII. Cf. § 34.

§ 157. ENDICOTT, ANNABEL M.: 'The Structure of George Herbert's *Temple*: A Reconsideration', *UTQ*, XXXIV (1965), 226–37.

§ 158. ENRIGHT, D. J.: 'George Herbert and the Devotional Poets', in *From Donne to Marvell*, ed. Boris Ford (1956), pp. 142–59.

§ 159. ERICSON, EDWARD E., JR.: 'A Structural Approach to Imagery', *Style*, III (1970), 227–47.

§ 160. ESCH, ARNO: 'Zum Gedichtaufbau von George Herbert', in his *Englische religiöse Lyrik des 17. Jahrhunderts* (Tübingen, 1955), Ch. III.

§ 161. FESTUGIÈRE, A. J.: *George Herbert, poète, saint, anglican* (Paris, 1971). Introductory.

§ 162. FISCH, HAROLD: 'Hebraic Poetry' [i.e. Herbert and the Psalter], in his *Jerusalem and Albion* (1964), pp. 56–62.

§ 163. FISH, STANLEY E.: *The Living Temple: George Herbert and Catechizing* (Berkeley, 1978). Cf. his *Self-Consuming Artifacts* (Berkeley, 1972), Ch. III.

§ 164. FREEMAN, ROSEMARY: *English Emblem Books* (1948). Includes in Ch. VI a revised form of 'George Herbert and the Emblem Books', *RES*, XVII (1941), 150–65.

§ 165. FREEMAN, ROSEMARY: 'Parody as a Literary Form: George Herbert and Wilfred Owen', *EC*, XIII (1963), 307–22.

§ 166. FREER, COBURN: *Music for a King: George Herbert's Style and the Metrical Psalms* (Baltimore, 1972).

§ 167. FRYXELL, LUCY D.: 'George Herbert: Anti-Metaphysical Poet?' *Discourse* (Concordia College), VI (1963), 293–9.

§ 168. GALLAGHER, MICHAEL P.: 'Rhetoric, Style, and George Herbert', *ELH*, XXXVII (1970), 495–516.

§ 169. HALEWOOD, WILLIAM H.: 'Herbert', in his *The Poetry of Grace: Reformation Themes and Structures in English 17th-Century Poetry* (New Haven, 1970), Ch. IV.

§ 170. HANLEY, SARA W.: 'Temples in *The Temple*: George Herbert's Study of the Church', *SEL*, VIII (1968), 121–35.

§ 171. HARPER, GEORGE M.: 'George Herbert's Poems', *Quarterly Review*, CCLXVII (1936), 58–73.

§ 172. HAYES, ALBERT M.: 'Counterpoint in Herbert', *SP*, XXXV (1938), 43–60. On Herbert's metrical technique.

§ 173. HOWARD, THOMAS T.: 'Herbert and Crashaw: Notes on Meditative Focus', *Gordon Review*, XI (1968), 79–98.

§ 174. HUGHES, RICHARD E.: 'Conceptual Form and Varieties of Religious Experience in the Poetry of George Herbert', *Greyfriar* (Siena College, N.Y.), III (1960), 3–12.

§ 175. HUGHES, RICHARD E.: 'George Herbert's Rhetorical World', *Criticism*, III (1961), 86–94.

§ 176. HUGHES, RICHARD E.: 'George Herbert and the Incarnation', *Cithara*, IV (1964), i, 22–32.

§ 177. HUNTER, JIM: 'George Herbert', in his *The Metaphysical Poets* (1965), Ch. VII. Elementary.

§ 178. HUTCHINSON, F. E.: 'George Herbert: A Tercentenary', *Nineteenth Century*, CXIII (1933), 358–68; and 'George

Herbert', in *Seventeenth Century Studies presented to Sir Herbert Grierson* (Oxford, 1938), pp. 148–60.

§ 179. ITRAT-HUSAIN: *The Mystical Element in the Metaphysical Poets* (Edinburgh, 1948), Ch. III.

§ 180. JENNINGS, ELIZABETH: 'The Lyric Intervention: Herbert and Vaughan', in her *Every Changing Shape* (1961), Ch. VII. Elementary.

§ 181. KNIEGER, BERNARD: 'The Religious Verse of George Herbert', *CLAJ*, IV (1960), 138–47.

§ 182. KNIEGER, BERNARD: 'The Purchase-Sale: Patterns of Business Imagery in the Poetry of George Herbert', *SEL*, VI (1966), 111–24. Cf. above, p. 24, note 12.

§ 183. KNIGHTS, L. C.: 'George Herbert', in his *Explorations* (1946), pp. 112–30; repr. from *Scrutiny*, XII (1944), 171–86.

§ 184. KRANZ, GISBERT: 'George Herbert: Ein Dichter des Anglikanertums', *Hochland*, LV (1962–3), 235–46.

§ 185. LEISHMAN, J. B.: 'George Herbert', in his *The Metaphysical Poets* (1934), pp. 99–144.

§ 186. LUCAS, F. L.: 'George Herbert', *Life and Letters*, I (1928), 548–61; repr. as 'The Poet of Anglicanism', in his *Studies French and English* (1934), pp. 138–50.

§ 187. MCGILL, WILLIAM J., JR.: 'George Herbert's View of the Eucharist', *Lock Haven Review*, VIII (1966), 16–24.

§ 188. MAHOOD, M. M.: 'Something Understood: The Nature of Herbert's Wit' (as above, § 15), Ch. V. Cf. § 330.

§ 189. MANGELSDORF, SANDRA R.: 'Donne, Herbert, and Vaughan: Some Baroque Features', *NEMLA Newsletter*, II (1970), i, 14–23.

§ 190. MARTZ, LOUIS L.: 'George Herbert: In the Presence of a Friend' (as above, § 74), Ch. VII.

§ 191. MARTZ, LOUIS L.: 'George Herbert: The Unity of *The Temple*' (as above, § 74), Ch. VIII.

§ 192. MILES, JOSEPHINE: 'Some Major Poetic Words', in *Essays and Studies*, University of California Publications in English, XIV (1943), 233–9. Also, with Hanan C. Selvin: 'A Factor Analysis of Poetry in the 17th Century', in *The Computer and Literary Style*, ed. Jacob Leed (Kent, Ohio, 1966), pp. 116–27. Cf. § 80.

§ 193. MOLLENKOTT, VIRGINIA R.: 'George Herbert's Epithet-Sonnets', *Genre*, V (1972), 131–7.

§ 194. MOLLENKOTT, VIRGINIA R.: 'Experimental Freedom in Herbert's Sonnets', *Christian Scholar's Review*, I (1971), 109–16.

§ 195. MONTGOMERY, ROBERT L., JR.: 'The Province of Allegory in George Herbert's Verse', *Texas Studies in Literature and Language*, I (1960), 457–72.

§ 196. MORE, PAUL ELMER: 'George Herbert', in his *Shelburne Essays*, 4th Series (1906), pp. 66–98.

§ 197. MULDER, JOHN R.: 'George Herbert's *The Temple:* Design and Methodology', *SCN*, XXXI (1973), 37–45. Cf. § 87.

§ 198. ORANGE, U. M. D.: 'The Poetry of George Herbert', *Poetry Review*, XXIV (1933), 118–27. One of several studies occasioned by the tercentenary of Herbert's death, and representative of now obsolete attitudes.

§ 199. OSTRIKER, ALICIA: 'Song and Speech in the Metrics of George Herbert', *PMLA*, LXXX (1965), 62–8.

§ 200. PARFITT, GEORGE A. E.: 'Donne, Herbert and the Matter of Schools', *EC*, XXII (1972), 381–95.

§ 201. PENNEL, CHARLES A., AND WILLIAM P. WILLIAMS: 'The Unity of *The Temple*', *Xavier University Studies*, V (1966), 37–45.

§ 202. POGGI, VALENTINA: *George Herbert* (Bologna, 1967).

§ 203. POLLOCK, JOHN J.: 'George Herbert's Enclosure Imagery', *SCN*, XXXI (1973), 55.

§ 204. RICKEY, MARY E.: *Utmost Art: Complexity in the Verse of George Herbert* (Lexington, Ky., 1966). Includes her essay 'Herbert's Technical Development', *JEGP*, LXII (1963), 745–60.

§ 205. RICKEY, MARY E.: 'Rhymecraft in Edward and George Herbert', *JEGP*, LVII (1958), 502–11.

§ 206. ROSS, MALCOLM M.: 'George Herbert and the Humanist Tradition', in his *Poetry and Dogma: The Transformation of Eucharistic Symbols in 17th Century English Poetry* (New Brunswick, N.J., 1954), Ch. VI; repr. from *UTQ*, XVI (1947), 169–82.

§ 207. ROWSE, A. L.: 'The Caroline Country Parson: George Herbert', in his *The English Spirit* (1944), Ch. XIX; repr. from *Country Life*, XCI (1942), 252–5 (illustr.). An appreciation.

§ 208. SANDERS, WILBUR: '"Childhood is Health": The Divine Poetry of George Herbert', *Melbourne Critical Review*, V (1962), 3–15.

§ 209. SANDERS, WILBUR: 'Herbert and the Scholars', *Melbourne Critical Review*, IV (1961), 102–11. A review of §§ 37, 74, 206, 219.

§ 210. SANDLER, FLORENCE: '"Solomon ubique regnet": Herbert's Use of the Images of the New Covenant', *PLL*, VIII (1972), 147–58.

§ 211. SELINCOURT, ERNEST DE: 'George Herbert', *Hibbert Journal*, XXXIX (1941), 389–97.

§ 212. STAMBLER, ELIZABETH: 'The Unity of Herbert's *Temple*', *Cross Currents*, X (1960), 251–66.

§ 213. STEIN, ARNOLD: *George Herbert's Lyrics* (Baltimore, 1968); includes his essays 'George Herbert: The Art of Plainness', in *The Poetic Tradition*, ed. D. C. Allen and H. T. Rowell (Baltimore, 1968), pp. 99–122, and 'George Herbert's Prosody', *Language and Style*, I (1968), 1–38.

§ 214. STEWART, STANLEY: 'Time and *The Temple*', *SEL*, VI (1966), 97–110. Cf. § 109.

§ 215. SUMMERS, JOSEPH H.: 'Gentlemen at Home and at Church: Henry King and George Herbert', in his *The Heirs of Donne and Jonson* (1970), Ch. III.

§ 216. SUMMERS, JOSEPH H.: *George Herbert: his Religion and Art* (Cambridge, Mass., 1954); includes his essay 'Herbert's Form', *PMLA*, LXVI (1951), 1055–72. One chapter ('The Conception of Form') repr. in *The Metaphysical Poets*, ed. Frank Kermode (Greenwich, Conn., 1969), pp. 230–51; another ('The Poem as Hieroglyph'), in *Seventeenth Century English Poetry*, ed. William R. Keast (1962), pp. 215–37.

§ 217. SWARDSON, H. R.: 'George Herbert's Language of Devotion', in his *Poetry and the Fountain of Light* (1962), Ch. III.

§ 218. TAYLOR, IVAN E.: 'Cavalier Sophistication in the Poetry of George Herbert', *Anglican Theological Review*, XXXIX (1957), 229–43.

§ 219. TUVE, ROSEMOND: *A Reading of George Herbert* (Chicago, 1952). Cf. § 113.

§ 220. TUVE, ROSEMOND: 'George Herbert and *Caritas*', in her *Essays*, ed. T. P. Roche (Princeton, 1970), pp. 167–206; repr. from *JWCI*, XXII (1959), 303–31.

§ 221. VENDLER, HELEN: *The Poetry of George Herbert* (Cambridge, Mass., 1975). Cf. §297, and *Forms of Lyric*, ed. Reuben A. Brower (1970), pp. 19–45.

§ 222. WALKER, JOHN W.: 'The Architectonics of George Herbert's *The Temple*', *ELH*, XXIX (1962), 289–305.

§ 223. WARREN, AUSTIN: 'George Herbert', in his *Rage for Order: Essays in Criticism* (Chicago, 1948), Ch. II; repr. from *American Review*, VII (1936), 249–71.

§ 224. WATSON, GEORGE: 'The Fabric of Herbert's *Temple*', *JWCI*, XXVI (1963), 354–8.

§ 225. WHITE, HELEN C.: 'George Herbert and the Road to Bemerton', and 'George Herbert and *The Temple*', in her *The Metaphysical Poets* (1936; repr. 1962), Ch. VI–VII.

§ 226. WHITLOCK, BAIRD W.: 'The Baroque Characteristics of the Poetry of George Herbert', *Cithara*, VII (1968), ii, 30–40.

§ 227. WILLIAMSON, GEORGE: 'The Sacred Line: Herbert, Crashaw, Vaughan', in his *The Donne Tradition* (Cambridge, Mass., 1930; repr. 1958), Ch. V.

§ 228. WILLIAMSON, GEORGE: 'George Herbert', in his *A Reader's Guide to the Metaphysical Poets* (1967; 1968), Ch. V.

§ 229. ZIEGELMAIER, GREGORY: 'Liturgical Symbol and Reality in the Poetry of George Herbert', *American Benedictine Review*, XVIII (1967), 344–53.

2. Studies of Individual Poems

In addition to the book-length studies by Rickey, Stein, Summers, and Tuve [§§ 204, 213, 216, 219], see:

§ 230. ADLER, JACOB H.: 'Form and Meaning in Herbert's "Discipline"', *N&Q*, CCIII (1958), 240–3.

§ 231. AKRIGG, G. P. V.: 'George Herbert's "The Caller"', *N&Q*, CXCIX (1954), 17. Should 'The Collar' read 'The Caller'? Cf. J. M. Bickham, in *Exp*, X (1951), No. 17.

§ 232. ALLEN, DON C.: 'George Herbert's "Sycomore"', *MLN*, LIX (1944), 493–5. See above, p. 100, note on 11.

§ 233. ALLEN, DON C.: *Image and Meaning: Metaphoric Traditions in Renaissance Poetry* (Baltimore, 1960), Ch. IV. On 'The Rose'.

§ 234. BENJAMIN, EDWIN B.: 'Herbert's "Vertue"', *Exp*, IX (1950), No. 12.

§ 235. BLAU, SHERIDAN D.: 'The Poet as Casuist: Herbert's "Church-Porch"', *Genre*, IV (1971), 142–52.

§ 236. BOWERS, FREDSON: 'Herbert's Sequential Imagery: "The Temper"', *MP*, LIX (1962), 202–13.

§ 237. BROWN, C. C., AND W. P. INGOLDSBY: 'George Herbert's "Easter Wings"', *HLQ*, XXXV (1972), 131–42.

§ 238. CARNES, VALERIE: (as above, § 143). On 'The Church-Porch'.

§ 239. CARPENTER, MARGARET: 'From Herbert to Marvell: Poetics in "A Wreath" and "The Coronet"', *JEGP*, LXIX (1970), 50–62.

§ 240. CHAMPION, LARRY S.: 'Body versus Soul in George Herbert's "The Collar"', *Style*, I (1967), 131–7.

§ 241. CLARK, IRA: (as above, § 146). On 'Love unknown'.

§ 242. COLLMER, ROBERT G.: 'Herbert's "Businesse"', 15–30', *Exp*, XVI (1957), No. 11.

§ 243. D., A.: 'Five Notes on George Herbert', *N&Q*, CXCVII (1952), 95–6.

§ 244. DAVIES, H. NEVILLE: 'Sweet Music in Herbert's "Easter"', *N&Q*, CCXIII (1968), 95–6.

§ 245. ELDREDGE, FRANCES: 'Herbert's "Jordan"', *Exp*, XI (1952), No. 3.

§ 246. EL-GABALAWY, SAAD: 'The Pilgrimage: George Herbert's Favourite Allegorical Technique', *CLAJ*, XIII (1970), 408–19. On 'The Pilgrimage', 'Peace' and 'Redemption'.

§ 247. EMPSON, WILLIAM: *Seven Types of Ambiguity* (1930; 3rd revised edn, 1953), pp. 118–19 (on 'Hope'), 129–31 (on 'The Pilgrimage'), 226–33 (on 'The Sacrifice'). Cf. § 219.

§ 248. EMSLIE, MACDONALD: 'Herbert's "Jordan I"', *Exp*, XII (1954), No. 35.

§ 249. FLETCHER, ANGUS: *The Transcendental Masque* (Ithaca, N.Y., 1971), pp. 201 ff. Antecedents to the use of the echo device in 'Heaven'.

§ 250. FRENCH, ROBERTS W.: 'Herbert's "Vertue"', *Exp*, XXVI
1967), No. 4.

§ 251. GASKELL, RONALD: 'Herbert's "Vanitie"', *Critical Quar-
terly*, III (1961), 313–5.

§ 252. GREENWOOD, E. B.: 'George Herbert's Sonnet "Prayer":
A Stylistic Study', *EC*, XV (1965), 27–45.

§ 253. HANDSCOMBE, R. J.: 'George Herbert's "The Collar":
A Study in Frustration', *Language and Style*, III (1970),
29–37.

§ 254. HANLEY, SARA W.: 'George Herbert's "Ana ⟨Mary
Army⟩ Gram"', *ELN*, IV (1966), 16–19.

§ 255. HARBINSON, M. J.: 'A Crux in Herbert's "The Sacrifice"',
N&Q, CCXIII (1968), 96–8. On ll. 121–4.

§ 256. HART, JEFFREY: 'Herbert's "The Collar" Re-read',
Boston University Studies in English, V (1961), 65–73.

§ 257. HASTINGS, ROBERT: '"Easter Wings" as a Model of Her-
bert's Method', *Thoth*, IV (1963), 15–23.

§ 258. HEDGES, JAMES L.: 'Thomas Adams, Robert Burton, and
Herbert's "The Collar"', *SCN*, XXXI (1973), 47–8.

§ 259. HILBERRY, CONRAD: 'Two Cruxes in George Herbert's
"Redemption"', *N&Q*, CCI (1956), 514. Also 'Herbert's
"Dooms-day"', *Exp*, XVI (1958), No. 24.

§ 260. HILL, D. M.: 'Allusion and Meaning in Herbert's "Jordan
I"', *Neophilologus*, LVI (1972), 344–51.

§ 261. HOLLANDER, JOHN: (as above, § 50), pp. 288–94. On
several poems with musical references.

§ 262. HUNTLEY, FRANK L.: 'A Crux in George Herbert's *The
Temple*', *ELN*, VIII (1970), 13–17. On 'Church-lock and
key'.

§ 263. JOHNSON, LEE ANN: 'The Relationship of "The Church
Militant" to *The Temple*', *SP*, LXVIII (1971), 200–6.

§ 264. KARETZ, GENE H.: 'The Rhyme Scheme in Herbert's
"Man"', *N&Q*, CCI (1956), 144–6.

§ 265. KIRKWOOD, JAMES I., and GEORGE W. WILLIAMS, '"An-
neal'd" as Baptism in Herbert's "Love-joy"', *American
Notes and Queries*, IV (1965), 3–5.

§ 266. KNIEGER, BERNARD: 'Herbert's "Redemption"', *Exp* XI
(1953), No. 24.

§ 267. LAMBA, B. P. AND R. J.: 'Herbert's "The Agonie", 9–10',
Exp, XXVIII (1970), No. 51. See also the replies by
Edgar F. Daniels and René Rapin, *Exp*, XXX (1971),
No. 16.

§ 268. LEIMBERG, INGE: 'George Herbert "The Sinner": Der
Tempel als Memoria-Gebäude', *Archiv für das Studium
der Neueren Sprachen und Literaturen*, CCVI (1970),
241–50.

§ 269. LEITER, LOUIS H.: 'George Herbert's Anagram [of the
Virgin Mary]', *CE*, XXVI (1965), 543–4. Cf. § 287.

§ 270. LEVANG, DWIGHT: 'George Herbert's "The Church

Militant" and the Chances of History', *PQ*, XXXVI (1957), 265–8. Notes that a Puritan preacher was punished in 1635 for remarking that religion 'stood on tiptoes ready to be gone' to America [cf. above, p. 199, note on 235–6].

§ 271. LEVITT, PAUL M., and KENNETH G. JOHNSTON: 'Herbert's "The Collar": A Nautical Metaphor', *SP*, LXVI (1970), 217–24.

§ 272. LEVITT, PAUL M., AND KENNETH G. JOHNSTON: 'Herbert's "The Collar" and the Story of Job', *PLL*, IV (1968), 329–30.

§ 273. LOW, ANTHONY: 'Herbert's "Jordan I" and the Court Masque', *Criticism*, XIV (1972), 109–18.

§ 274. MCGUIRE, PHILIP C.: 'Herbert's "Jordan II" and the Plain Style', *Michigan Academician*, I (1969), iii–iv, 69–74.

§ 275. MCLUHAN, HERBERT M.: 'Herbert's "Virtue"', *Exp*, II (1943), No. 4.

§ 276. MANNING, STEPHEN: 'Herbert's "The Pearl", 38', *Exp*, XIV (1956), No. 25.

§ 277. MERRILL, THOMAS F.: '"The Sacrifice" and the Structure of Religious Language', *Language and Style*, II (1970), 275–87.

§ 278. MINER, EARL: (as above, § 81), pp. 231–46. On 'The Flower'.

§ 279. MOHANTY, HARENDRA P.: 'George Herbert's "The Collar"', *Indian Journal of English Studies*, VI (1965), 114–6.

§ 280. MOLESWORTH, CHARLES: 'Herbert's "The Elixir": Revision towards Action', *Concerning Poetry*, V (1972), 12–20.

§ 281. MOLLENKOTT, VIRGINIA R.: 'George Herbert's "Redemption"', *ELN*, X (1973), 262–7.

§ 282. MOLLENKOTT, VIRGINIA R.: 'The Many and the One in George Herbert's "Providence"', *CLAJ*, X (1966), 34–41.

§ 283. MOLONEY, MICHAEL F.: 'A Suggested Gloss for Herbert's "Box where sweets..."', *N&Q*, CXCIX (1954), 50. Cf. above, p. 103, note on 10.

§ 284. NAYLOR, E. W.: 'Three 17th-Century Poet-Parsons and Music', in his *The Poets and Music* (1928), pp. 73–9; repr. from *Proceedings of the Musical Association*, LIV (1927–8), 93–113.

§ 285. NORTON, DAN S.: 'Herbert's "The Collar"', *Exp*, II (1944), No. 41, and III (1945), No. 46.

§ 286. PATRIDES, C. A.: (as above, § 91), pp. 82–3. On 'The Collar'.

§ 287. REITER, ROBERT E.: 'George Herbert's "Anagram"', *CE*, XXVIII (1966), 59–60. Cf. § 269.

§ 288. SCHEUERLE, WILLIAM H.: 'A Reading of George Herbert's "Content"', *Language Quarterly*, IV (1965), i–ii, 37–9.

§ 289. SCHWARTZ, HELEN J.: 'Herbert's "Grief"', *Exp*, XXXI (1973), No. 43.

§ 290. STANWOOD, P. G.: 'The Liveliness of Flesh and Blood: Herbert's "Prayer I" and "Love III"', *SCN*, XXXI (1973), 52–3.

§ 291. STEADMAN, JOHN M.: 'Herbert's Platonic Lapidary: A Note on "The Foil"', *SCN*, XXX (1972), 59–62.

§ 292. STEWART, STANLEY: (as above, § 109), pp. 52–9. On 'Paradise' and other poems.

§ 293. THORNTON, ROBERT D.:   'Polyphiloprogenitive: The Sapient Sutlers', *Anglican Theological Review*, XXXV (1953), 28–36. On 'The Windows', in relation to T. S. Eliot's 'Sunday Morning Service'.

§ 294. TUVE, ROSEMOND: 'On Herbert's "Sacrifice"', *Kenyon Review*, XII (1950), 51–75. Cf. William Empson, 'George Herbert and Miss Tuve', *ibid.*, 735–8.

§ 295. TUVE, ROSEMOND: 'Sacred "Parody" of Love Poetry, and Herbert', in her *Essays*, ed. T. P. Roche (Princeton, 1970), pp. 207–51; repr. from *SR*, VIII (1961), 249–90. On 'A Parodie'.

§ 296. UNRAU, JOHN: 'Three Notes on George Herbert', *N&Q*, CCXIII (1968), 94–5.

§ 297. VENDLER, HELEN: 'George Herbert's "Vertue"', *Ariel: A Review of International English Literature*, I (1970), ii, 54–70. Also above [§ 221] on a number of other poems.

§ 298. VON ERDE, FREDERICK: 'George Herbert's "The Sonne": In Defense of the English Language', *SEL*, XII (1972), 173–82.

§ 299. WEINBERGER, G. J.: 'George Herbert's "The Church Militant"', *Connecticut Review*, IV (1971), ii, 49–57.

§ 300. WEST, MICHAEL: 'Ecclesiastical Controversy in George Herbert's "Peace"', *RES*, XXII (1971), 445–51.

§ 301. WHITING, PAUL R.: 'Two Notes on George Herbert', *N&Q*, CCX (1965), 130–1.

§ 302. WILLIAMS, R. DARBY: 'Two Baroque Game Poems on Grace: Herbert's "Paradise" and Milton's "On Time"', *Criticism*, XII (1970), 180–94.

§ 303. WILSON, F. P.: 'A Note on George Herbert's "The Quidditie"', *RES*, XIX (1943), 398–9.

§ 304. WOLFE, JANE E.: 'George Herbert's "Assurance"', *CLAJ*, V (1962), 213–22.

3. *Studies of the Latin Poetry*

Herbert's Latin poems are translated in *LPH*. Other modern translations are listed below [§§ 305, 311]. In the 17th century the 'Aethiopissa ambit Cestum' was freely translated by Henry Reynolds as 'A Blackmore Mayd wooing a faire Boy', and published in Henry King's *Poems* (1657), with the latter's 'The Boy's

Answere to the Blackmore' (both in *The Poems of Henry King*, ed.
Margaret Crum [Oxford, 1965], p. 151).

§ 305. BLUNDEN, EDMUND: 'George Herbert's Latin Poems',
E&S, XIX (1933), 29–39. Includes translations of 'In
honorem illustr. D.D. Verulamij', 'Triumphus mortis'
(i.e. *Lucus* XXXII), and parts of *Memoriae matris
sacrum*.

§ 306. BRADNER, LEICESTER: *Musae Anglicanae: A History of
Anglo-Latin Poetry, 1500–1925* (1940). The context of
Herbert's Latin poems, themselves discussed briefly
(pp. 96–7).

§ 307. BRADNER, LEICESTER: 'New Poems by George Herbert:
The Cambridge Latin Gratulatory Anthology of 1613',
RN, XV (1962), 208–11. Prints two poems on the
marriage of the Elector Palatine Frederick to Princess
Elizabeth.

§ 308. GARDNER, HELEN: 'Donne's Latin Poem to Herbert and
Herbert's Reply', in her edition of *The Divine Poems* of
Donne (Oxford, 1952), App. G.

§ 309. GIBBS, J.: 'An Unknown Poem of George Herbert', *TLS*,
30 December 1949 (p. 857). The complete version of a
poem known only from its first two lines [*FEH*, p. 459].

§ 310. STORY, G. M.: 'George Herbert's *Inventa Bellica*: A New
Manuscript', *MP*, LIX (1962), 270–2. On 'Triumphus
mortis' (i.e. *Lucus* XXXII).

§ 311. SUMMERS, JOSEPH H.: in *Quarterly Review of Literature*,
VI (1951), 211–2. Translates 'Homo, statua', 'Patria',
'In angelos' (i.e. *Lucus* I, II, XXIV), and 'Horti,
deliciae Dominae' (*Memoriae matris sacrum* V).

4. Studies of the Prose Works

The first edition of *Herbert's Remains. Or, Sundry Pieces of that
sweet Singer of The Temple, Mr George Herbert* (1652) is available in
facsimile from the Scolar Press (1970); it contains Oley's biography
[*BO*], the text of both *A Priest to the Temple: or, The Country
Parson*, and *Jacula Prudentum. Or Outlandish Proverbs, Sentences,
&c.*, and some minor pieces. The *Priest* has been published several
times, usually in editions intended for the preacher (e.g. by Hugh
Martin, in 'A Treasury of Christian Books', 1956). Two notable
exceptions are the responsible editions by H. C. Beeching (Oxford,
1898), and *FEH*, pp. 223 ff.

§ 312. ENDICOTT, ANNABEL M.: '"The Soul in Paraphrase":
George Herbert's "Library"', *RN*, XIX (1966), 14–16.

§ 313. BOTTRALL, MARGARET: 'George Herbert and *The Country
Parson*', *Listener*, XLVII (1952), 558–62; expanded in
her *George Herbert* (1954), Ch. IV.

§ 314. LIEVSAY, JOHN L.: *Stefano Guazzo and the English Renais-
sance* (Chapel Hill, 1961), pp. 141–4. On the Guazzian
proverbs in Herbert's collection.

§ 315. LUKE, STANLEY: 'An Old Handbook on the Pastoral Office',
  London Quarterly Review, CLXII (1937), 198–206.
  Outlines the contents of *A Priest to the Temple*.

§ 316. WILSON, F. P.: 'English Proverbs and Dictionaries of
  Proverbs', *Library*, 4th Series, XXVI (1946), 51–71.
  Herbert's collection in context.

§ 317. WRIGHT, HERBERT G.: 'Was George Herbert the Author of
  Jacula prudentum?' *RES*, XI (1935), 139–44. The 1651
  edn is authentic.

5. Studies of Herbert's Reputation and Influence

Herbert's poems have often been reduced to hymns,[1] from the
single one—inevitably 'The 23rd Psalme'—contained in Joseph
Boyse's *Sacramental Hymns* (1693), to the several poems in *Select
Hymns taken out of Mr Herbert's Temple* (1697; facsimile edn,
Augustan Reprint Society, 1962), or Henry Playford's *The Divine
Companion* (1701), or Samuel Bury's *Collection of Psalms, Hymns
and Spiritual Songs* (1707), but especially in John Wesley's *Hymns
and Sacred Poems* (1739) which includes no fewer than forty-two
poems from *The Temple*. It is hardly surprising that studies of the
development of hymnody rarely fail to mention Herbert: e.g.
John Julian, ed., *A Dictionary of Hymnology*, 2nd edn (1907);
Louis F. Benson, *The English Hymn* (1915); Frederick J. Gillman,
The Evolution of the English Hymn (1927); C. S. Phillips, *Hymnody
Past and Present* (1937); H. A. L. Jefferson, *Hymns in Christian
Worship* (1950); etc. See also below, §§ 321, 325, and 328. Poems
which are still sung as hymns include 'Antiphon I', 'Vertue',
'The Call', 'The 23rd Psalme', 'The Elixer', and 'L'Envoy'.

§ 318. BANZER, JUDITH: '"Compound Manner": Emily Dickin-
  son and the Metaphysical Poets', *American Literature*,
  XXXII (1961), 417–33.

§ 319. BRITTIN, NORMAN A.: 'Emerson and the Metaphysical
  Poets', *American Literature*, VIII (1936), 1–12.

§ 320. DAVIES, ANEIRIN T.: *Dylan* [Thomas]: *Druid of the
  Broken Body* (1964), pp. 40 ff.

---

[1] I say 'reduced' advisedly, where others have used 'mutilated' [§ 343].
Bury's *Collection*, mentioned above, includes a version of 'Prayer I'
which begins:

> Prayer the Church's Banquet is,
> Prayer's the Devil's rage,
> Prayer's the Soul in Paraphrase . . .

and ends:

> Prayer exalted Mannah is,
> And Gladness of the best,
> Prayer in Heaven in ordinary,
> Prayer is Man well drest.

§ 321. DUCKLES, VINCENT: 'John Jenkins's Settings of Lyrics by George Herbert', *Musical Quarterly*, XLVIII (1962), 461–76. The settings are among the earliest known examples of Herbert lyrics with music. There are six of them: one each from 'Christmas' and 'The Dawning', and two each from 'The Starre' and 'Grieve not the Holy Spirit'.

§ 322. DUNCAN, JOSEPH E.: *The Revival of Metaphysical Poetry* (Minneapolis, 1959), pp. 43–5 (on John Keble), 102–9 (on Francis Thompson), etc. Cf. Above, p. 103, note on 15.

§ 323. DUNCAN-JONES, ELSIE: 'Benlowes's Borrowings from George Herbert', *RES*, n.s., VI (1955), 179–80.

§ 324. HOWELL, A. C.: 'Christopher Harvey's *The Synagogue* (1640)', *SP*, XLIX (1952), 229–47.

§ 325. HUTCHINSON, F. E.: 'John Wesley and George Herbert', *London Quarterly and Holborn Review*, CLXI (1936), 439–55.

§ 326. HUTCHINSON, F. E.: '[Herbert's] Contemporary and Later Reputation', in *FEH*, pp. xxxix–l.

§ 327. JOSELYN, SISTER M.: 'Herbert and Muir: Pilgrims of their Age', *Renascence*, XV (1963), 127–32.

§ 328. LEACH, ELSIE A.: 'John Wesley's Use of George Herbert', *HLQ*, XVI (1952–3), 183–202.

§ 329. LEACH, ELSIE A.: 'More Seventeenth-Century Admirers of Herbert', *N&Q*, CCV (1960), 62–3.

§ 330. MAHOOD, M. M.: 'Two Anglican Poets', in her *Poetry and Humanism* (1950), Ch. II. On Herbert and Christina Rossetti.

§ 331. NETHERCOT, ARTHUR H.: 'The Reputation of the "Metaphysical Poets" during the 17th Century', *JEGP*, XXIII (1924), 173–98; 'The Reputation of the "Metaphysical Poets" during the Age of Pope', *PQ*, IV (1925), 161–79; and 'The Reputation of the "Metaphysical Poets" during the Age of Johnson and the "Romantic Revival"', *SP*, XXII (1925), 81–132.

§ 332. PETTET, E. C.: *Of Paradise and Light: A Study of Vaughan's 'Silex Scintillans'* (Cambridge, 1960), Ch. III. On Herbert's influence.

§ 333. RAUTER, HERBERT: 'Eine Anleihe Sternes bei George Herbert', *Anglia*, LXXX (1962), 290–4. See above, p. 39, note on 239–40.

§ 334. REESE, HAROLD: 'A Borrower from Quarles and Herbert', *MLN*, LV (1940), 50–2. The unacknowledged use of 'Providence' in a 1669 volume.

§ 335. RICKEY, MARY E.: 'Vaughan, *The Temple* and Poetic Form', *SP*, LIX (1962), 162–70.

§ 336. SLOANE, WILLIAM: 'George Herbert's Reputation, 1650–1710: Good Reading for the Young', *N&Q*, CCVII (1962), 213.

§ 337. SPARROW, JOHN : 'George Herbert and John Donne among
        the Moravians', in *Hymns Unbidden*, by Martha W.
        England and John Sparrow (1966), pp. 1–29. On the
        adaptation of thirty poems by Herbert in the Moravian
        hymnal of 1754.

§ 338. STANFORD, DONALD E. (ed.): *The Poems of Edward Taylor*
        (New Haven, 1960). On Herbert's 'pervasive influence',
        see Louis L. Martz's Foreword (pp. xiii ff.) and the
        annotation (*passim*).

§ 339. SUMMERS, JOSEPH H.: 'Time and *The Temple*', in his
        George Herbert (Cambridge, Mass., 1954), Ch. I.

§ 340. SWANSTON, HAMISH: 'The Second *Temple*', *Durham
        University Journal*, n.s., XXV (1963), 14–22. On
        Crashaw's *Steps to the Temple* (1646).

§ 341. THOMPSON, ELBERT N. S.: '*The Temple* and [John Keble's]
        The Christian Year', *PMLA*, LIV (1939), 1018–25.

§ 342. WARD, DAVID: *T. S. Eliot between Two Worlds* (1973),
        pp. 283–5.

§ 343. WILLIAMSON, KARINA: 'Herbert's Reputation in the 18th
        Century', *PQ*, XLI (1962), 769–75.

6. Addenda

Studies published since 1974 include Roberts's *Bibliography* and
the DiCesare-Mignami *Concordance* (above, p. 223), Amy Charles's
Life and facsimile of *W* (pp. 223, 224), the two books by Fish (§163)
and Vendler (§221), and the following essays among several other
performances:

BELL, ILONA: ' "Setting Foot into Divinity": George Herbert and
    the English Reformation', *MLQ*, XXXVIII (1977), 219–41.

GALLAGHER, PHILIP J.: 'George Herbert's "The Forerunners" ',
    ELN, XV (1977), 14–18.

HARNACK, H. ANDREW: 'George Herbert's "Aaron": The Aesthetics
    of Shaped Typology', *ELN*, XIV (1976), 25–32.

HIGBIE, ROBERT: 'Images of Enclosure in George Herbert's *The
    Temple*', *Texas Studies in Literature and Language*, XV (1974),
    627–38.

KELLIHER, W. HILTON: 'The Latin Poetry of George Herbert', in
    The Latin Poetry of English Poets, ed. J. W. Binns (1974), pp.
    26–57.

LEWALSKI, BARBARA K.: 'Typology and Poetry: A Consideration of
    Herbert, Vaughan and Marvell', in *Illustrious Evidence*, ed. Earl
    Miner (Berkeley, 1975), pp. 41–69.

MCLAUGHLIN, ELIZABETH, and GAIL THOMAS: 'Communion in *The
    Temple*', *SEL*, XV (1975), 111–24.

TAYLOR, MARK: *The Soul in Paraphrase: George Herbert's Poetics*
    (The Hague, 1974).

Index of Titles

Index of First Lines